IMAGES
of America

BOONE COUNTY

On the Cover: Crowned Mrs. Liberty in the 1959 inaugural pageant, Ann Graham (center) passes the honor, bejewelled crown, and updated title to Laurie Banton, Mrs. Boone County 1960, as runner-up Ruth Hungate (left) looks on. (Ralph W. Stark Heritage Center.)

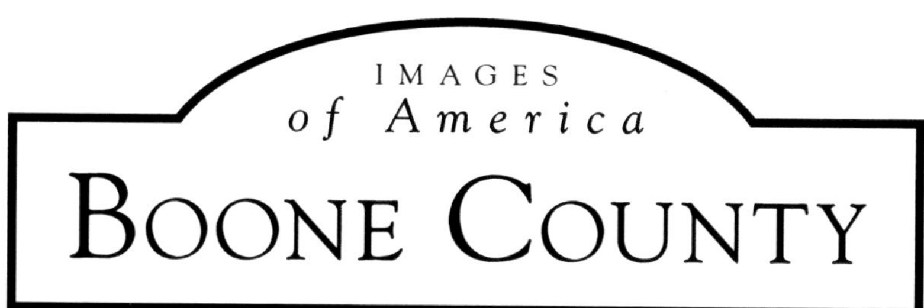

Kassie Ritman

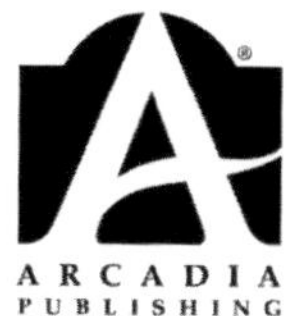

ISBN 978-1-4671-1731-9

Published by Arcadia Publishing
Charleston, South Carolina

Printed in the United States of America

Library of Congress Control Number: 2016932220

For all general information, please contact Arcadia Publishing:
Telephone 843-853-2070
Fax 843-853-0044
E-mail sales@arcadiapublishing.com
For customer service and orders:
Toll-Free 1-888-313-2665

Visit us on the Internet at www.arcadiapublishing.com

Dedicated to Lebanon schoolteachers B.J. Goodwin (English), and Paul Tauer (history). Yes, I was listening.

Contents

ACKNOWLEDGMENTS

I extend a heartfelt thanks to all Boonites near and far who helped with the compilation of this book, especially Jamey Hickson, Eric Spall, Phyllis Myers, the volunteers at Tri-Area Library, Cathy Hungate-Winteregg, Kathy and Patty Hedges, Rick Robertson, Steve Anderson, John Glendenning, Karen Seager-Everett, Becky Merritt, Susan Bennett, Joette Cross, Toby McClain, Tom Santelli, Dick Birge, Debbie Graham, the Coahran family, Ruth Everett, Kevin and Judy Thompkins Coon, Linda Mansfield, Gene Crucean, Rod Sutphin, the staff at Zionsville Bentley (especially Greg Albers), the Miller family, Brett Skipper, Sally Dickerson, Pandora Woodward, and Marcia Mustin. Also, thank you to Bob Guernsey for his extensive writing on the history of agriculture and 4-H in the county. Perhaps my deepest debt of gratitude goes to Ralph Stark for tending to every thread of each of Boone County's stories so lovingly with an unwavering enthusiasm over the years.

Sources consulted for this book include Hon. L.M. Crist's *History of Boone County Indiana* (1914), Samuel Harden and John Spahr's *Early Life and Times in Boone County, Indiana* (1887), and Toby McDaniel's *Honk if You're a Hoosier* (2001).

Unless otherwise noted, all images come from the Ralph W. Stark Heritage Center at the Lebanon Public Library.

INTRODUCTION

On January 29, 1830, the Indiana General Assembly passed an act for the formation of a new county north of already thriving Marion and Hendricks Counties. The county, which contained 423 square miles of swamp and ancient hardwood groves, was to be named in honor of frontiersman Daniel Boone and was ordered to be surveyed within the year.

Though many considered the newly chartered county untillable and thus unlivable, on April 1, 1830, Boone County was officially formed. Twelve townships were surveyed, with 20 sections of 80 acres each. Exceptions were Perry Township, which was smaller than the rest and had an oddly shaped border when platted, and Worth Township, which seemed to have been an oddly carved afterthought. Many residents of Indiana nicknamed the new county "Frog Land" or the "Hog Swamp;" some went so far as to call the newly surveyed area "The State of Boone"—rather than Boone County—to figuratively set it aside from the rest of verdant Indiana.

Upon the county's founding, census-takers counted just over 600 white and freedmen settlers. The new settlers joined an uncounted number of Lenape (or Delaware) people already residing on the land who had been trading with French furriers from Canada since the 1700s. Archaeological digs later conducted by Col. Eli Lilly and others revealed that people had made their homes in the area in times predating the arrival of Europeans to the New World. Artifacts such as Adena arrowheads (thought to be roughly 1,000 years old) have been excavated, as have Abasolo arrowheads dating back 5,000 years.

On June 7, 1830, representatives of the area met at the cabin of Austin Davenport in Eagle Township, where they elected Jamestown, located at the new county's southwestern edge, as the county seat. At the time, the village of Jamestown comprised a settlement of about a dozen cabins. Serving as the primary stagecoach stop between Indianapolis and Crawfordsville made Jamestown the most heavily populated place in Boone County.

Jamestown's reign as the county seat was short-lived. Two years after its designation, a state legislative act required that all cities serving as county seats had to be at or within two miles of the geographic center of the county. So, during the first week of May 1831, a survey party was formed to stake the center point of Boone County. A small hill surrounded by a ring of willow ponds was selected. The survey party then hastily laid out sections and blocks. A one-room log cabin on Lot 1, Block 16 became the first residence of the new county seat. The name of the new city came from Adam Miller French, the youngest member of the survey party. It is widely reported that French looked at all the towering hickory trees around him and was reminded of the biblical "cedars of Lebanon." Feeling inspired by the sight, he recommended Lebanon as the new city's name. However, it is rumored that he may instead have grown tired of the endless debate surrounding the team's last task; as a young man (about 26 at the time), he likely longed to finish the survey and head out of the mosquito-infested backwoods and back home to the comforts of civilization. If this is true, he may have offered this inspirational tale along with the name to speed things along. This alternative scenario is especially plausible since Lebanon happened to be the name of French's hometown in Ohio.

In anticipation of the state's first centennial, Leander Mead Crist wrote a remarkably comprehensive book in 1914. The 577-page account—*History of Boone County, Indiana: With biographical sketches of representative citizens and genealogical records of old families*—is an invaluable resource that gives a sweeping account of early life in the region. Filled with reported evidence of prehistoric peoples, land surveys, grants, and treaties, the book also recorded the surnames of settlers and their personal histories organized by township. Although much of the content was extracted from an 1887 work by Harden and Spahr (*Early Life and Times of Boone County Indiana*), Crist was a well-educated man, both a lawyer and a teacher, who knew the county well after serving as principal of Thorntown's high school for many years. After starting from the material Harden and Spahr had gathered and published as a compilation, Crist meticulously organized and verified the content while also adding considerable new information.

In 2016, Indiana celebrates its statehood bicentennial, and Boone County citizens are looking forward to their own 200-year anniversary as an official county. The estimated population has exploded to over 60,000 people who call the State of Boone home. Big-city neighbor Indianapolis has certainly grown, too, stretching to blur the line between Marion and Boone Counties. Despite the encroaching suburban creep, perhaps what continues to bind Boone County residents together in a sense of community is the unusually stable population. Though former residents may live and work across the globe, most of the original surnames recorded in 1830 still populate the county today.

Presented here amid some of the area's earliest photographs is an overview of Boone County from its most primitive years into more modern times. The first chapter seeks to illustrate the events that affected the lives of Boone County citizens during those hard pioneer times. In the second chapter, Boone County is shown struggling to establish towns and enough commerce to step out of the swamp and catch up with neighboring communities. Chapter three gives a sampling of those who are at rest in Boone County and takes a look at the somewhat controversial ways the dead have been memorialized or forgotten here. The fourth chapter ushers in a new wave of modern times. Businesses were booming, and advances in transportation, communication, and new fuels and machinery allowed all communities to make headway—which changed the lives of country and city folk alike. Chapter five examines what care means to the people of Boone County, with images representing a spectrum that ranges from serving the nation to caring for those at home who are frail or without family. The sixth chapter includes stories about Boone County's strong and varied agricultural heritage. Of course, hand in glove with farming, this section also touches on the farmer's constant struggle against Indiana weather when raising animals and/or crops. Chapter seven aims to stir musings and memories as schools, sports, and all the activities of youth are revisited. Chapter eight showcases the celebrations that Boone County cannot resist, from Independence Day festivities to 4H fairs, festivals, centennial celebrations, and courthouse crowds gathering to watch the laying of cornerstones. Clearly, celebrating has been a time-honored high priority for Boone County residents. The ninth and final chapter is all about being famous. Fame is a broad term in the State of Boone. Some people and businesses here are known only to those who have spent time in the area; others are known around the globe. Either way, each of them makes Boone County proud, and each is a part of the history that makes Boone County a great place to live.

One

The Pioneer Years

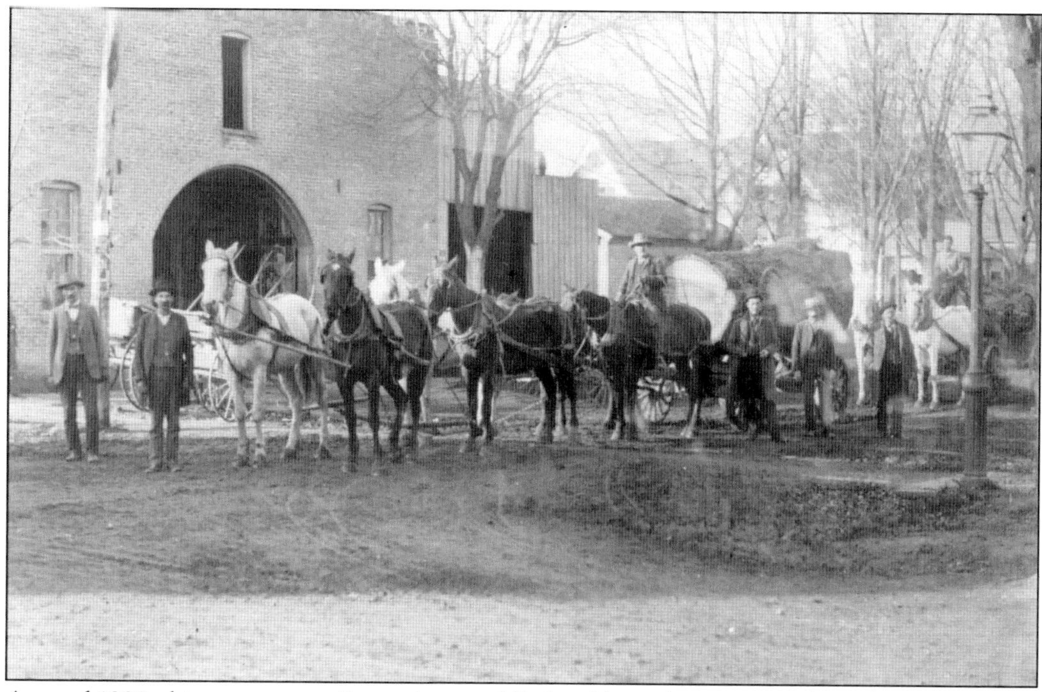

Around 1888, this enormous tulip poplar was felled and brought into town for milling into usable lumber. The *Lebanon Pioneer* reported in 1873 that a similar poplar tree, 33 feet in circumference, was taken down at the Jackson township farm of William Coombs. The *Patriot* newspaper told of another ancient tree—a sycamore from Chauncy Canine's property in Washington Township—presented in 1902 at A.N. Holloway's mill. These may have been the last few giant trees felled in the area.

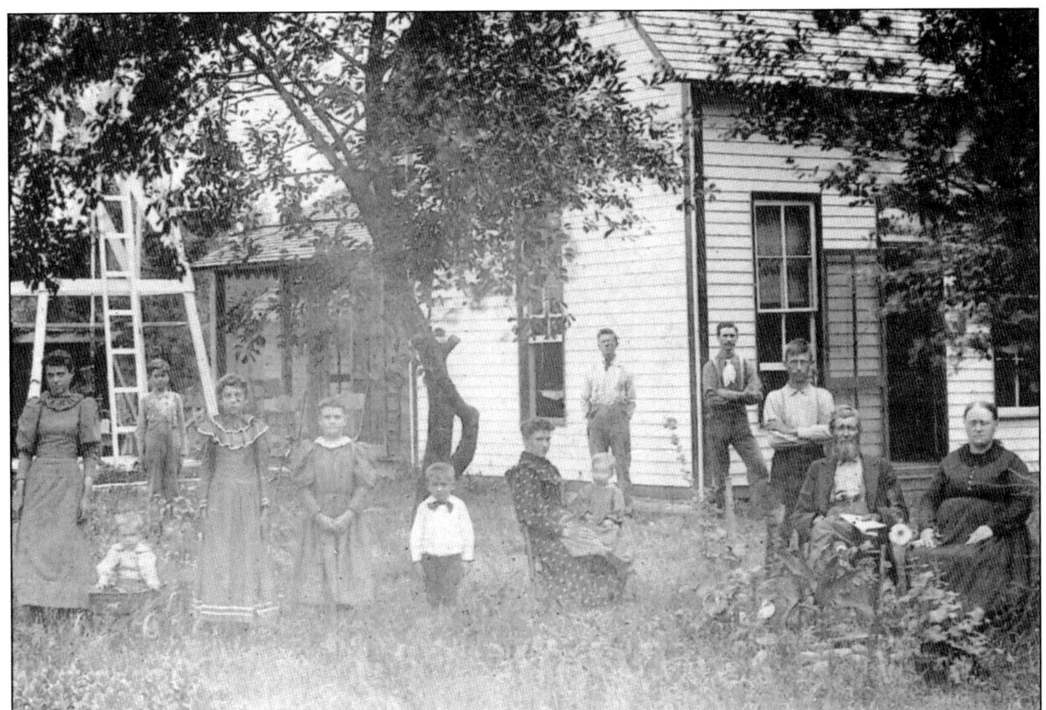

Silvester and Elizabeth Robertson came to Harrison Township in 1858. There, he built a log cabin and eventually this fine house. While teaching in a nearby one-room schoolhouse, he acquired 100 acres, enabling him to both farm and establish a field tile factory. Drainage tiles were in high demand. Eventually, Silvester built the two-story home shown in this 1894 photograph of his family, likely taken after services at New Brunswick Church of Christ. Six generations later, the farm is still owned by Silvester's family. (Rick Robertson.)

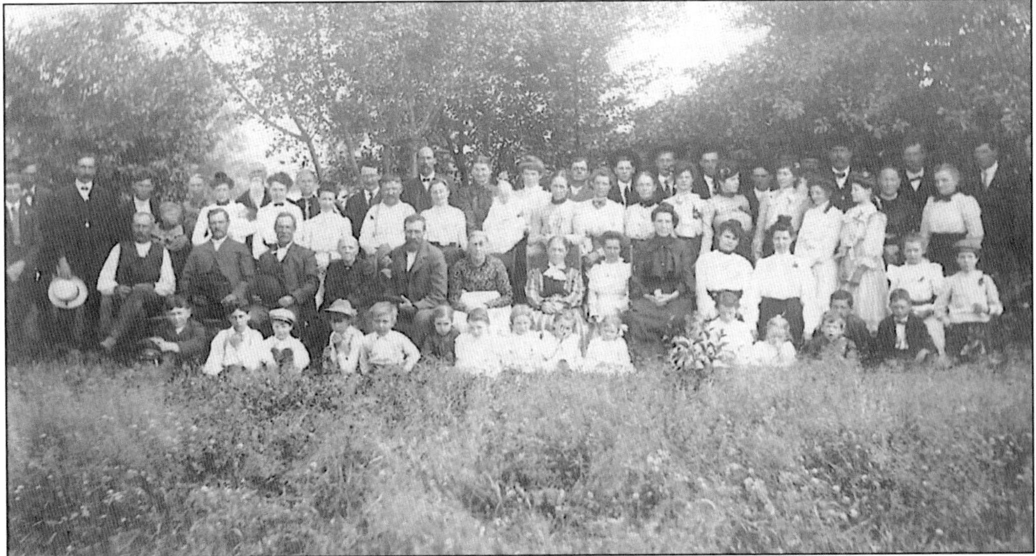

Despite the constant hardships of pioneer life, this 1909 photograph shows English immigrant and early settler Susan White Everett (second row, fourth from the left) at age 84. She is surrounded by more than 60 of her American-born descendants. (Everett family.)

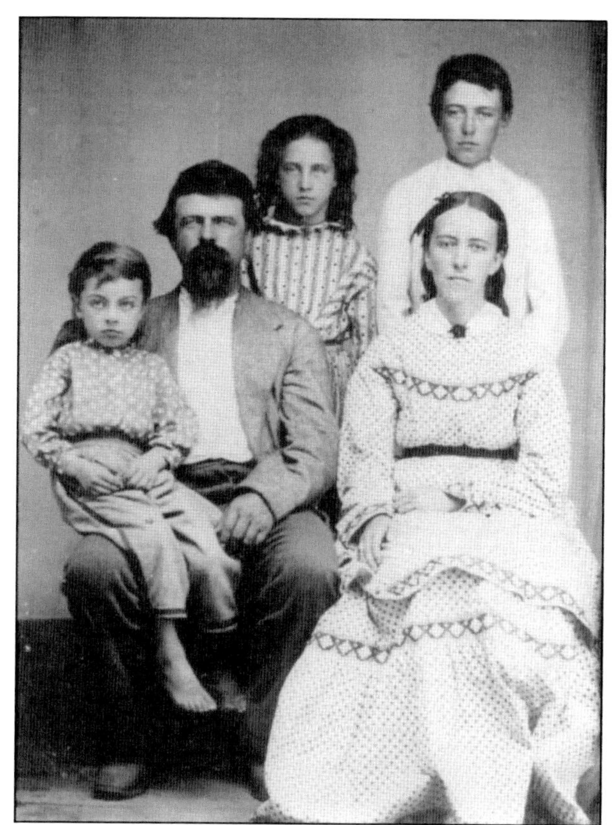

This 1870 photograph shows pioneers John and Jane Edwards with their young family. Listed among the first settlers in the Whitelick area, the Edwards family lived a life of ceaseless work, rarely seeing others in the early years except at church services provided by circuit-riding preachers who led services about once per month, usually at a farmhouse. (Everett family)

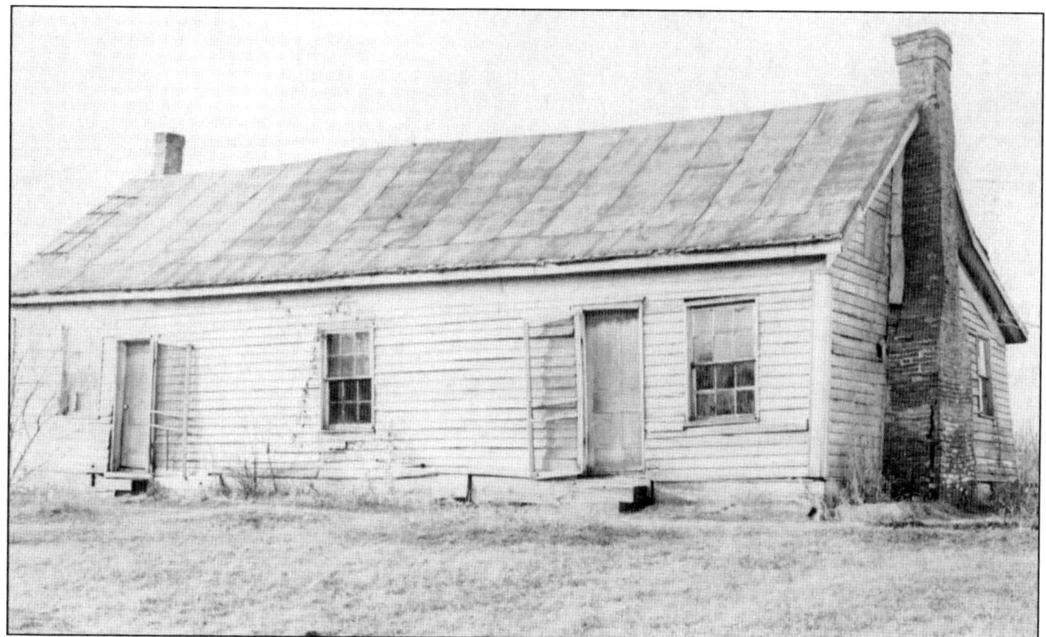

Isaac Leap's cabin was typical of those built in Boone County. Though his home seems quite modest, he owned 80 acres and also kept a store at nearby Rosston. He also served as a Baptist minister. Leap's 1837 land grant title was signed by Pres. Martin Van Buren.

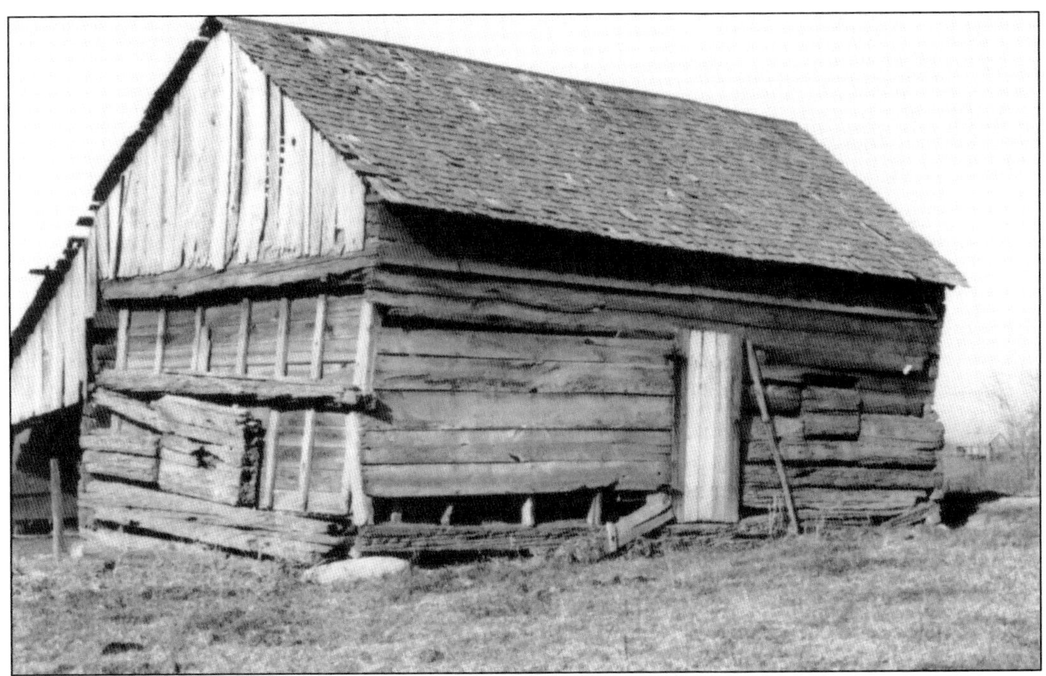

The Charles Schooler cabin (in use at the time of this 1966 photograph as a farmer's outbuilding) was a sturdy log structure built about two miles south of Whitestown. The Schooler family settled here in the early 1830s. Part of their property contained three low spots used by bison as wallows. The buffalo would go to these swampy depressions to roll in mud to deter flies and other insects.

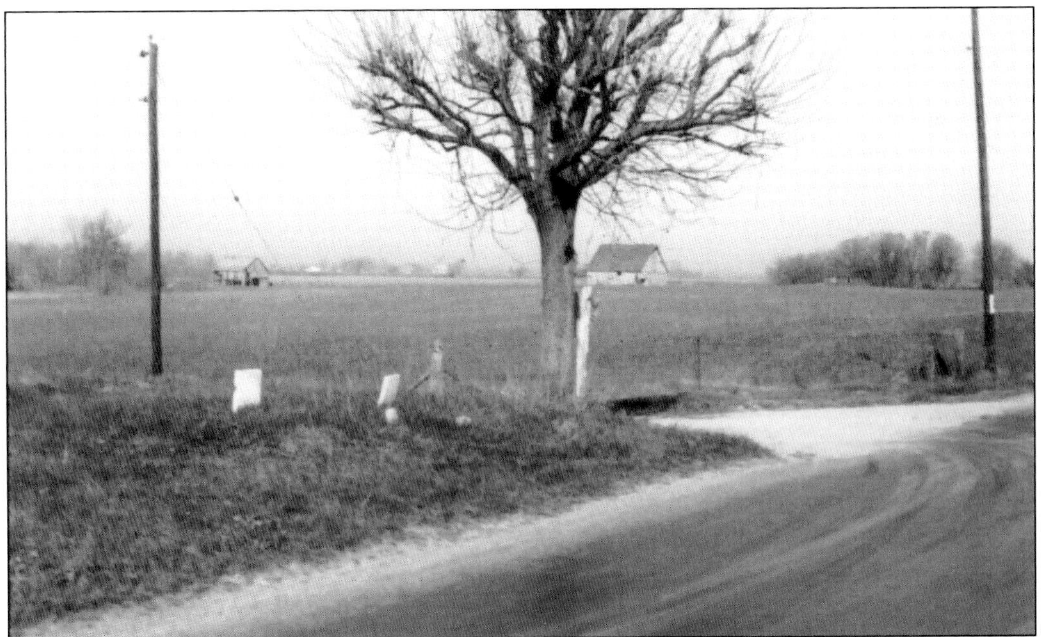

At the corner of the Schooler property, a 28-square-foot plot was reserved for family burials. Only three markers remain in the unfenced cemetery. The oldest one belongs to the Schoolers' young son Andrew, who died in 1839 at eight months of age.

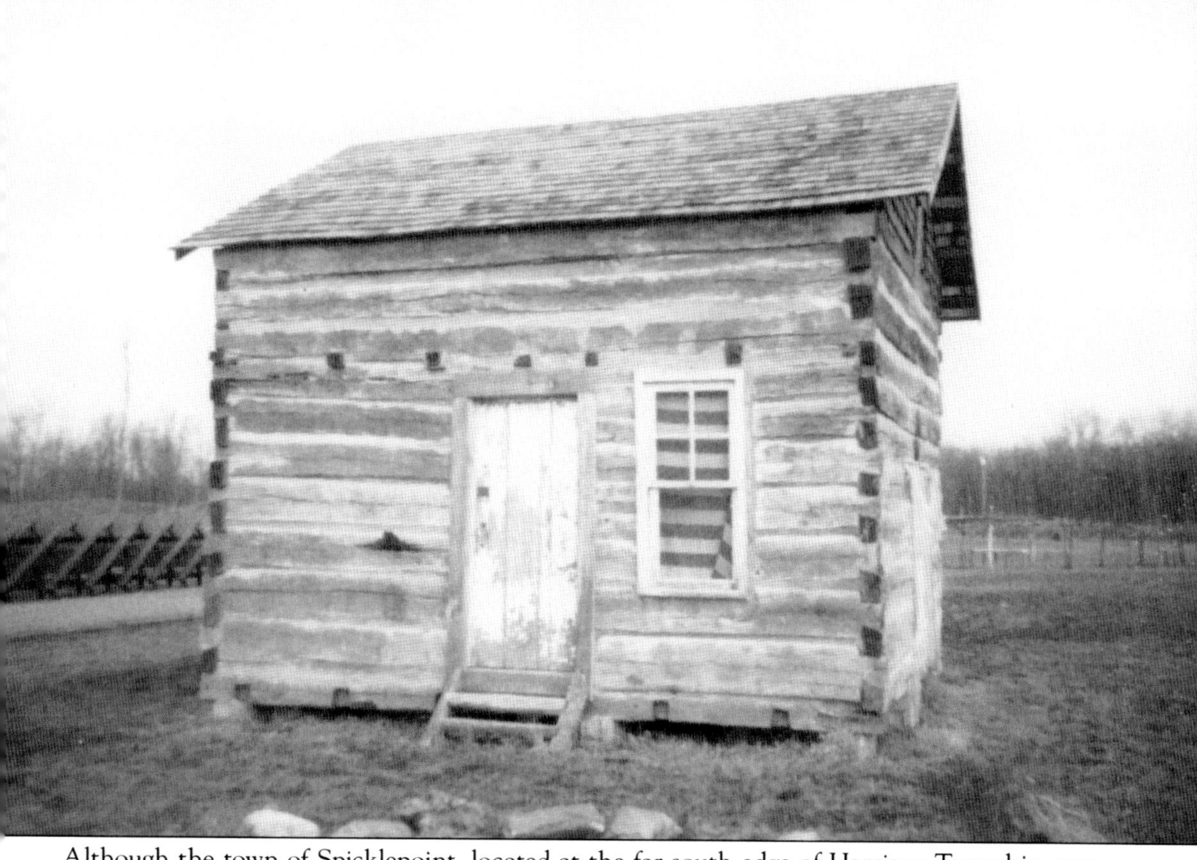

Although the town of Spicklepoint, located at the far south edge of Harrison Township, was only a cornfield and vague memory after about 1905, it once was home to a store, a schoolhouse, three residences, two doctors' offices (Dr. Parrish and Dr. Stevens), and a sawmill and corn-grinding operation. When the tiny town was "discontinued," this one-room cabin—built in 1834 by James Logan, and which once housed the Acton family and their nine children for an entire winter)—was moved and used as part of a much larger home. When that home was razed in the 1970s, the cabin was rediscovered in a well preserved state. The Society for the Preservation of Our Indian Heritage carefully removed it and reassembled it on the grounds of Old Mill Run Park for display.

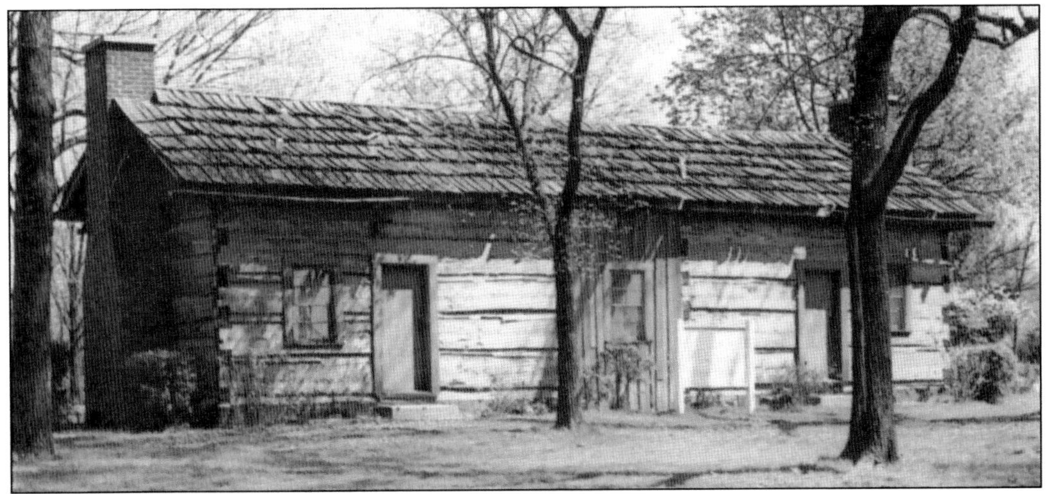

This substantially larger log cabin was built north of James Logan's cabin by the Herr family in Perry Township. Many settlers from neighboring Hendricks County followed an old trail, known as Buzzard's Trail, into Boone County. The path was used by Indians who traded with William Conner's post along the White River in Hamilton County. Wildlife also used the path to travel through the heavily swamped and forested area. The cabin was gifted to the James Hill chapter of the Daughters of the American Revolution (DAR) in 1937 and moved to Memorial Park in Lebanon, where it is maintained as a historic site and rented out for private events.

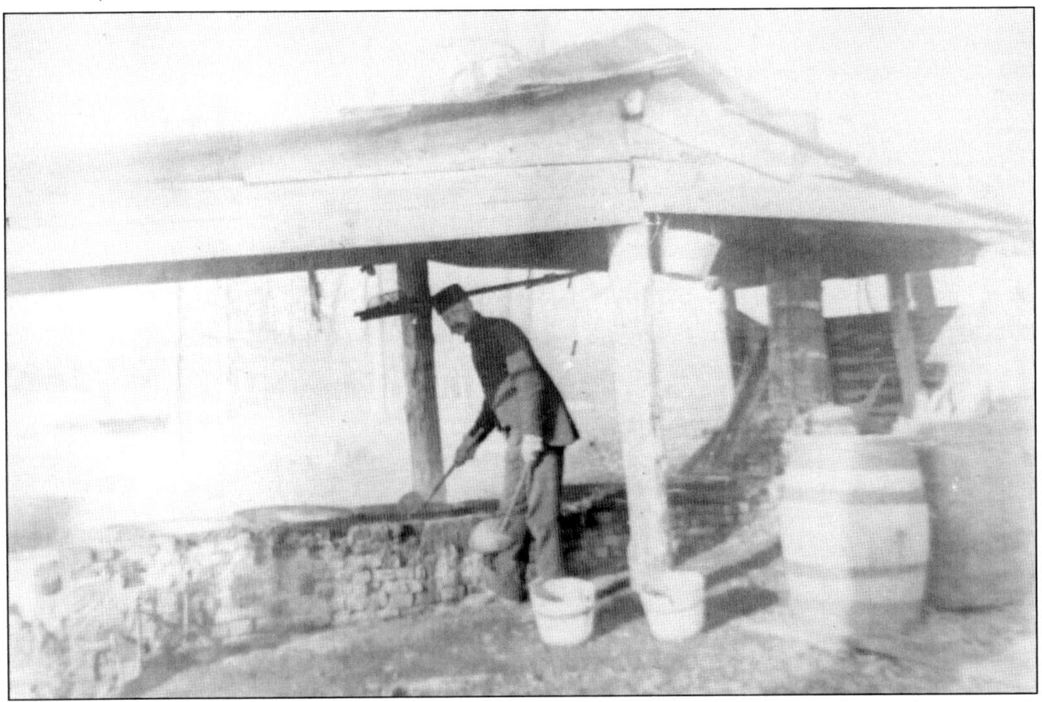

This c. 1880 photograph shows Theodore (Dora) Caldwell working in the sugar camp he ran each spring. Caldwell collected sap from the many maple trees on his property along Sugar Creek, near Brown's Wonder. He produced about 100 gallons of maple syrup each season. Another famous sugar camp, called Uncle Johnny's, was near Whitestown at the current site of the Whitestown Lions Club Park.

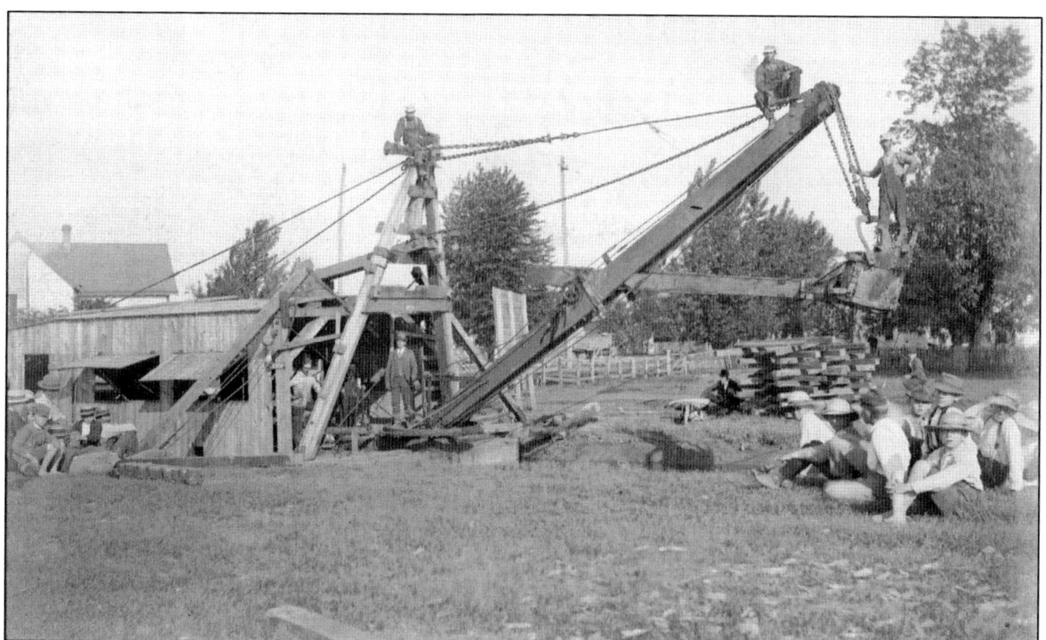

In 1904, this large dredging sled attracted a daily crowd of onlookers at Lebanon's Prairie Creek. Until the creek was dredged, rerouting much of the waterlogged drainage areas, "swamp rattlers" (Massasauga rattlesnakes) were a constant threat. The deadly reptiles found a safe haven and endless food supplies in the chicken houses and grain bins of the damp county's farmland. Men baling hay to store for winter livestock feed were always on the lookout for "snake bales." When the last of the drainage problem areas was remedied, the rattler population died off.

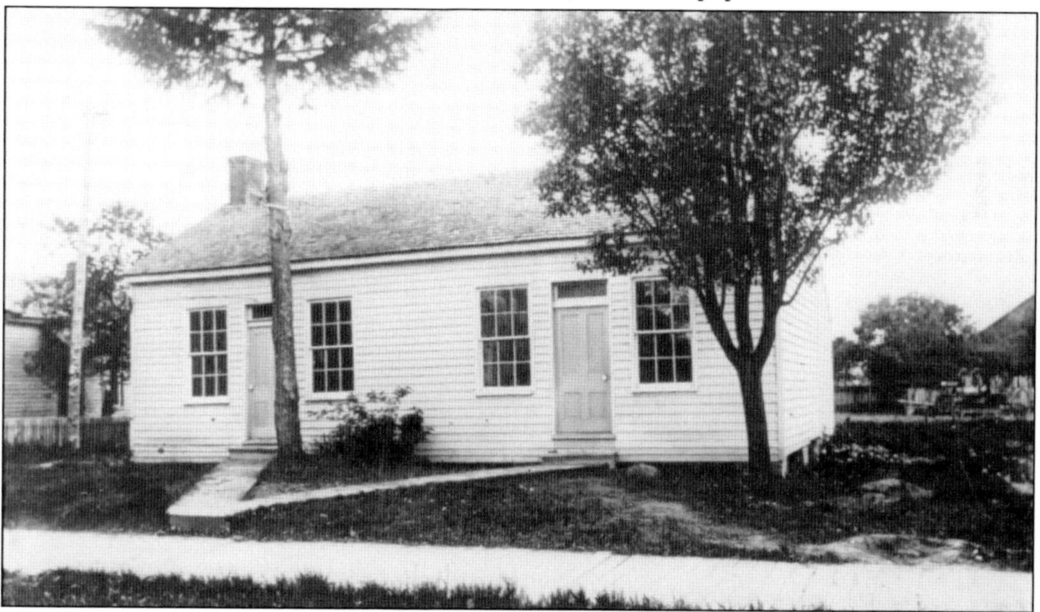

This c. 1890 photograph shows the early Lebanon City Building, which was constructed as a home in 1839. The city added a barn and additional rooms for the fire department. The simple, wood-frame structure served the county seat until it was replaced with a larger, brick building in 1903. Note the wooden sidewalk in the foreground.

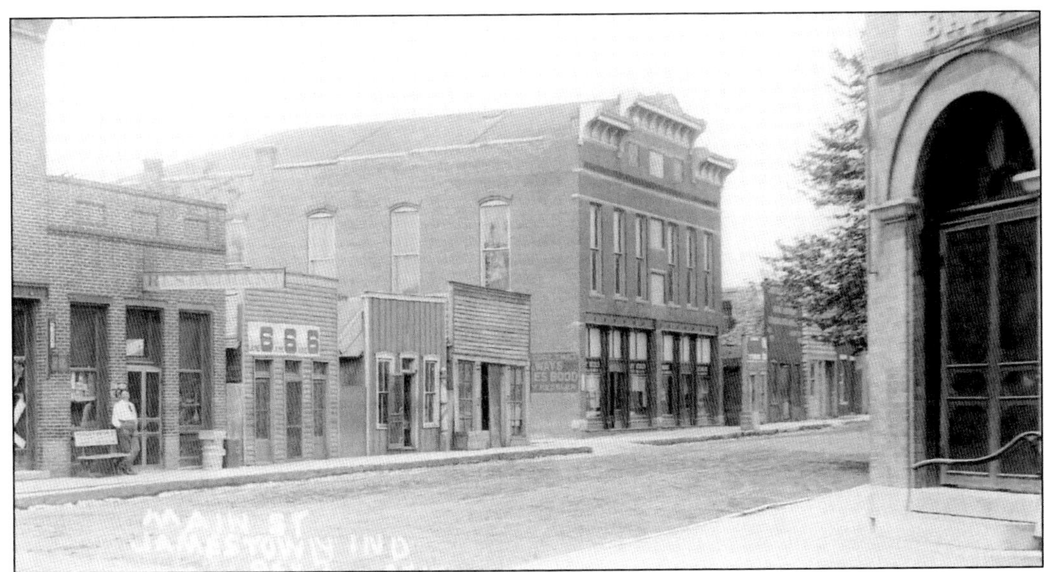

John Gipson and James Matlock laid out a 16-lot town for a new settlement along the stagecoach route from Indianapolis to Crawfordsville. Gipson had purchased 80 acres in the area in 1828. The two flipped a coin to decide who would name the new town. Matlock, having won the toss, immediately pronounced it to be Jamestown. Locals often use the more familiar name of "Jimtown," to the confusion of those new to the area. In the 1920s, banners lined Main Street commemorating the town's not-to-be forgotten distinction: "Jamestown, Boone's First County Seat." (Tri-Area Library History Vault.)

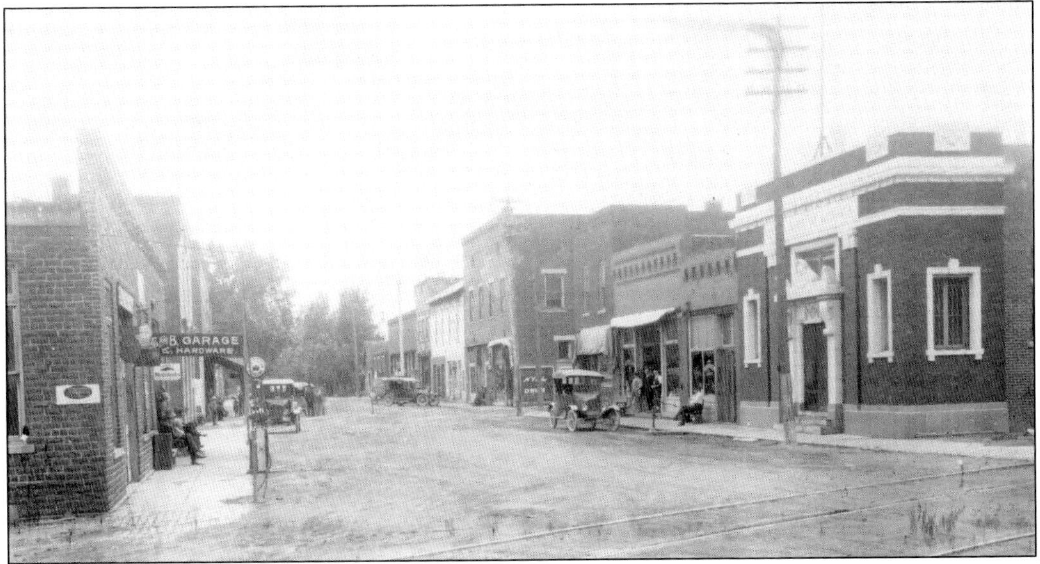

The town originally named Osceola—but changed to Advance, perhaps due to great hopes of economic gains from the coming railroad station—was once home to a mineral spring. This scene shows the old downtown around 1918, when Red Harlis and Oty Walls used to drive sheep up and down Main Street to switch pastures on a regular schedule. Advance has hit hard times, but, true to its name, is struggling to go forward. The abandoned bank building at right is now a community library. The general store houses Boone County Uniques, a thriving antiques business. The railroad tracks are visible in the foreground.

Groves of thorn-covered honey locust trees once blanketed the area where Thorntown was settled. There are several versions of how the town got its name. In the second volume of *Boone Magazine*, published in March 1974, Ralph Stark tells of a beautiful Indian maiden courted by two competing young warriors. When the two men fought to the death, the maiden was so distraught she pierced her own heart with a deadly honey locust thorn, then died from the self-inflicted wound and the grief of heartbreak. (Author's collection.)

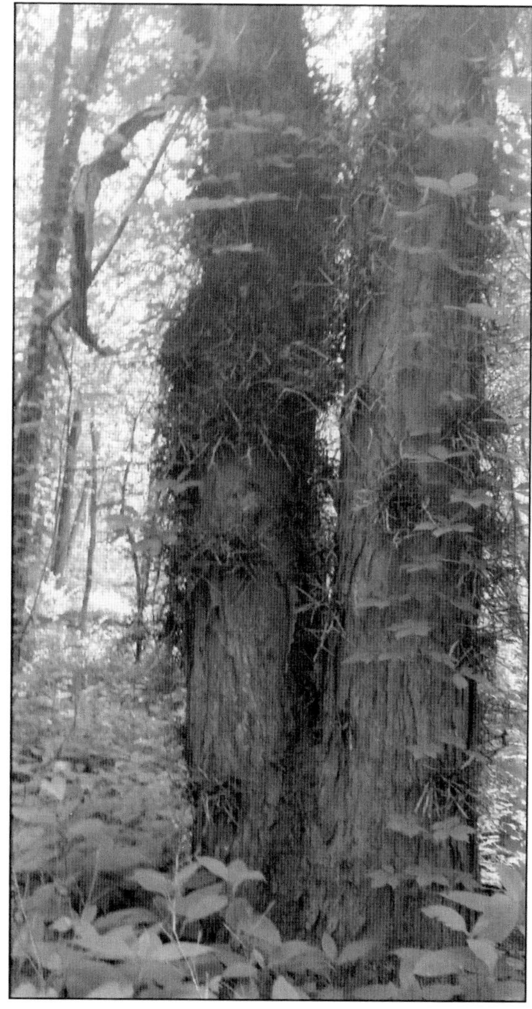

In 1852, telegraph lines and the Indianapolis, Cincinnati & Lafayette Railroad came to Boone County. Also that year, Henry Hill launched a weekly newspaper called *The Lebanon Pioneer.* Two prominent citizens of the day also happened to be heavy promoters of the new railway. William Zion immediately laid out sections for the sale of building lots and a station stop on property he owned in Eagle Township, naming the development Zionsville after himself. The old depot, shown here around 1900, was removed in 1921. Meanwhile, fellow railroad stockholder Harvey Hazelrigg laid out a similar new station at the corner of his farm in the north section of the county. Hazelrigg Station was well positioned between Lafayette and Indianapolis and provided lumber and water to fuel the steam engines.

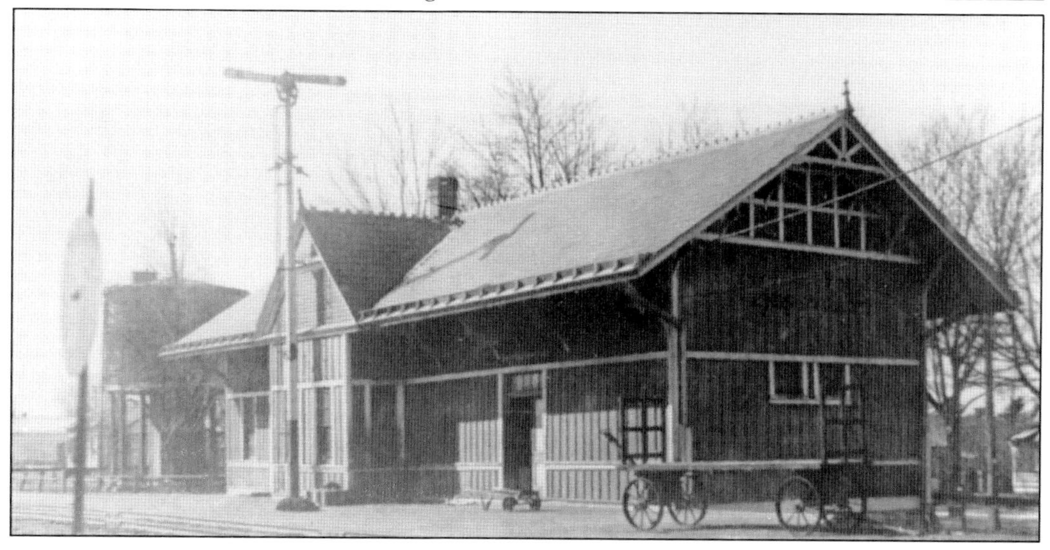

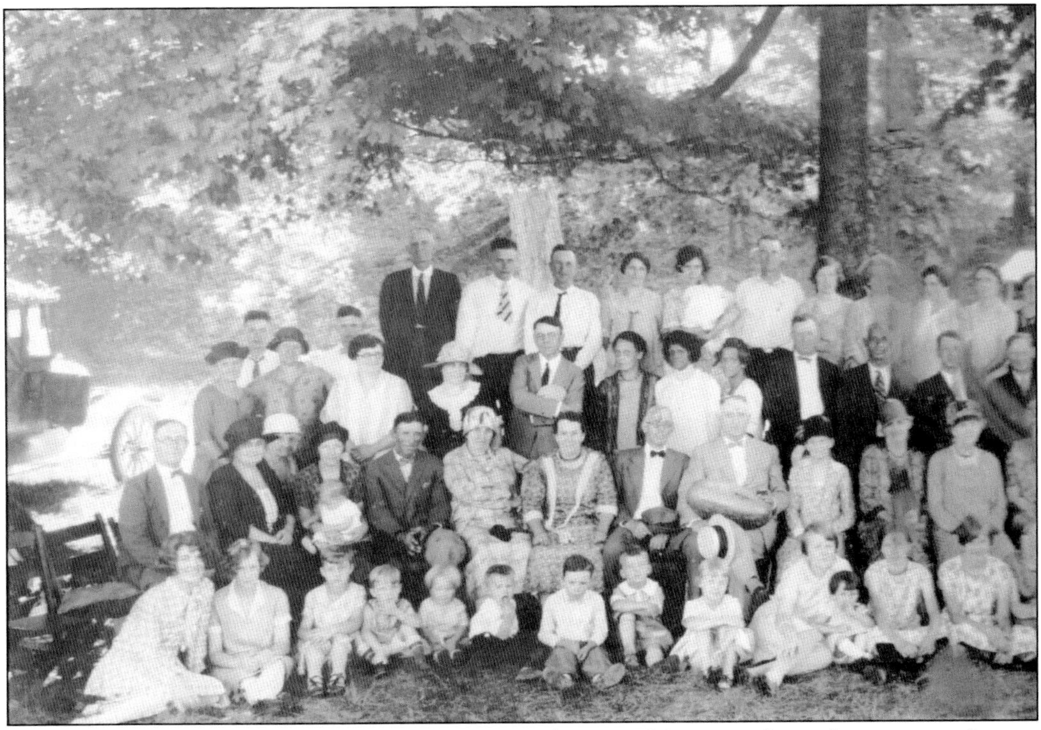

Boone County had a diverse population in its early years. Many attribute this to several areas being settled by generally liberal and accepting Quakers. This photograph from an unidentified church picnic near Thorntown shows individuals with white, black, Native American, and mixed heritages enjoying an afternoon together. (Thorntown History Museum.)

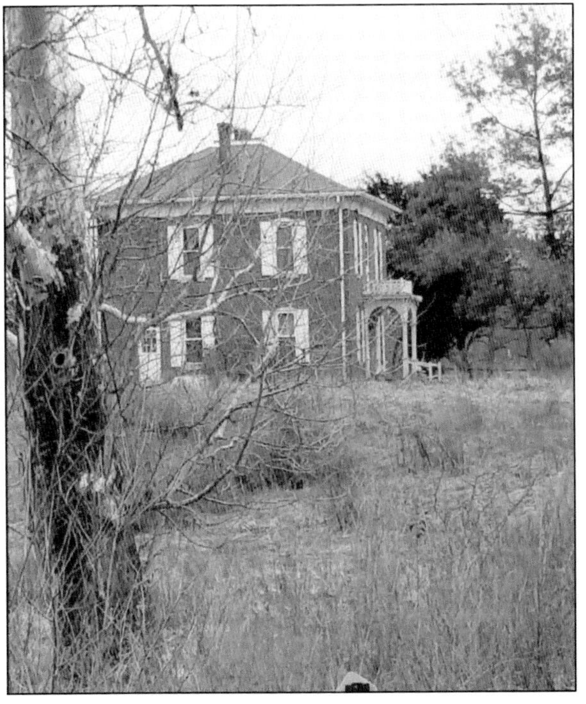

The brick Caldwell family home is pictured here in the 1880s. An earlier version of the house was at the center of some excitement in the 1850s. The father of neighbor Edward Shepard came to Alexander Caldwell's home one afternoon ill and needing help crossing through the heavily wooded half-mile between the Caldwell homestead and the Shepard property on nearby Lost Road. Caldwell's oldest son, Alvin, was sent along to help the man. The next day, two of the Caldwell daughters, Maranda and Armilda, crossed the woods, tending to the elderly Shepard until he died just before midnight. Upon returning home, the Caldwell sisters told their father that the younger Shepard was also quite ill. (Author's collection.)

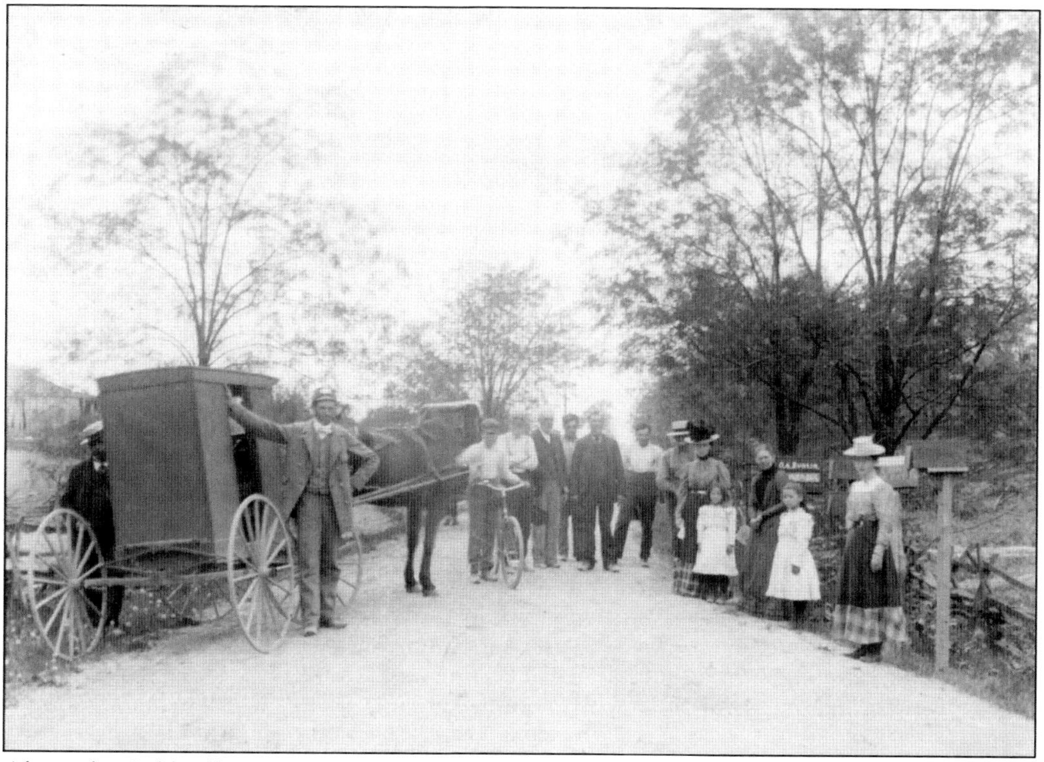

Alexander Caldwell sent word to Mechanicsburg ordering a casket and a grave digger for the deceased. Gathering the aid of his brothers, he then rushed to the Shepard homestead, sending Mrs. Shepherd and her children away from the house as he cared for Edward. By morning, doctors had diagnosed the ailment as cholera, and panic ensued. Onlookers gathered at the roadside, holding their noses to avoid breathing in the deadly "vapors." This photograph was taken near the site about 50 years later.

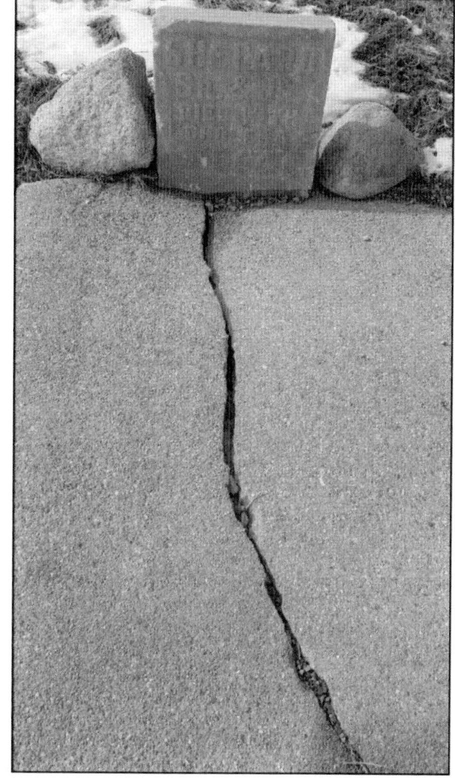

When Edward Shepard died, the exhausted Caldwell brothers went home to rest. In a panic over transferring the two deceased men, the roadside onlookers hastily dug a wide grave. Finally, William Hopkins volunteered to go into the home and carry out one Shepard man in the coffin and the other in its shipping box. Both father and son were hastily buried at the roadside. Modern reviews of the case indicate that the two likely died of ptomaine poisoning (a deadly though noncontagious food-borne illness). The grave marker reads "Shepard, Sr. & Jr., died with Cholera, 1854." The accuracy of the date on the stone is debatable.

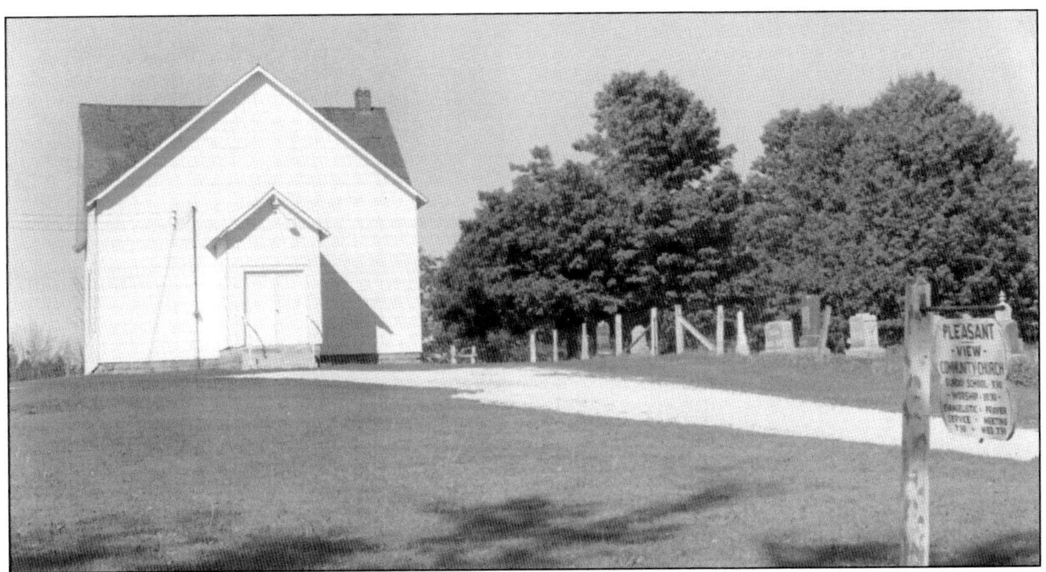

Pleasant View Community Church was formed in 1860 in the area near Eagle Creek and the old John Shelburne farm. Before then, the only convenient Sunday services were held at Hard Shell Baptist Church and officiated by Noah Gifford, an area farmer who did not believe in Sunday school or musical instruments; Gifford preached predestination sermons with frightfully depressing themes. After one springtime sermon in which Gifford spoke of places in hell filled with "infants not a span high," most folks had reached their limit. Led by church members Washington St. Clair and George Dodson, some of the congregation funded and erected a new church. Perhaps holding a more optimistic view on reaching the kingdom of heaven, the new church was named Pleasant View. In an odd twist, 113 years later, Pleasant View was discontinued and removed via deliberate burning. Gifford is not, of course, in the adjoining cemetery.

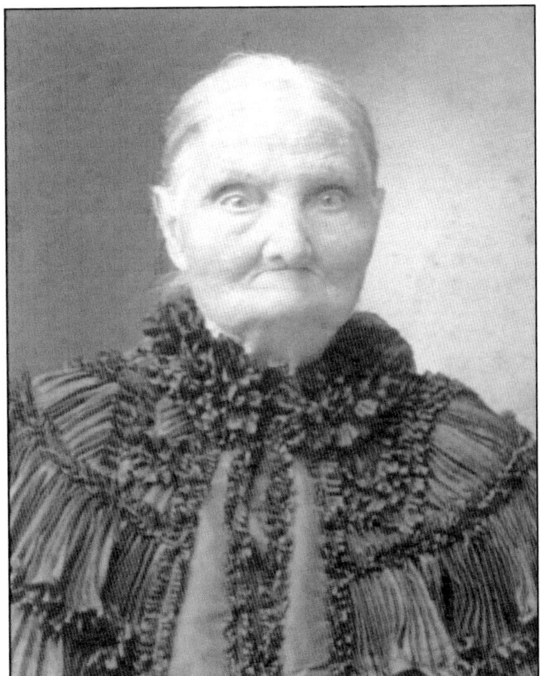

As reported by county newspapers, Sarah Powell McCann earned the title of "oldest in the county" during the 1912 Fourth of July celebrations. That year, she was 92; she lived to be almost 97.

Two

Out of the Swamp

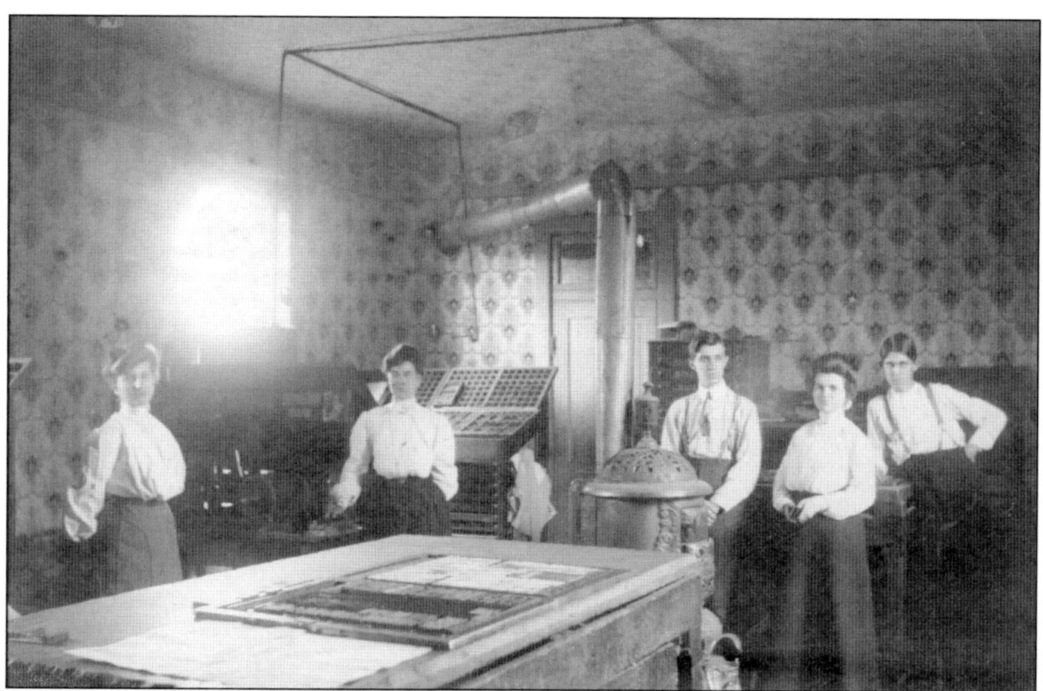

The *Lebanon Reporter* opened shop in 1891. This is the composition room of the newspaper as it appeared around 1900. Some competitors of note were *The Patriot* (founded in 1866), *Advance Hustler* (1899), *Jamestown Press* (1894), *Boone County Pioneer* (1852), *Thorntown Argus* (1881), *Whitestown Enterprise* (1894), and the *Zionsville News* (1870). Only the *Lebanon Reporter* remains in operation today.

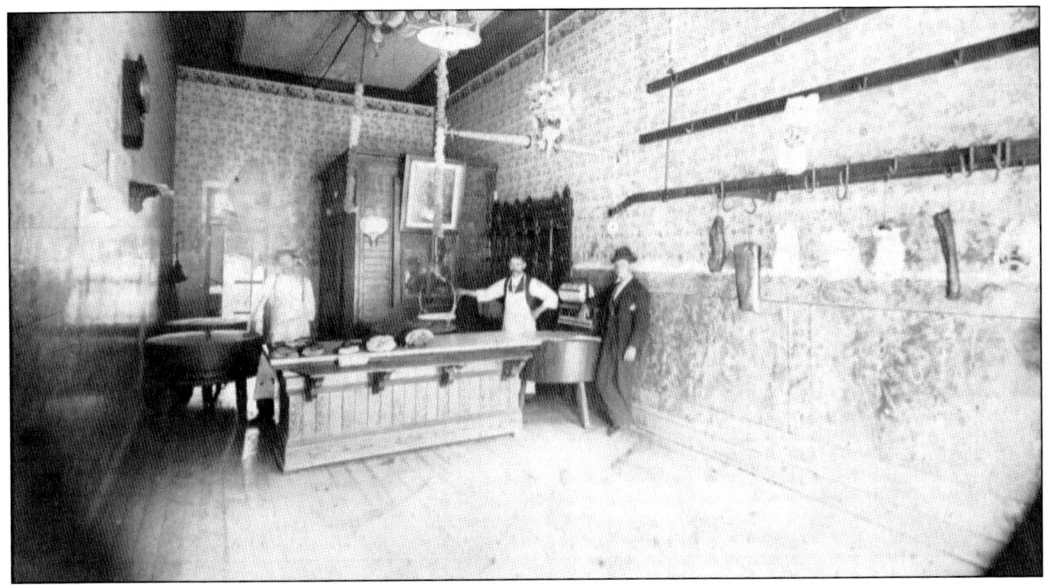

By modern standards, the interior of the Overleese butcher shop, pictured in 1897, does not look very appetizing. The three men in the photograph are brothers—Andy (left) and Dora (center) were butchers at the shop, and Otus was employed elsewhere.

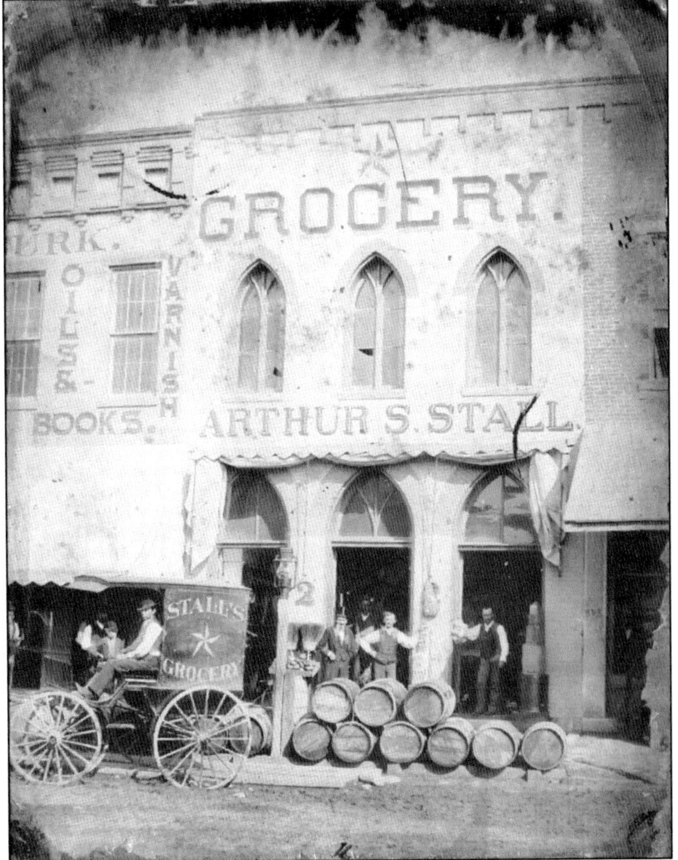

This photograph of Arthur St. Clair Stall's general store and post office in Thorntown is thought to be from its earliest days of operation. Stall and his wife, Elizabeth, moved from neighboring Clinton County in 1865. The new store was stocked with a modern assortment of items essential to daily life. (Thorntown History Museum.)

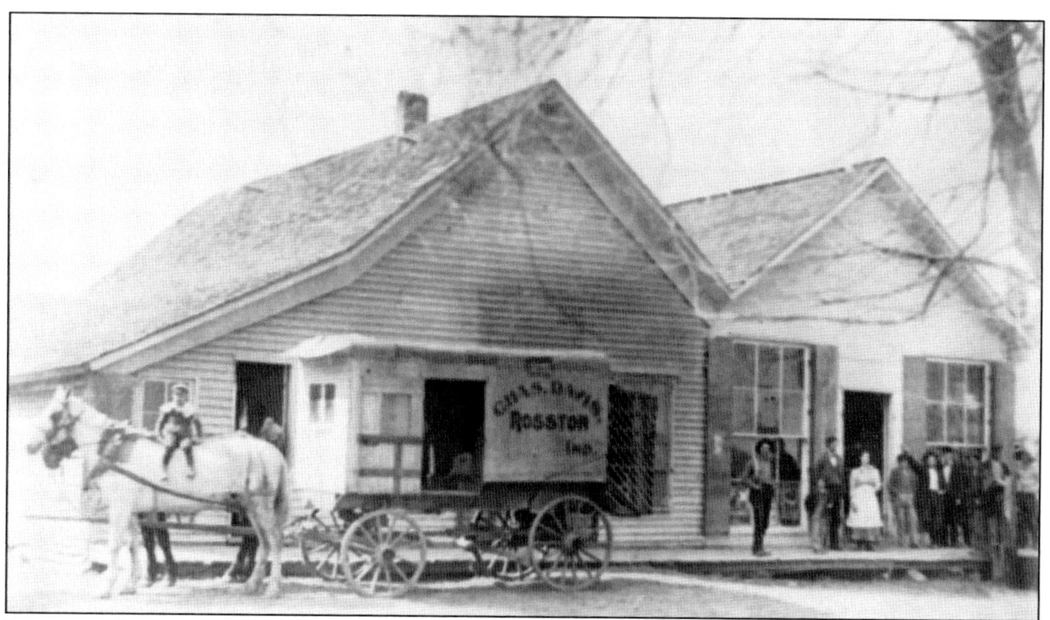

Most small towns had at least one of four things to center them as a settlement: a church, a general store, a mill, or a postmaster's office. Charles Davis ran his Rosston store for many years with a small corner set aside for postal business. He also had a "huckster" wagon that delivered his goods to people beyond village limits.

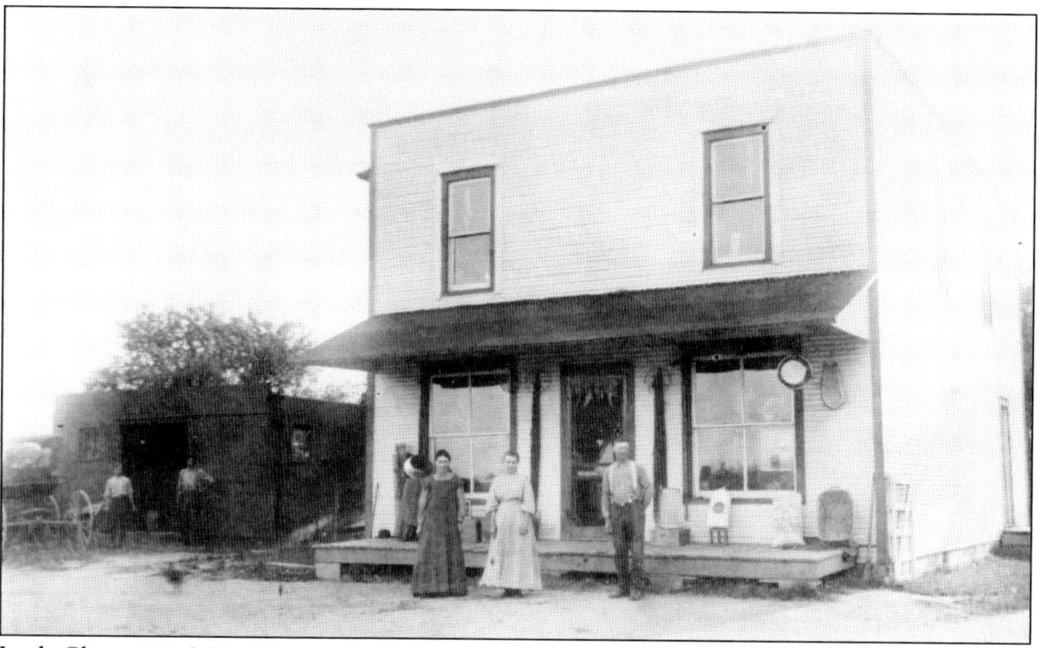

Little Chicago, in Marion Township about two miles southeast of Elizaville, was home to the James French General Store. Town boundaries blurred with other areas and names such as Swampdoodle, Dot, Center, and Buzzard's Roost. Of these, only Dot was briefly awarded designation as a postal stop. Eventually, French left Little Chicago and bought a shoe store on the courthouse square in Lebanon. Shown here in front of French's store in 1896 are, from left to right, Mrs. Albert Murray and Frannie and James French.

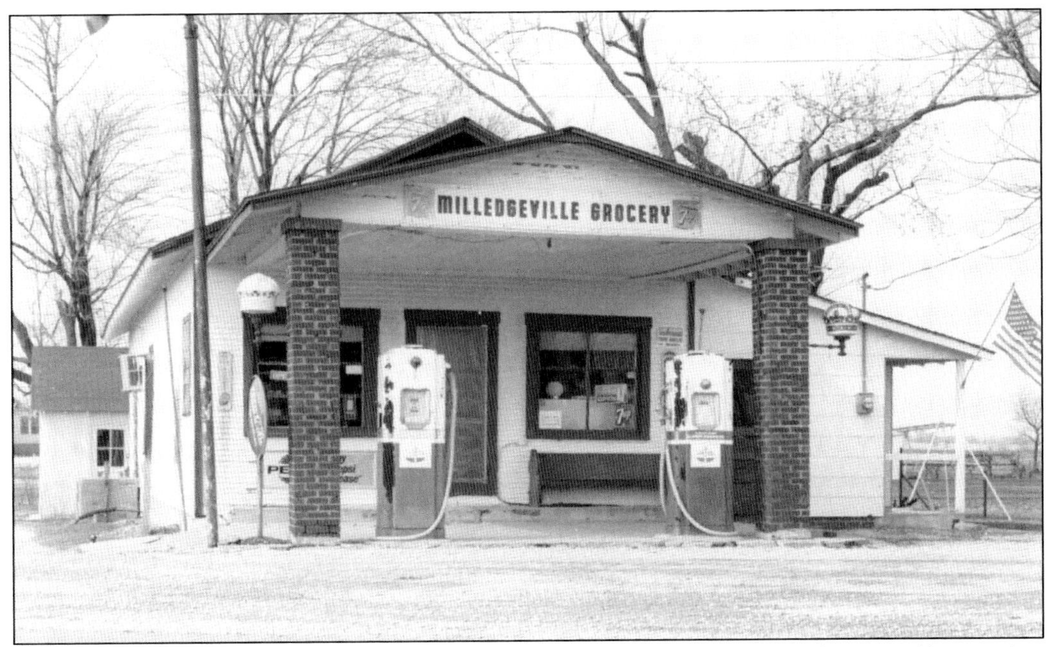

Milledgeville had a general store, a church, several homes, and at least one doctor's office. Today, only the general store building stands perfectly preserved, with the small church behind it. Since the store was located on the Pittsboro and Lebanon Road, traffic gave it an ample supply of customers. Most of the businesses disappeared or were abandoned once Interstates 65 and 74 were built in the 1960s, routing travelers away from this winding stretch of county highway.

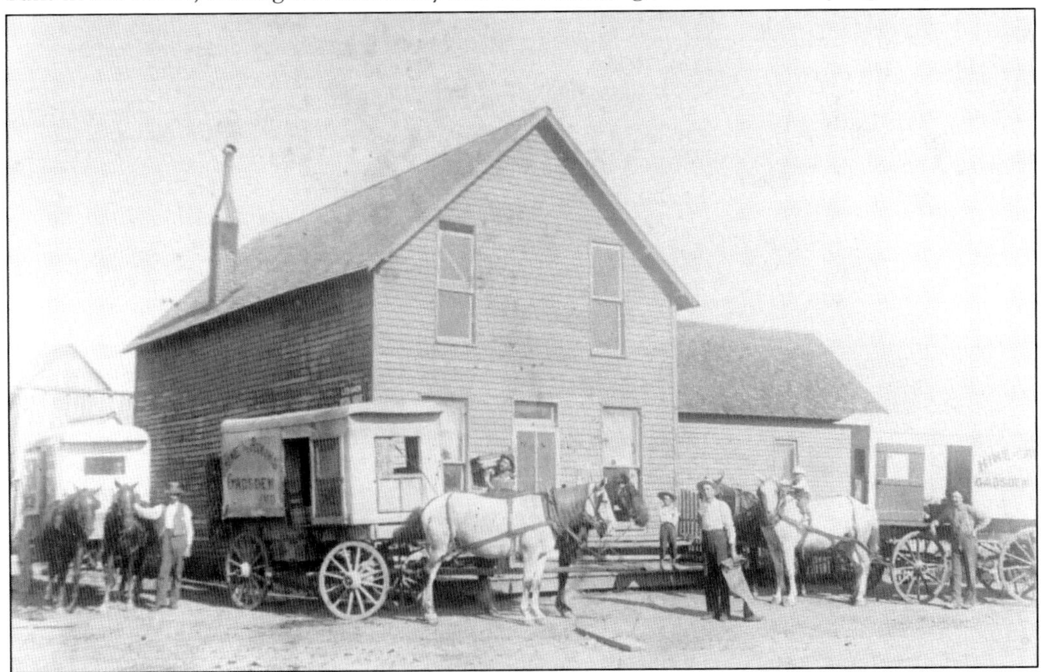

The Gadsden General Store, owned by William J. Hine and Samuel T. Atkins, is pictured here in 1896 as they load up a huckster with goods to take out on a daily route. Nearby are the orchards and greenhouses of the Buren Jones family.

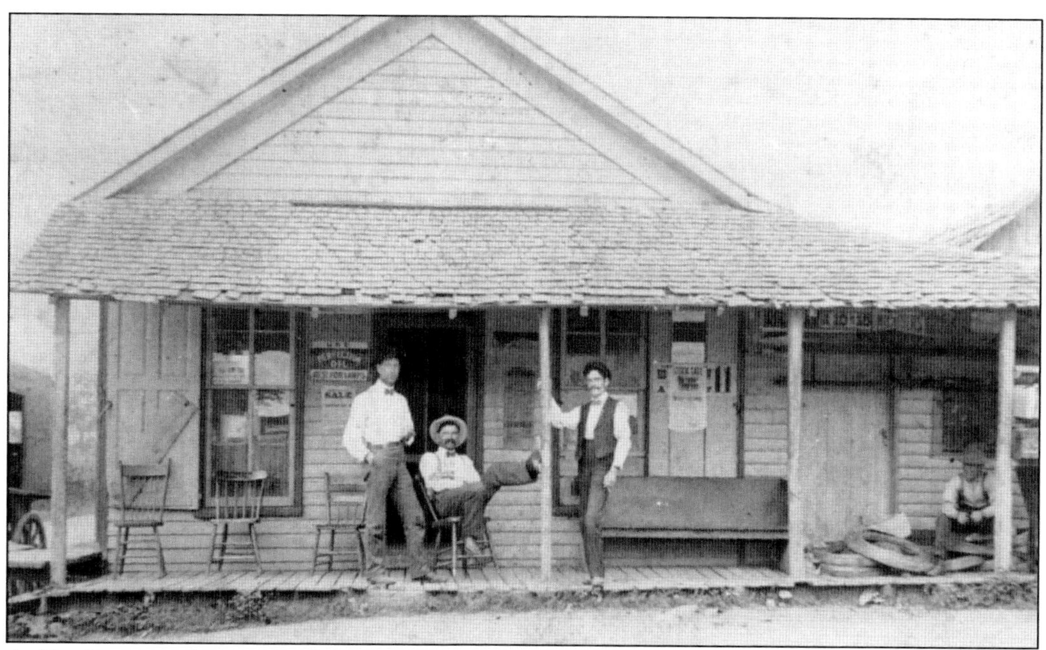

At Big Springs, the porch of the Ed Fowler Store seemed to attract loafers. Men often gathered at community stores to gossip, play cards, or discuss news.

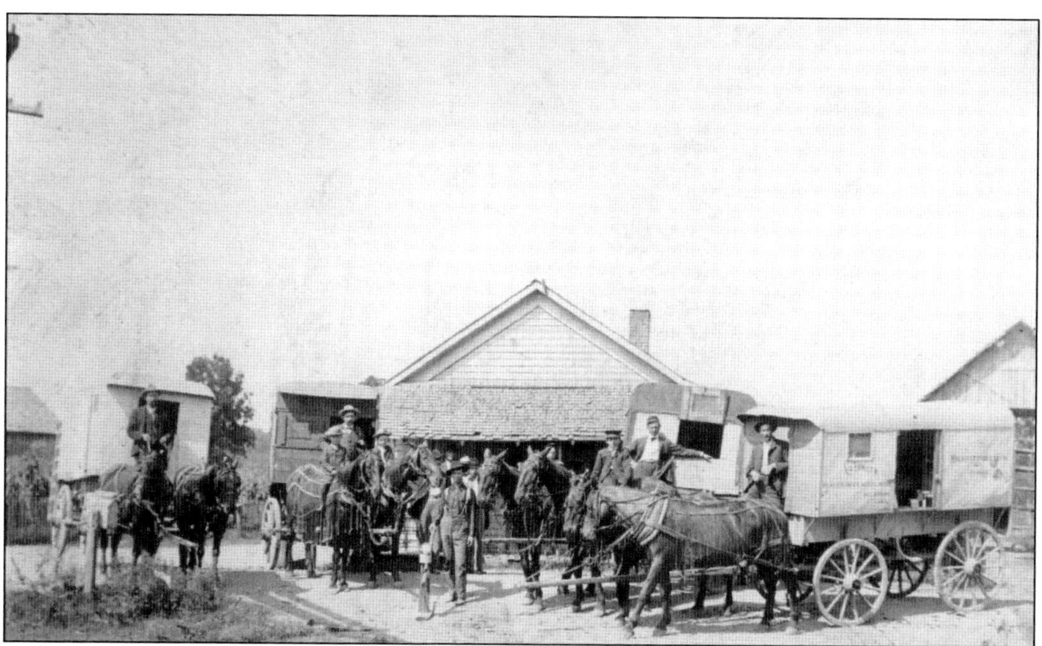

Ed Fowler ran several huckster trucks. Perhaps the loafers pictured here were just resting between loading wagons.

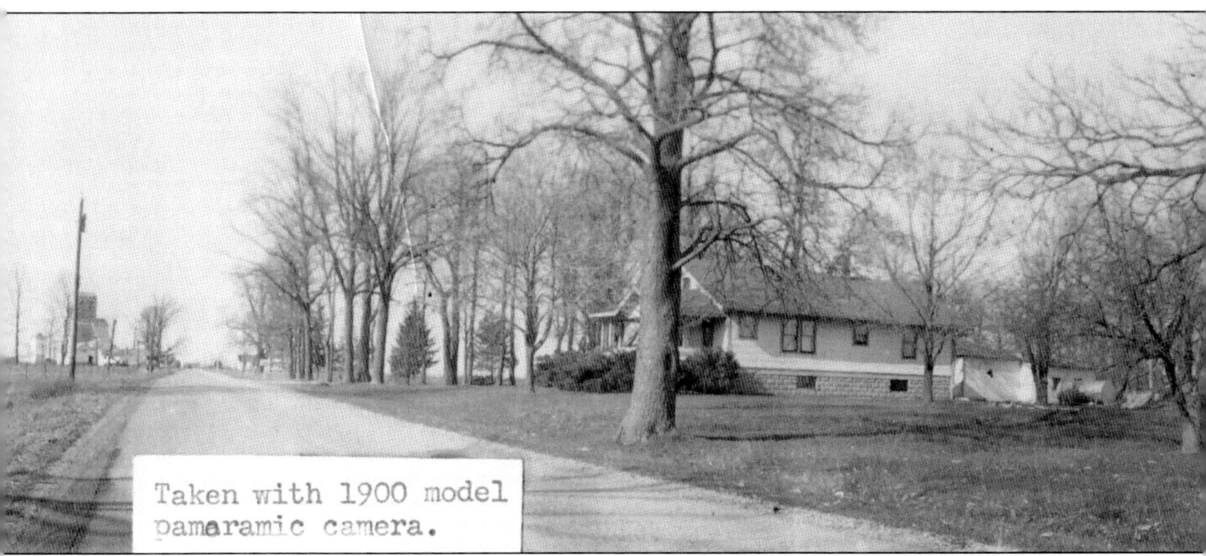

The small village of Shepherdsville was granted a post office in 1886 under the abbreviated name of Shepherd. Brothers Henry, John, Samuel, and James Glendenning had a grocery store there. Henry also served as the postmaster. The brothers operated a huckster wagon, taking turns traveling in pairs to drive the weeklong routes. They bought and sold goods while handling mail and delivering news. Although nothing marks the existence of Shepherdsville, a neighboring burg with an elevator and train stop, Herr, is within sight and is still noted on road maps.

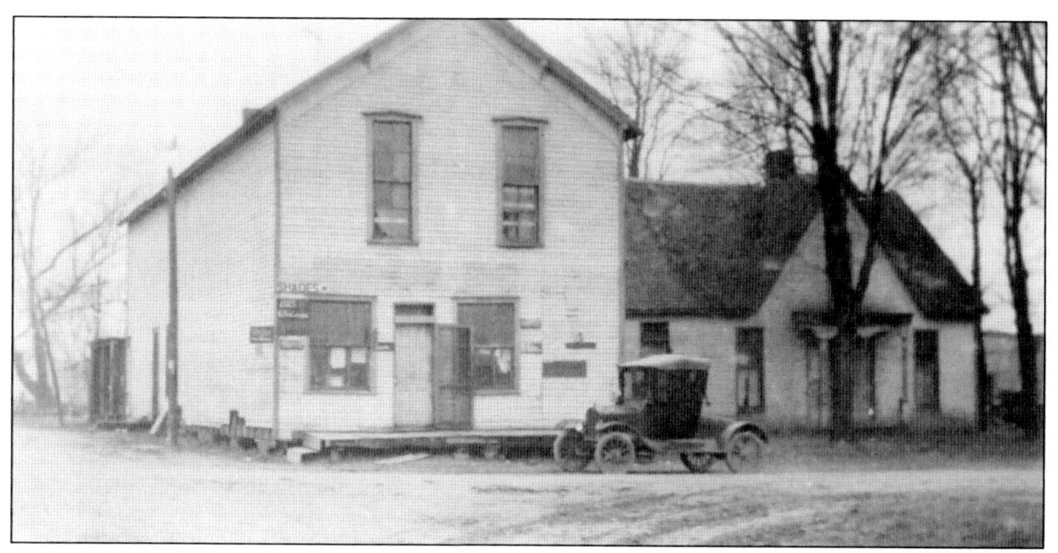

Dover—also at times known as Crackaway, Scarce, and Cason—was the location of this store owned by the Bennington family in 1918. It is unknown when it was originally built. By 1939, John and Laura Utley owned the store. They expanded and modernized the business, adding gasoline pumps out front.

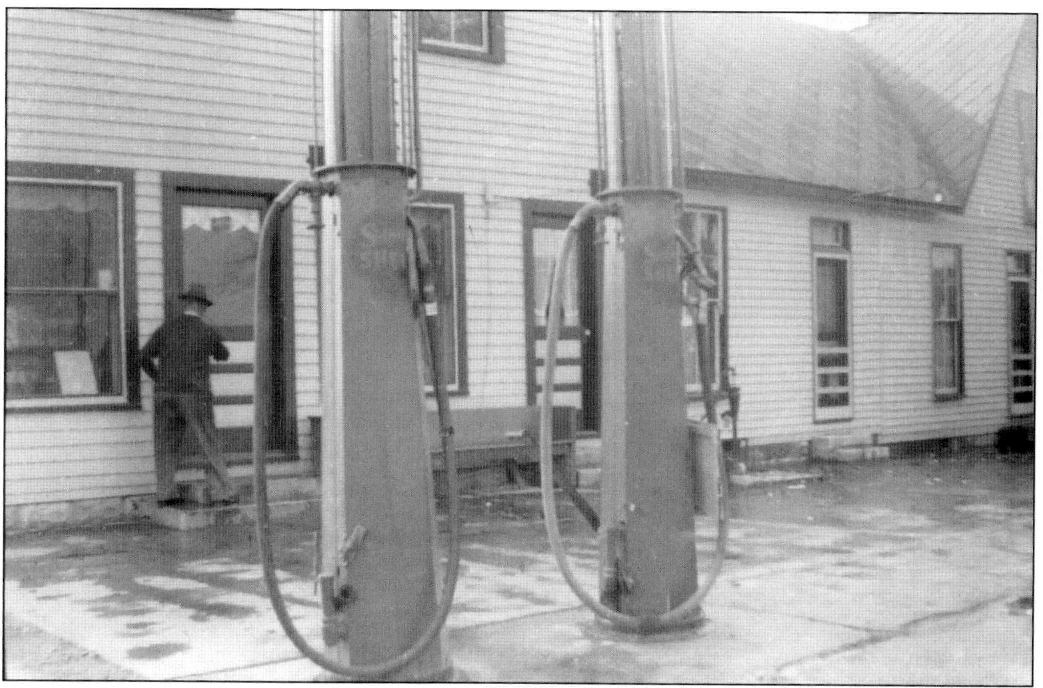

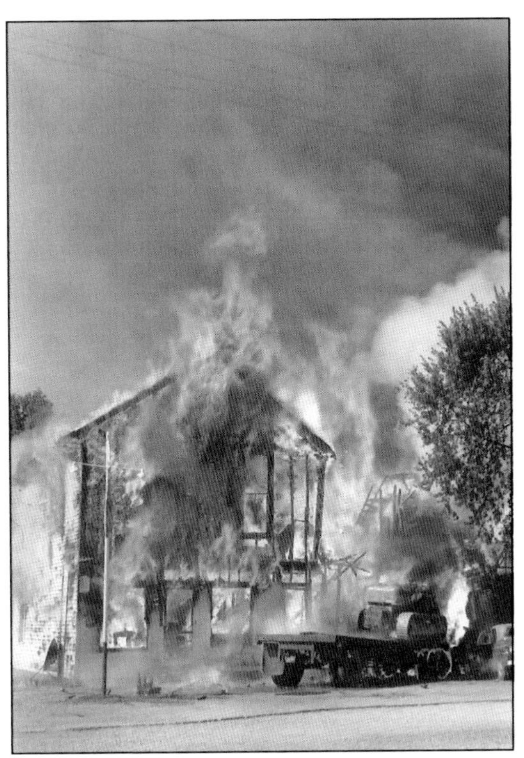

In the mid-1950s, a car failed to stop at the crossroads in front of the Dover store, hitting an oncoming flatbed truck hauling a bulldozer. The truck sheared off the store's gas pumps at their bases, and both vehicles careened into the building, setting ablaze everything in sight. The store and the house next door were a total loss. The truck driver died immediately. (Toby McDaniel.)

Just after the Civil War ended, banker Philander Anderson's wife complained to him that their modest house was too small. So, in 1868, he began building a three-story brick octagonal home on five acres at the edge of Zionsville. The home had 22 rooms, heavy carved oak paneling, and an impressive spiral staircase at its center. In 1880, desiring to move to Kansas, Anderson sold the home for $1,000 cash to a man named Mr. Stultz, from a nearby town, whom he had met earlier that day. Over the years, the home changed ownership a half-dozen times. In 1951, it was torn down and the property was redeveloped into a new neighborhood.

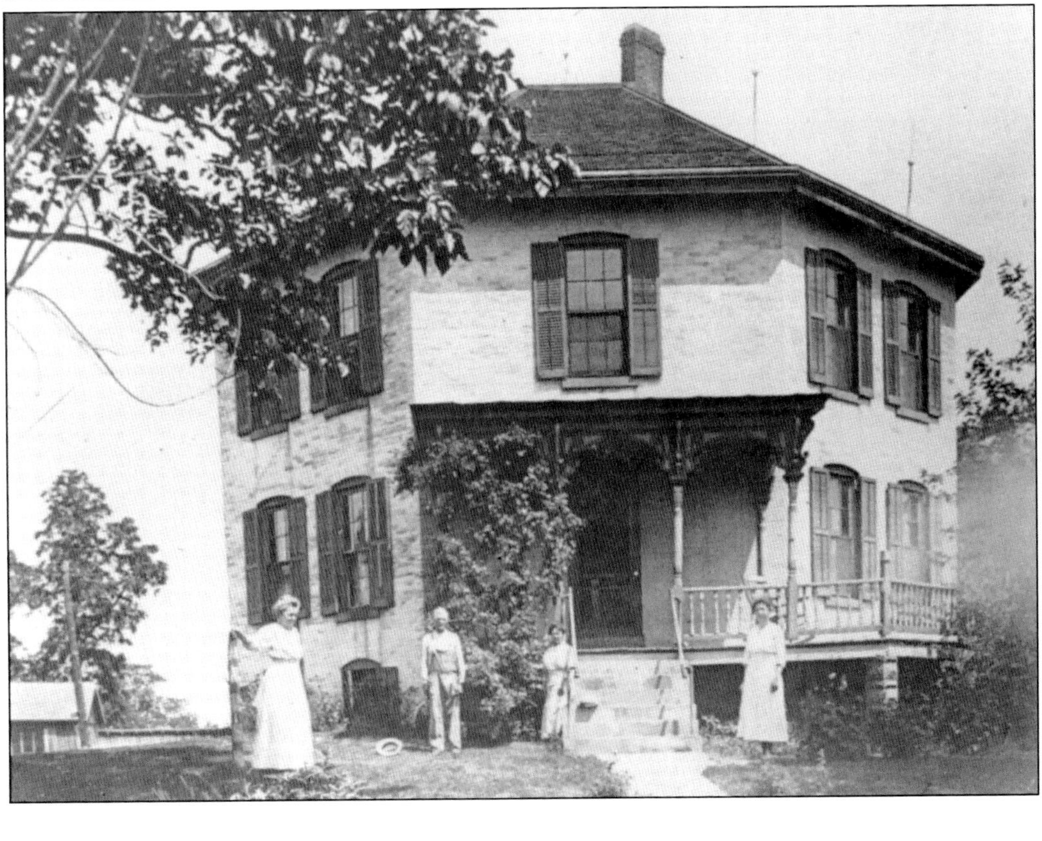

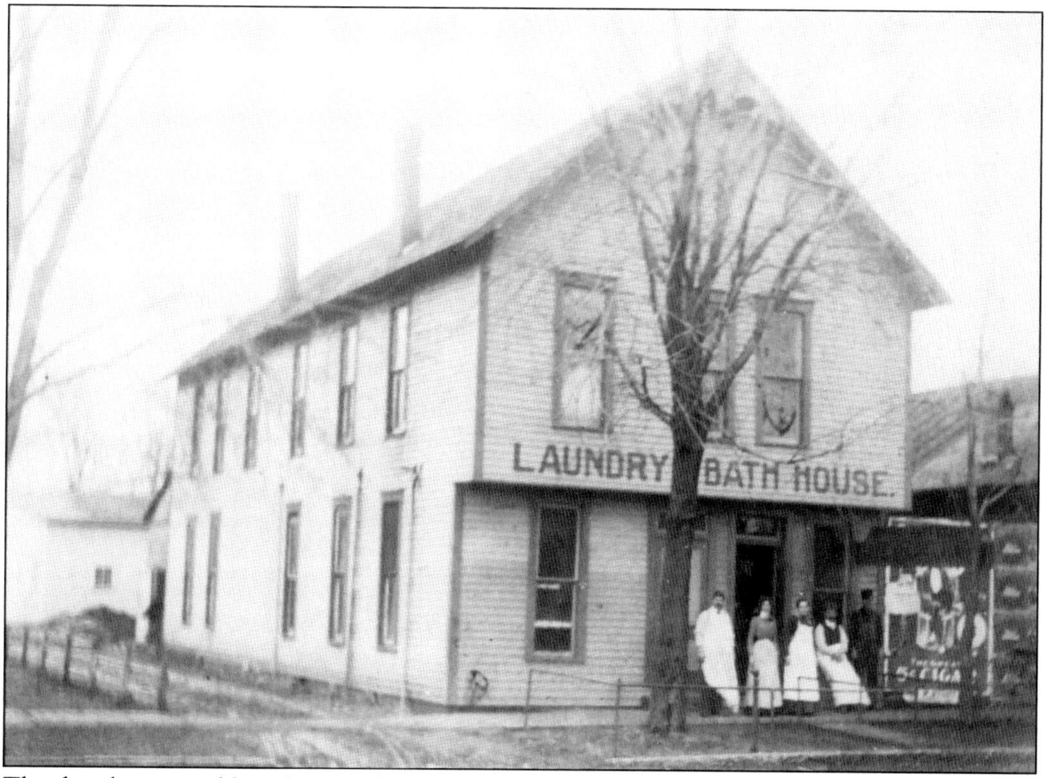

The dry cleaner and laundry now known as Royal Cleaners got its start as a steam laundry and bathhouse in 1889. Known as Elite Steam Laundry, this two-story structure caught fire and burned in 1913. The massive fire also destroyed the livery next door, as well as the adjoining sale barn, or auction house. The Cain and McClain residences across the street were heavily damaged. The laundry was rebuilt and continued in business.

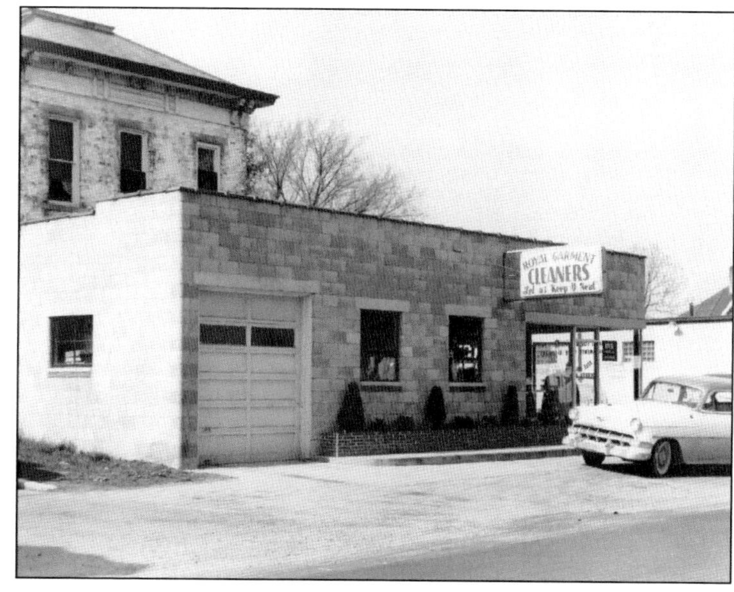

A few owners and two locations later, Art Dickerson bought the Elite Steam business in 1957. He immediately updated the rundown equipment and moved the operation to a well ventilated building. As of this writing, Elite Steam/Royal Cleaners has been in business for 127 years. Dickerson and his wife, Theda, work daily in what is believed to be the county's oldest continuously run business. (Dickerson family.)

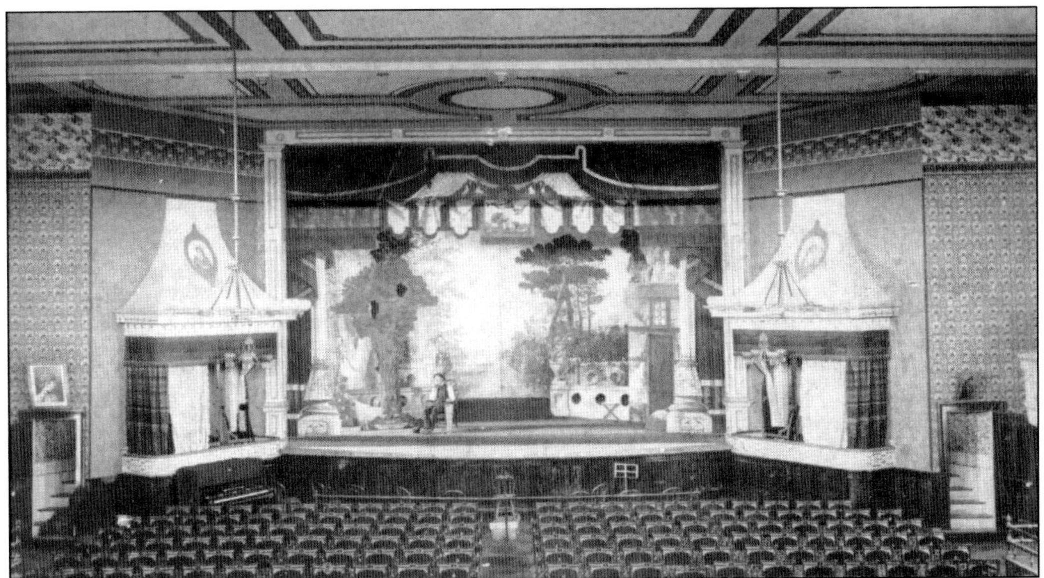

In 1885, J.C. Brown constructed a three-story building with hopes of using the ground floor for his hardware and implement business and adding an opera house on the second and third floors. However, he changed his mind after watching two other opera houses fail in the city. The enterprising businessman refitted the flooring on the second story and opened a roller rink. After a couple of years, the roller rink failed to turn a profit, so the ever-adaptable Brown went forward with plans to finish the third story as balcony seating and opened the 1,000-seat Brown's Grand Opera House without the threat of competition.

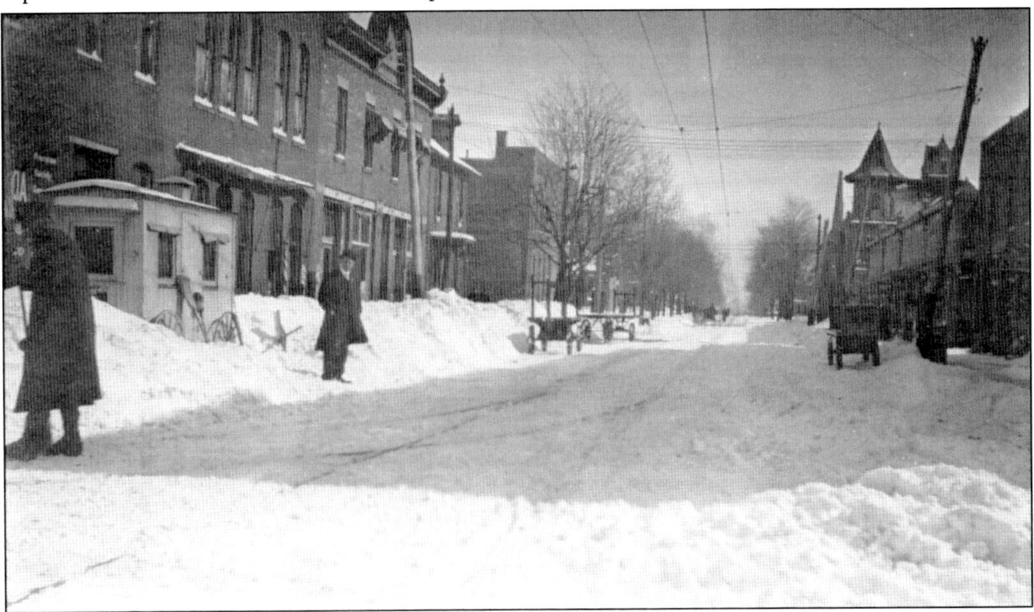

Perhaps the first "food truck" in Boone County came long before the modern craze. Ruben Coxen McIntyre, a veteran of the Union Army, was an enterprising man well ahead of his time. Shown here the day after the big blizzard of 1912, McIntyre's sandwich wagon—affectionately known as the "One Horse Hotel"—is open and ready to sell lunches to hungry shovelers. McIntyre sold hamburgers and locally bottled soda from around 1908 until his retirement in 1916.

Lost Road connects Boone and bordering Clinton County via Scotland Bridge, a one-lane, triple-arch stone bridge built in 1901 and spanning Sugar Creek. Though it is in fragile condition and widely reported to be haunted, it is still open to traffic and is listed in the National Register of Historic Places.

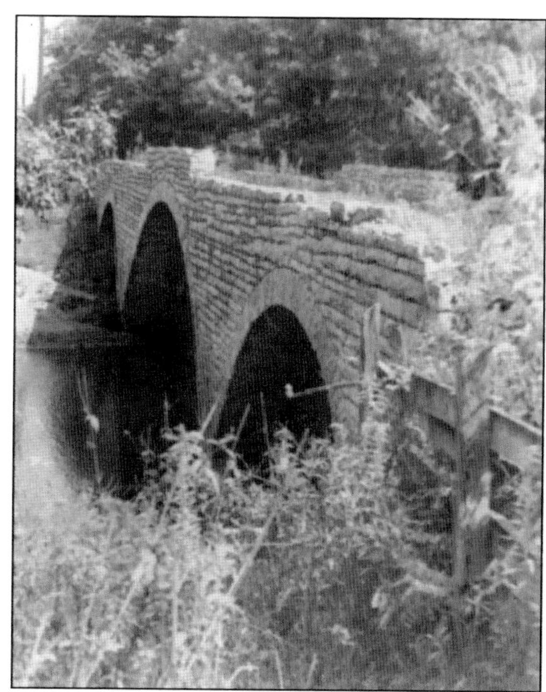

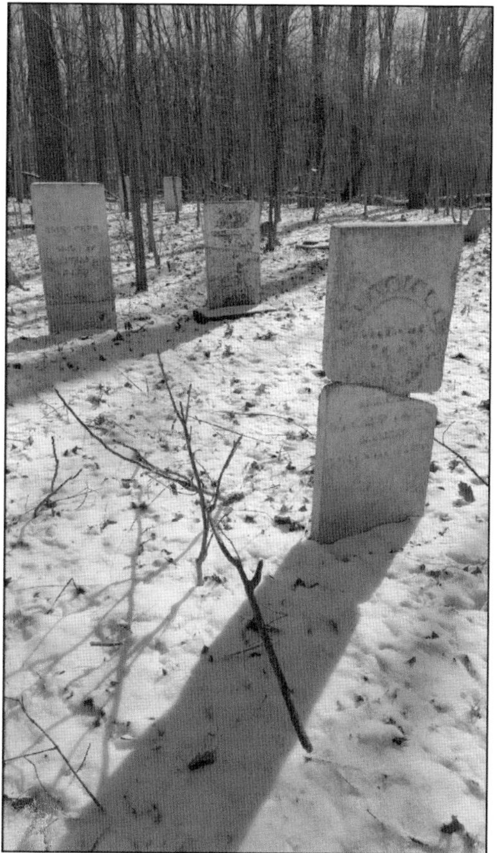

The only local bridge older than Scotland Bridge and still in use is Holiday Bridge, which spans Big Eagle Creek near Zionsville. Built in 1892, this bridge is also rumored to be haunted. The historic single-lane trestle bridge was structurally renovated in 2008. Allegedly the site of a KKK lynching, Holiday Bridge is near this spooky graveyard—the Cox/Old Eagle Cemetery, which terrifies teenagers and thrill-seekers on their way to visit the haunted bridge.

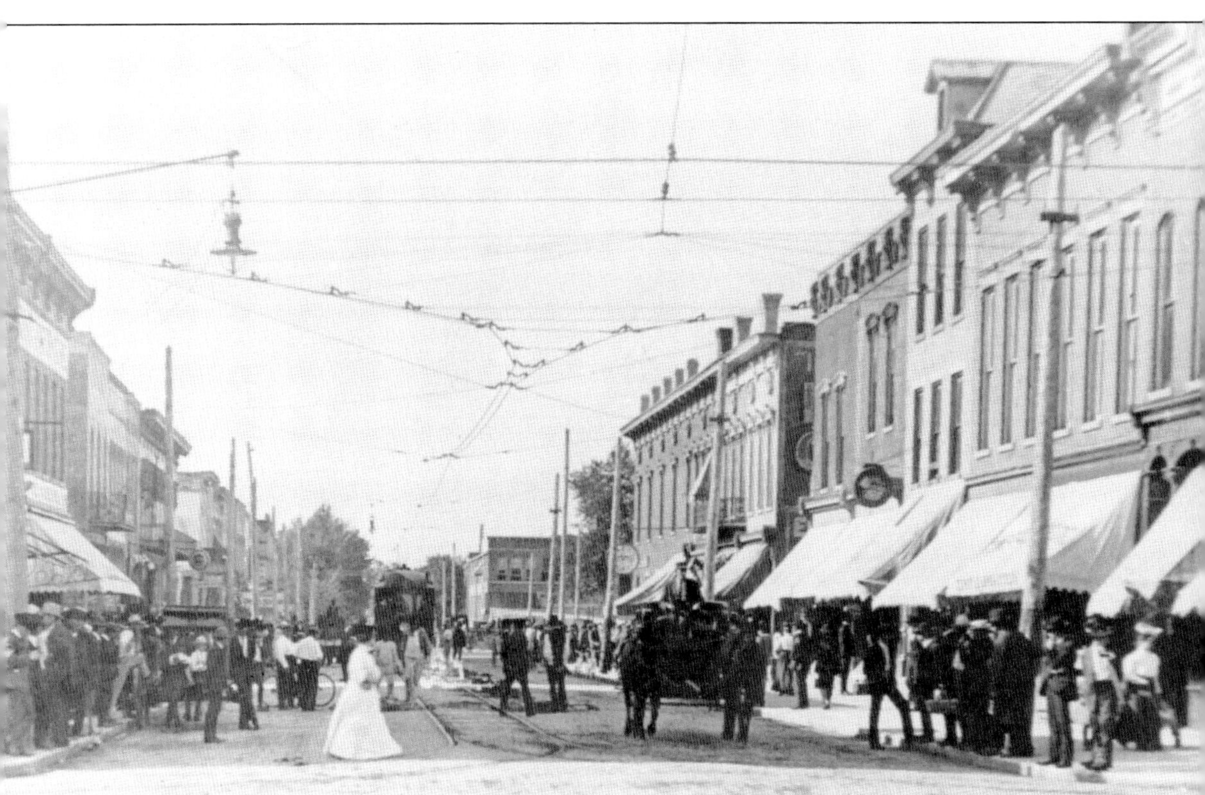

This busy street scene shows the many modernizations in Lebanon by around 1905. The overhead wires powered telephone service, telegraph messaging, traction cars, and electrical lights inside homes and businesses near downtown. Gas lights continued to illuminate the square until 1937. The city was also crisscrossed with railroad tracks, and most of the main streets were paved.

Three

At Rest in Boone

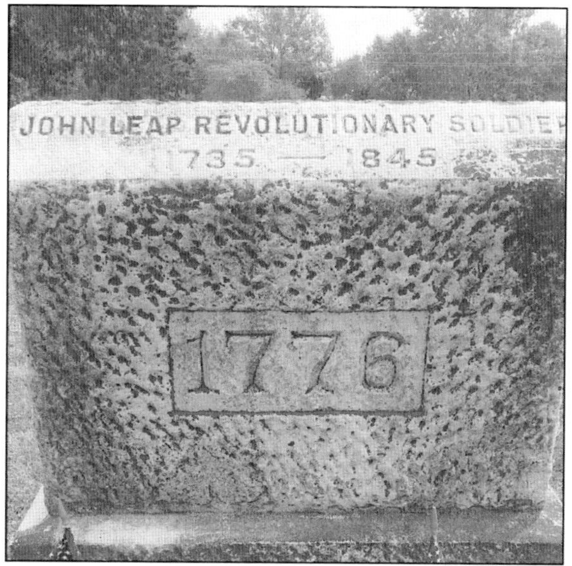

John Wesley Leap, father of Isaac Leap, is one of the 19 Revolutionary War soldiers believed to be interred in Boone County. John Leap settled near Fayette along the White Lick Creek in 1832. His grave is at the Mount Tabor Baptist Church cemetery. In 1896, the county began placing large monuments at each of these gravesites. The 18 others believed to be scattered across small and large cemeteries in the county include John Aldridge, Arthur Andrews, Francis Brown, Samuel Dooley, John Ferguson, Jacob Foreman, William Gipson, George W. Grimes, James Hill, Henry Johns Sr., John Kersey, John McMannis, William Pauley, Elias Plew, John Roberts, Jesse Robertson, Abraham Utter, and Joseph Wheatley. (Author's collection.)

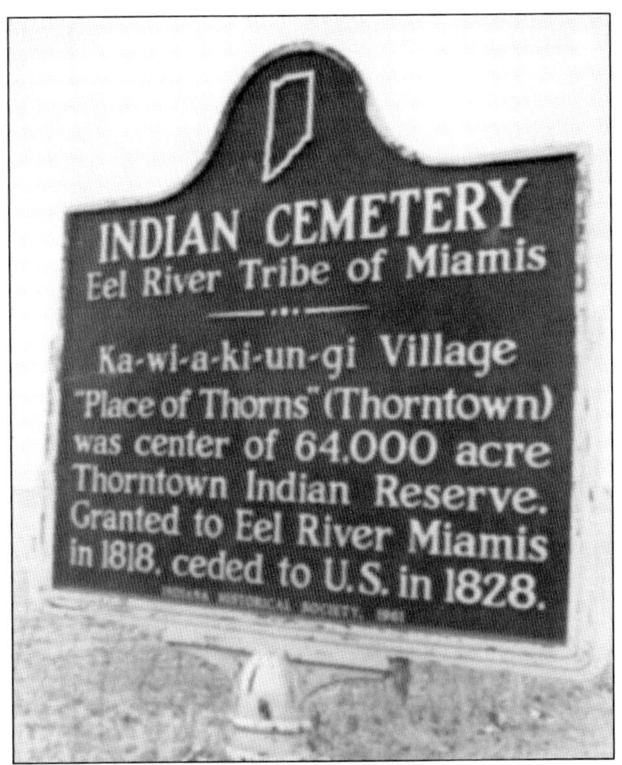

Thorntown had been settled by tribes of Miami Indians since the late 1700s. They had a thriving trade with French trappers who visited regularly. This sign was erected at the legendary burial site of two chiefs just outside of the town limits. During excavating to upgrade city water and sewer services in the first years of the 20th century, several Indian graves were found. One, reported in 1914 by the *Lebanon Patriot*, was in Thorntown near the corner of Pearl and Church Streets and only 18 inches deep. Another was found near Whitestown in October 1908, when the *Indianapolis Star* reported the discovery as a "Goliath Indian Skeleton." No one knows what became of either group of remains.

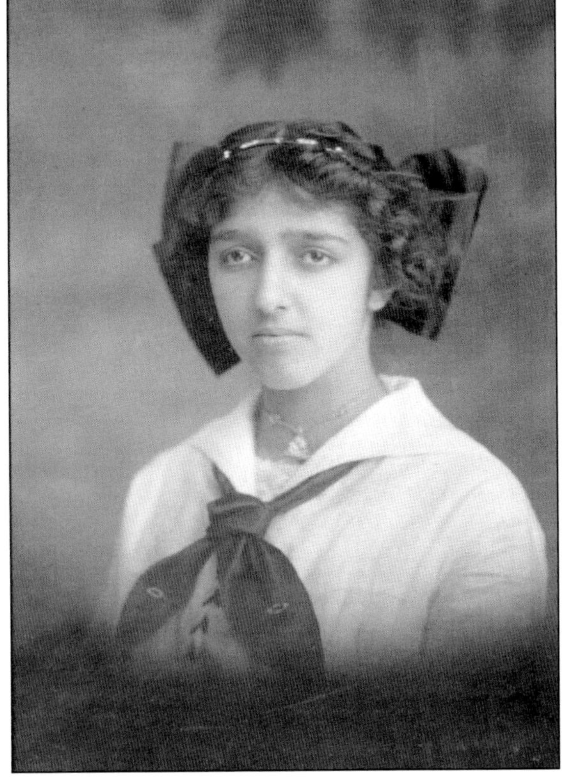

Ruth Johnson was the daughter of freedmen parents who came to Thorntown to farm and live peacefully after the Civil War. In 1866, the Colored School and an African Methodist Episcopal church were built in Thorntown. Along with Lebanon, Thorntown had a large concentration of Quakers, and both were considered welcoming and safe places to settle. The Negro Masonic Lodge was organized in 1868 at Thorntown, and the Elizaville post office was noted as having a large settlement of freedmen. The Colored Cemetery was laid out in 1869 and attracted burials from across the state—many noted only as "burial at Thorntown." (Thorntown History Museum.)

This photograph shows the remaining markers at the Colored Cemetery. Elisha Derricks and another Union soldier whose name has been lost to time are buried here. Only one marker remains with legible markings, recording the death of 17-year-old James L. Shad in 1878. Parts of three more stones remain but are broken and illegible. A tasteful blue-and-gold-enameled marker was placed in the grassy area by the Society for the Preservation of Our Indian Heritage to mark the graveyard. The family who owns the surrounding farm field respectfully keeps the lawn in good repair amid the crops growing around it.

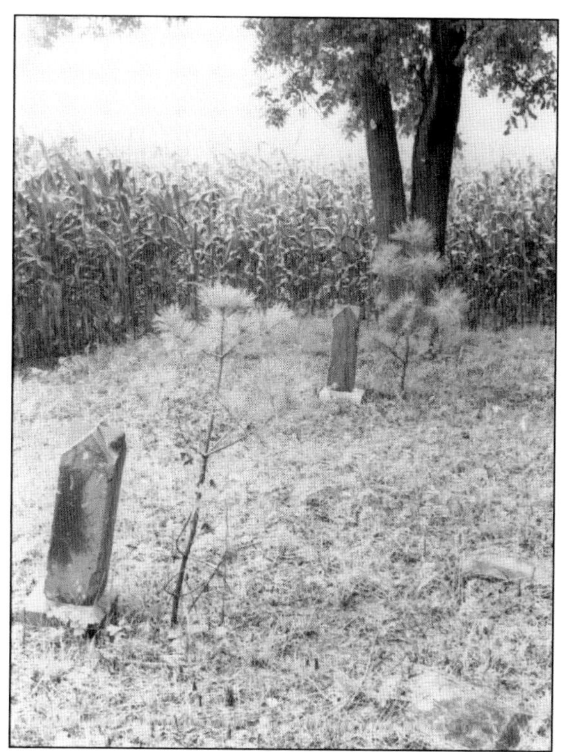

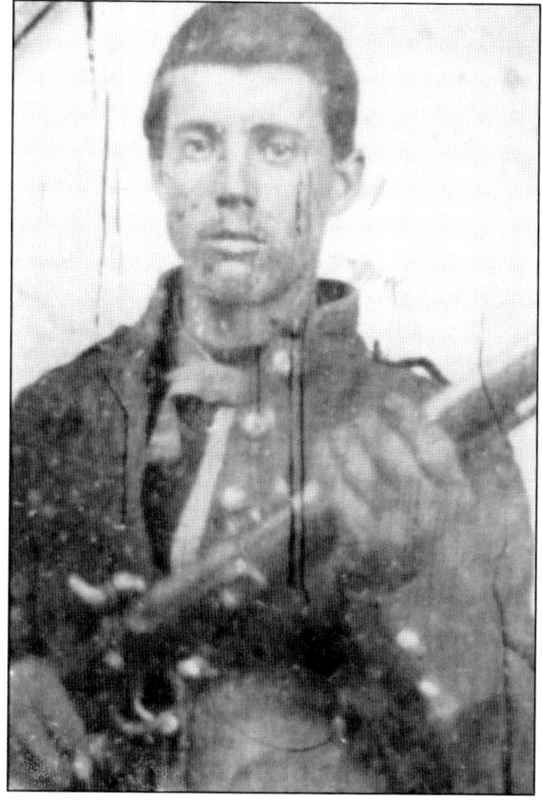

On March 1, 1862, Daniel O'Connel Neal, son of Judge Stephen Neal, died at the young age of 20. Stricken with typhoid fever while serving as a corporal in the Indiana Volunteer Infantry at Somerset, Kentucky, Daniel Neal was brought back to Lebanon and laid to rest in the old Cedar Hill cemetery.

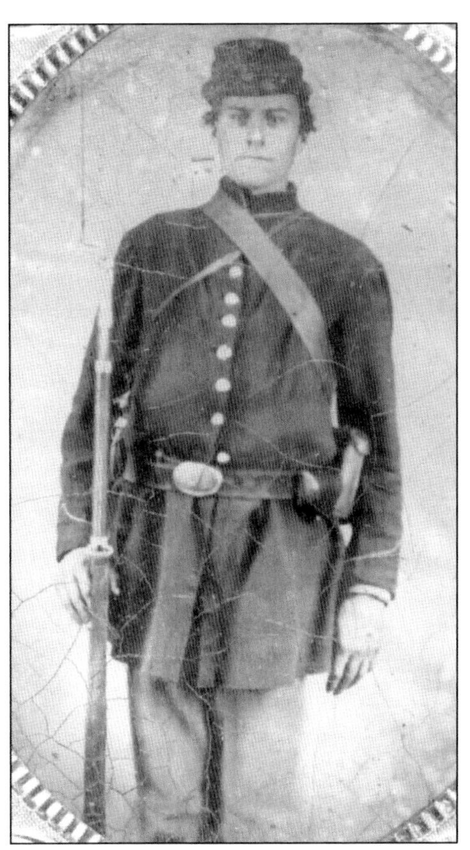

Uriah J. Mavity enlisted in August 1862. He was eventually captured and spent the rest of the war at the infamous Andersonville prison. Finally released and transported up the Mississippi River on the steamship *Sultana*, Mavity must have felt very relieved to be freed from the horrors of Andersonville. However, the ship made for carrying 376 was loaded up that day in April 1865 with more than 2,100 released men heading north. The ship's boiler exploded, killing about 1,800 passengers and crew. Mavity was unharmed and eventually made his way home. Later, he wrote a gruesome and gripping account of his experience on the ill-fated river steamer. He lived into his 60s, dying in 1910 at his home.

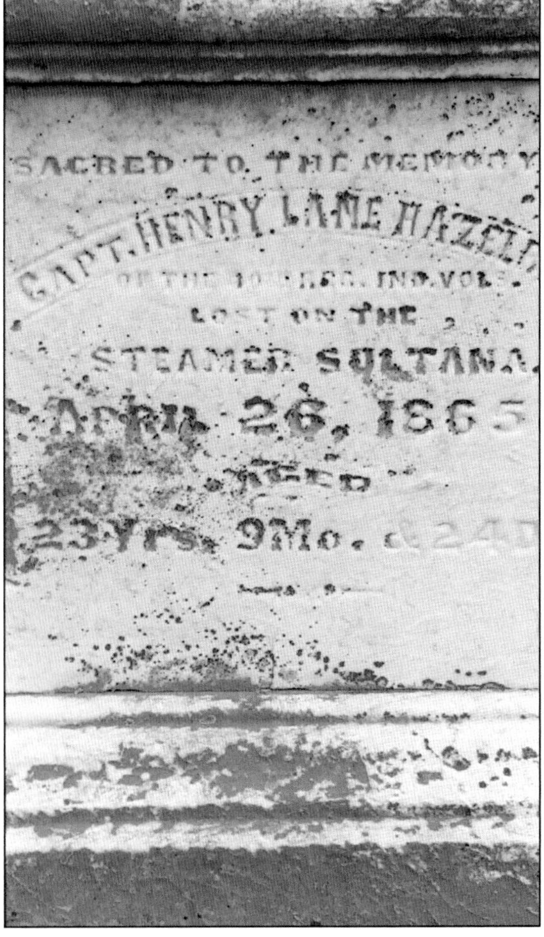

Henry Lane Hazelrigg was also captured in action and held within the confines of Andersonville prison camp. Released with all other Northern prisoners, he boarded the overloaded *Sultana* bound for home. Hazelrigg did not survive the explosion, and his body was not recovered. Although the loss of life was immense on April 27, 1865, the catastrophe went mostly unnoticed—likely because Lincoln's assassin, John Wilkes Booth, had been gunned down the day before. Even the engraver of Captain Hazelrigg's impressive cenotaph (a marker for an empty tomb) must have been caught up in the news of Booth's end, as the date of Henry Hazelrigg's death was errantly carved as April 26, 1865—the day before he died. (Author's collection.)

John M. Conyers was a two-term veteran of the Civil War, serving under Lew Wallace, the author of *Ben-Hur*. He then came home and served his community as postmaster of Reese's Mill for a time. Oddly, he did not lose his leg until a horseshoeing accident in 1885 resulted in amputation above the knee. Shortly after this, the man who had fought Confederates without serious injury lost the sight in his right eye when a hot cinder flew off of a piece of metal he was smithing.

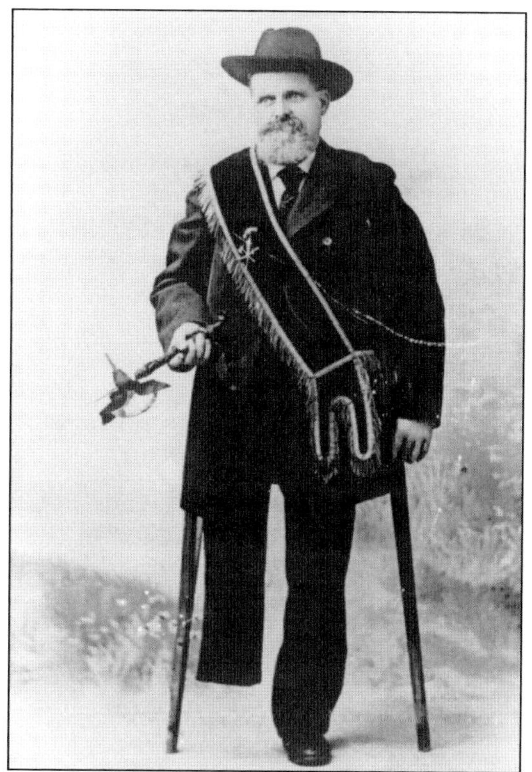

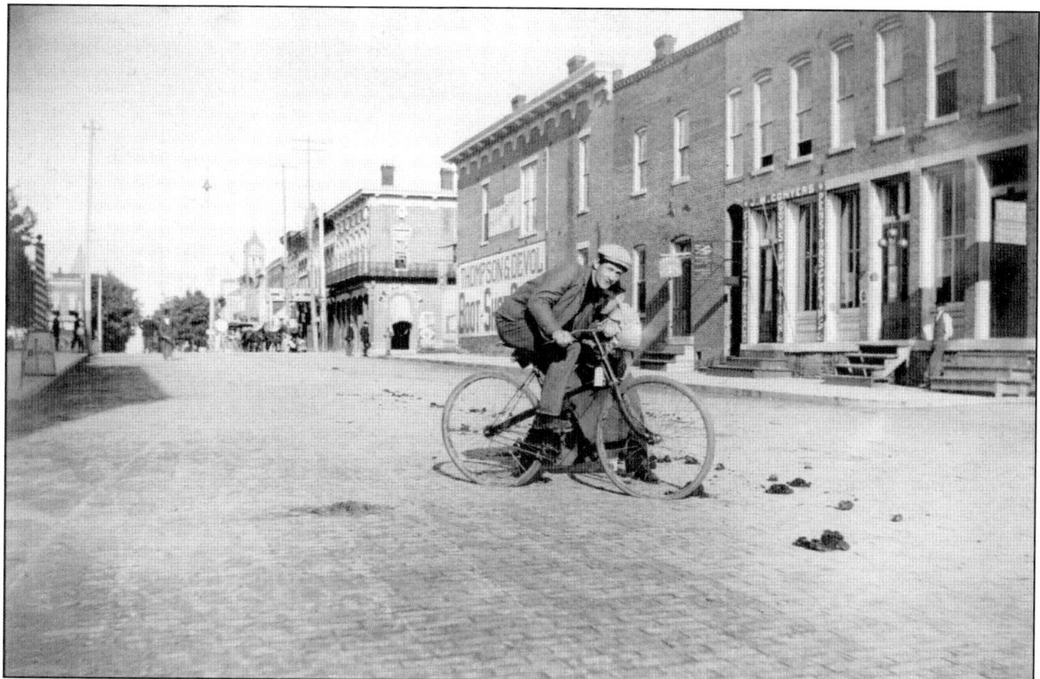

In later years, John M. Conyers became a gunsmith and pension agent who represented veterans, eventually opening an office in Lebanon. His storefront is shown behind these two people trying their hands at maneuvering a newfangled bicycle while dodging the hazards of horse "residue."

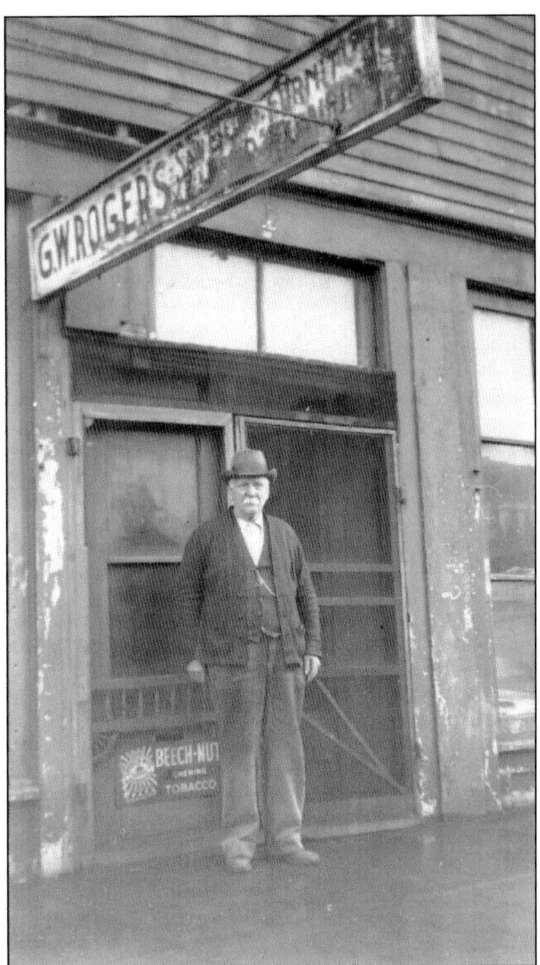

George W. Rogers was known around Thorntown as an Indian fighter and Civil War veteran. After the war, he came home and opened a furniture and carpentry store. He used the store both to sell his wares and as a place to relate harrowing tales of his adventures.

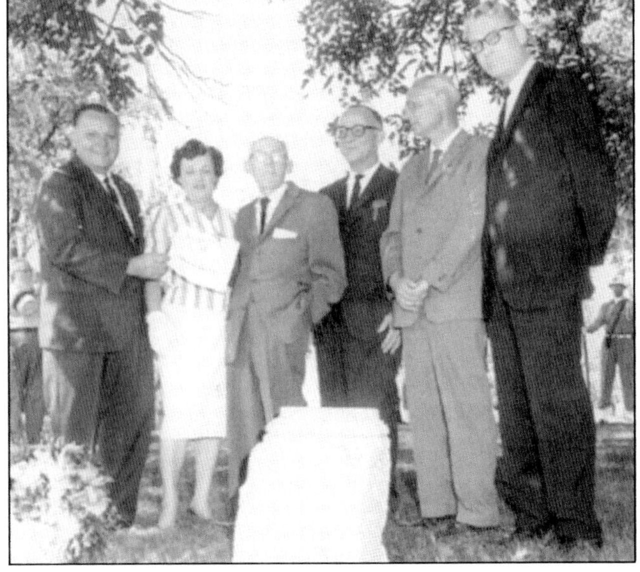

Col. Orville S. Hamilton was said to have died of a broken heart due to an Army clerical error. On Independence Day 1964, Rep. Richard L. Roudebush granted Hamilton the honorable discharge he deserved, about 100 years after the errant dishonorable one he received. Pictured from left to right are Roudebush; Mrs. Charles Forbes, great-granddaughter of Hamilton, receiving the official discharge; grandson Ben Combs Sr.; great-grandsons Ben Combs Jr. and James McIntyre; and Sen. Keith McCormick, who served as master of ceremonies.

After being captured in mid-June 1864 at Mt. Sterling, Kentucky, Confederate Army forage master John Bush was put on a train headed north to the Douglas prison encampment at Chicago. On July 17, when the train stopped at Thorntown for supplies, Bush attempted to flee. He was felled by one shot and left alongside the tracks. Eventually, his body was removed and placed in an unmarked grave at the Old Thorntown Cemetery. After the war, Union veteran James Bell used his own money to buy a headstone for Bush's grave. (Author's collection.)

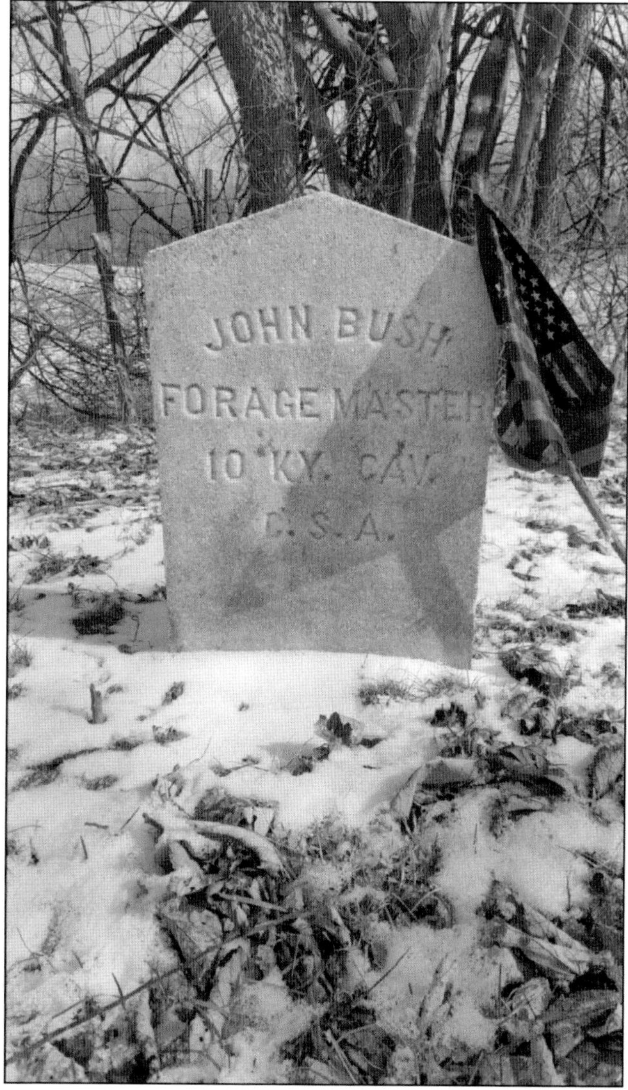

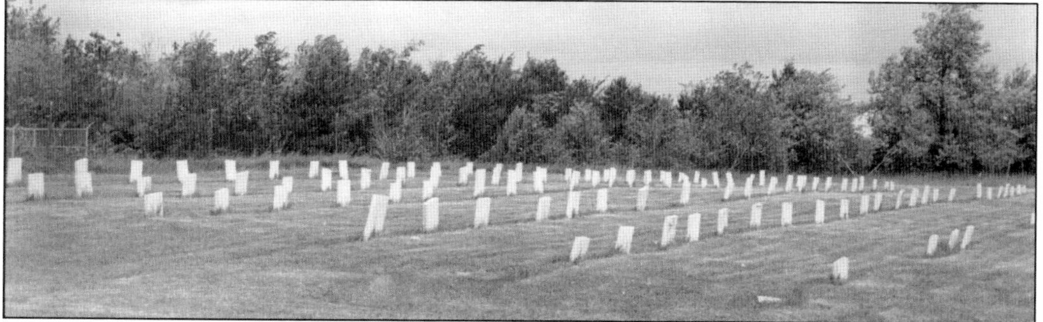

This potter's field cemetery is still used by the county and is now sharing space as the front lawn of the newest county jail. Originally founded to bury those who died at the Boone County Infirmary (the county poor farm), the potter's field has always offered dignified rest to the poor, unclaimed, and unidentified. There are currently no plans to move or discontinue this cemetery.

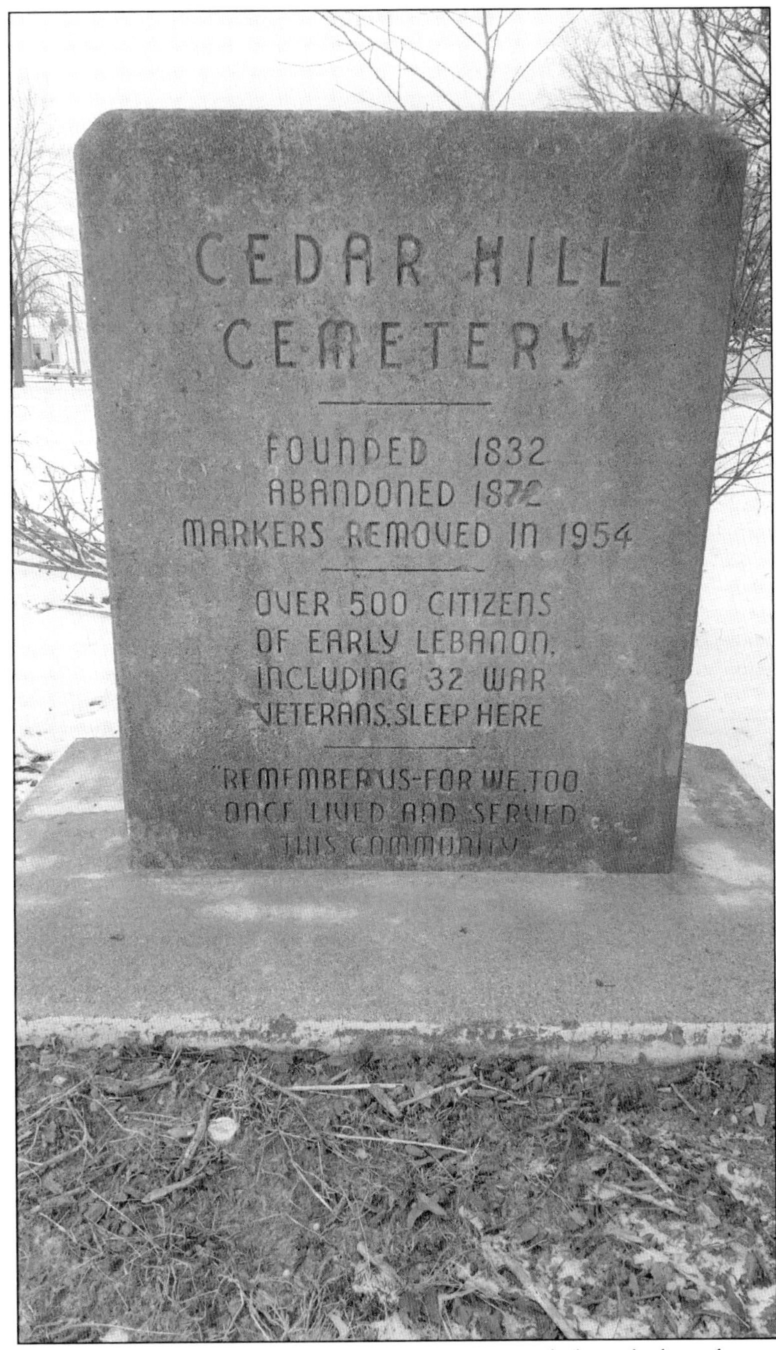

Much controversy surrounds the original community graveyard platted when the city of Lebanon was laid out. Called Cedar Hill, it was not officially named until about 1907 and is mostly referred to as "the old cemetery." The burial space was full to the brim only 40 years after opening. Eventually, it became impossible to dig a grave without finding the space already occupied. Adding to the confusion were the many graves that were either unmarked or marked by quick-to-decay wood. The number originally interred—and the number of those still resting at the old cemetery (now a city park in Lebanon)—is still unclear. (Author's collection.)

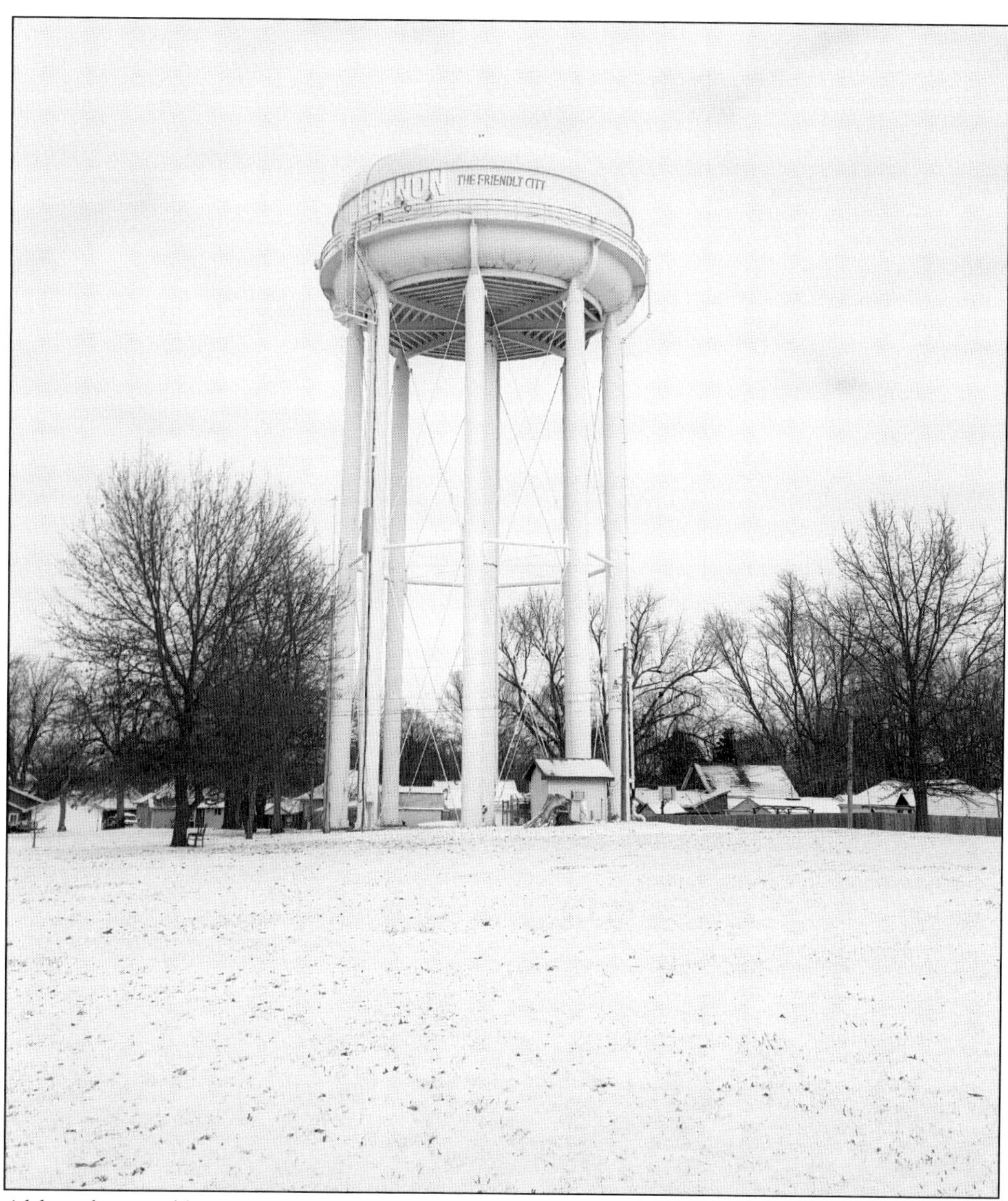

Although record keeping was not meticulous, one Revolutionary War soldier is verifiably buried at Cedar Hill Cemetery. James Hill rests here, along with at least 30 other veterans of the Civil War, Spanish-American War, and the War of 1812. Virtually abandoned after the 1872 opening of Rodefer Cemetery, the neglected graveyard was taken up as a project of the local James Hill Chapter of the DAR in 1954. The women had the heavy tangle of underbrush removed and found that most of the remaining markers were misplaced or badly damaged. In a controversial move, they ordered all the stones to be collected and displayed off-site, where ancestors and interested parties could claim them. Then, they erected a flagpole and two new monuments. They renamed the yard James Hill Park, and the city took over maintenance of the property, eventually making it home of the Lebanon water tower. No one knows what became of the unclaimed grave markers. (Author's collection.)

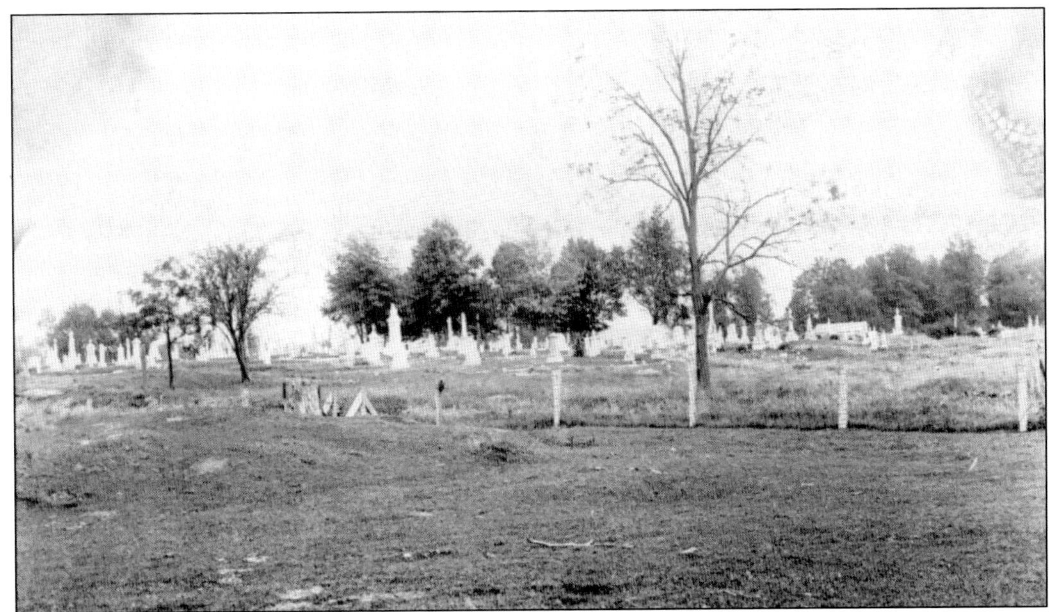

By 1890, the new Rodefer Cemetery was widely considered an eyesore. Oak Hill Cemetery Association formed in 1899 to buy out Rodefer and oversee the needed care and improvements. The name Oak Hill, inspired by the large oak tree shown just to the right of center in this photograph, was suggested by Charles F.S. Neal and unanimously agreed upon. Neal led the way, installing a sundial surrounded by a walking path in honor of his mother.

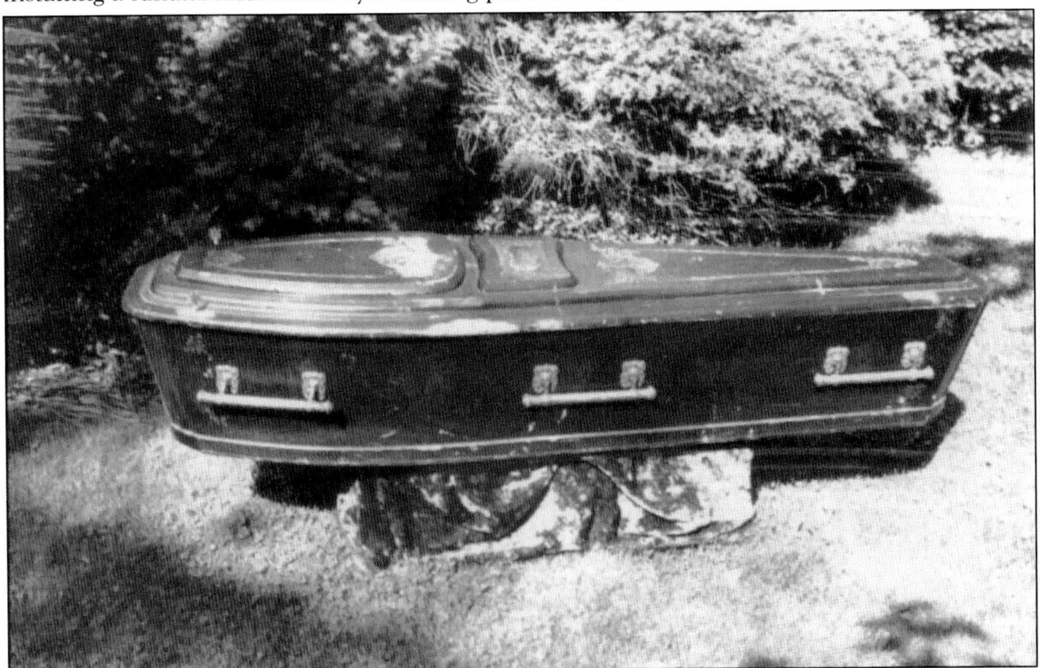

Upon the opening of the new cemetery, given the cramped and unkempt status of Cedar Hill, there was a rush of business for Rodefer's. Families of means immediately began making arrangements to have loved ones moved from Cedar Hill to the new place of rest. Even the Hazelrigg family moved the marker of their son Henry, who had been memorialized by an empty tomb on their farm.

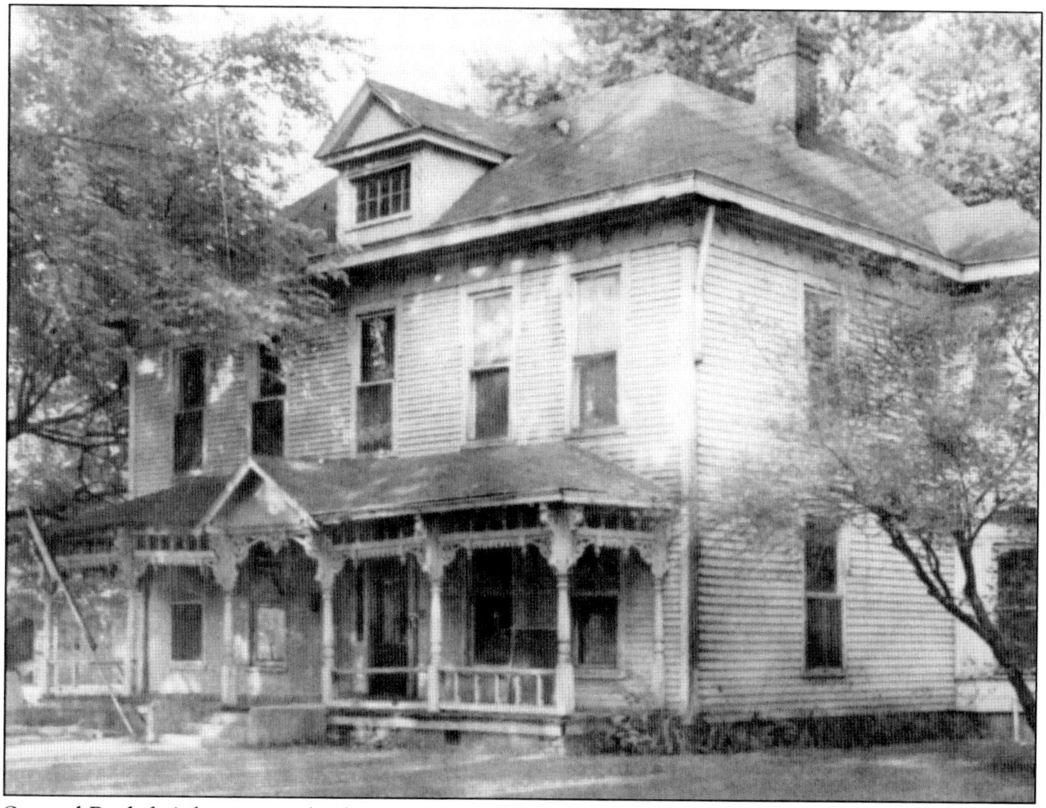

Samuel Rodefer's home was built in 1859. The 10-room house was evidence of his success in business. In March 1872, he purchased 9.2 acres on the eastern outskirts of Lebanon and established a new cemetery named the Rodefer Cemetery. Two weeks later, the first grave was opened for five-year-old Fannie Earhart, daughter of an area blacksmith; she had suffered an excruciating death by scalding. The man reported to have dug that first grave, William H. Ellis, was buried near her in 1910.

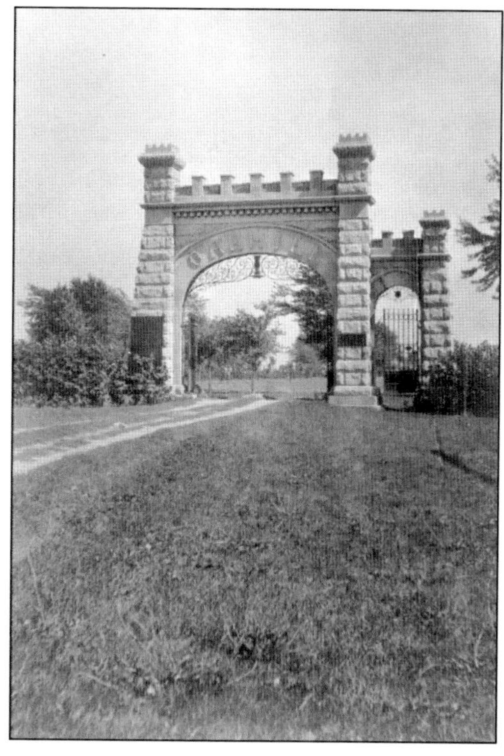

A caretaker's cottage was built on the Oak Hill property, along with the Victorian-style Powell chapel and a large greenhouse. A much-needed gate was donated by The Federation of Women's Clubs in 1903. Today, Oak Hill has grown to encompass more than 35 acres, with a section in use as the St. Joseph's Catholic Church cemetery. One hundred years after opening, the cemetery's memorial count was at just over 10,000.

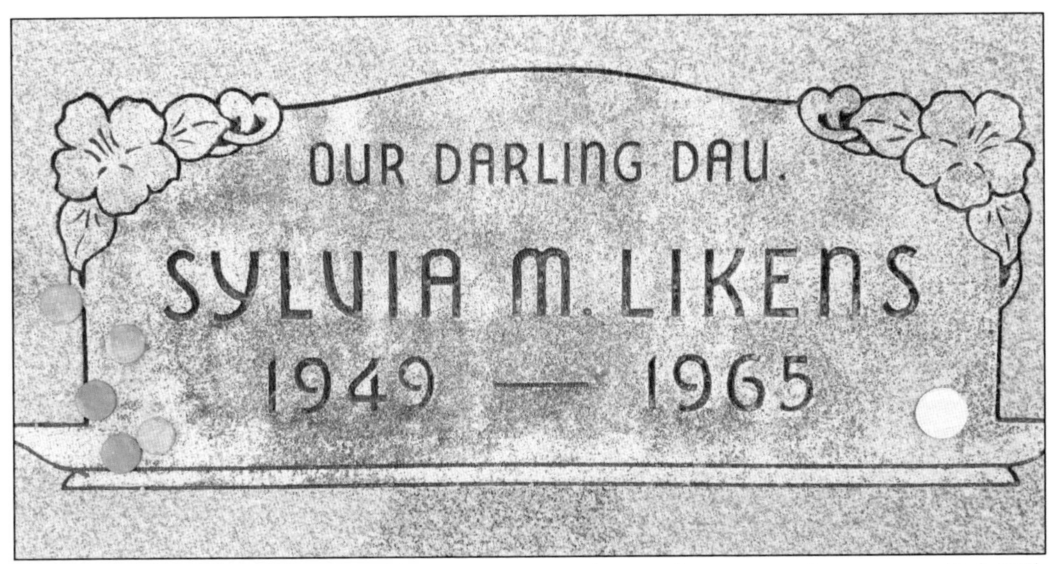

Many graves are planted in sadness, but one in particular stands out more than most at Oak Hill. The remains of 16-year-old Sylvia Likens are buried here. Likens was the victim of a 1965 torture slaying at the hands of a sadistic and neglectful caretaker. Perhaps even more shockingly, other children in the neighborhood participated in harming the teen. Although the murder took place in Indianapolis, Likens was born in Lebanon, and her family frequently moved between Marion and Boone Counties. At times, the family lived in Fayette. For a while, Likens and her sister attended school at Stokes Elementary. (Author's collection.)

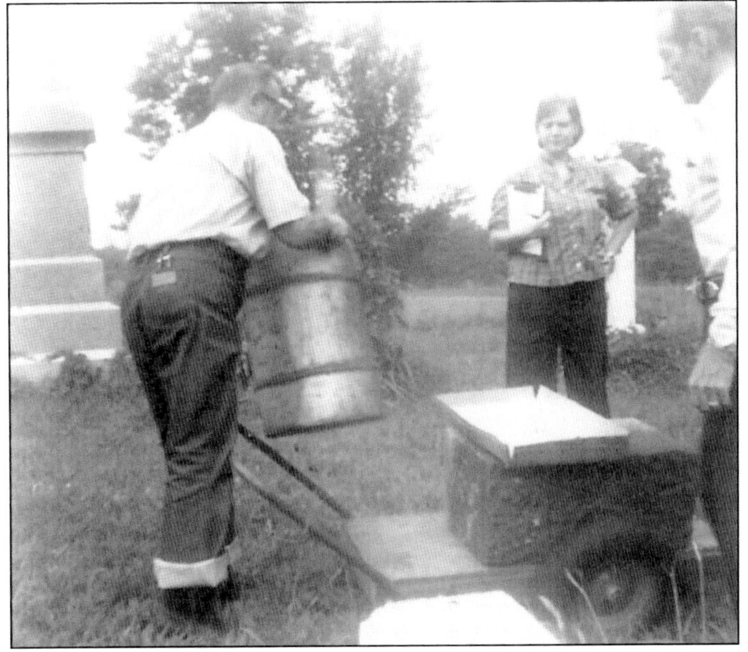

An estimated 90–100 separate cemeteries and small graveyards have been identified in Boone County. Beginning in about 1954 with the reclamation efforts of the old Cedar Hill cemetery by the local James Hill Chapter of the DAR, many of the long-abandoned sites were cleaned. Although some were treated to nothing more than a good mowing and removal of nuisance saplings, others, like this marker base at Mt. Tabor cemetery, were totally refurbished. (Ruth Everett.)

Four

NEWFANGLED BOONE

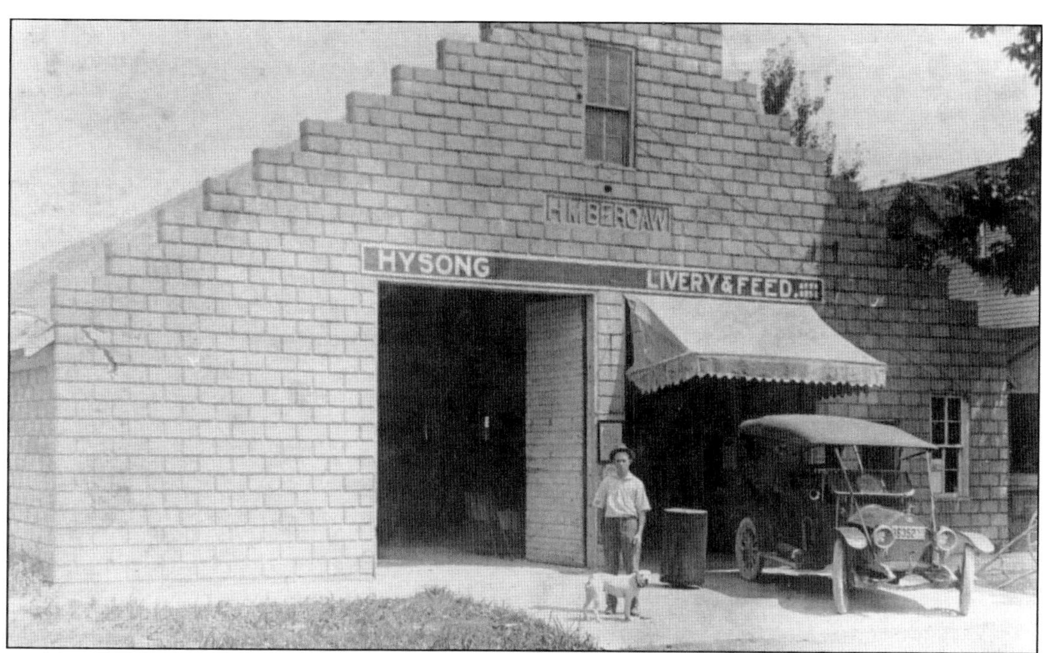

This c. 1916 photograph may be rather prophetic for Hysong Livery and Feed. The owner, John Hysong, seems to be standing between the past and the quickly overarching future. A short while after this scene was captured, the livery building was sold; it was then used for many years as a sale barn. It was sold again around 1940, and the facade was given a facelift to become a grocery store. It has been in continuous use as the Lebanon IGA grocery (now Railer's) since the switch, selling feed to a different clientele.

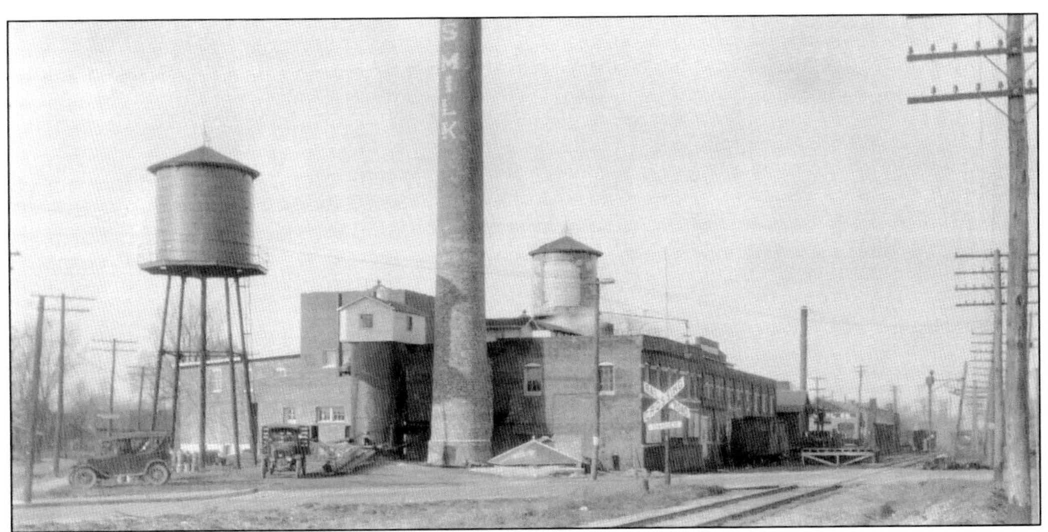

The Indiana Condensed Milk plant was connected to just about every family in Boone County when it was built around 1916. Most area farmers with dairy operations sold their milk to the company. An army of nearly 1,500 sellers was reported by 1917. Route haulers were hired to transport raw milk from farms into the plant, and chemists, packers, and processors worked in the factory. The plant was sold numerous times and finally saw its last days under ownership of the Kraft Company. Production at the factory ceased in 1968. Currently, the former plant is home to Lebanon's Theatre at the Milk Building.

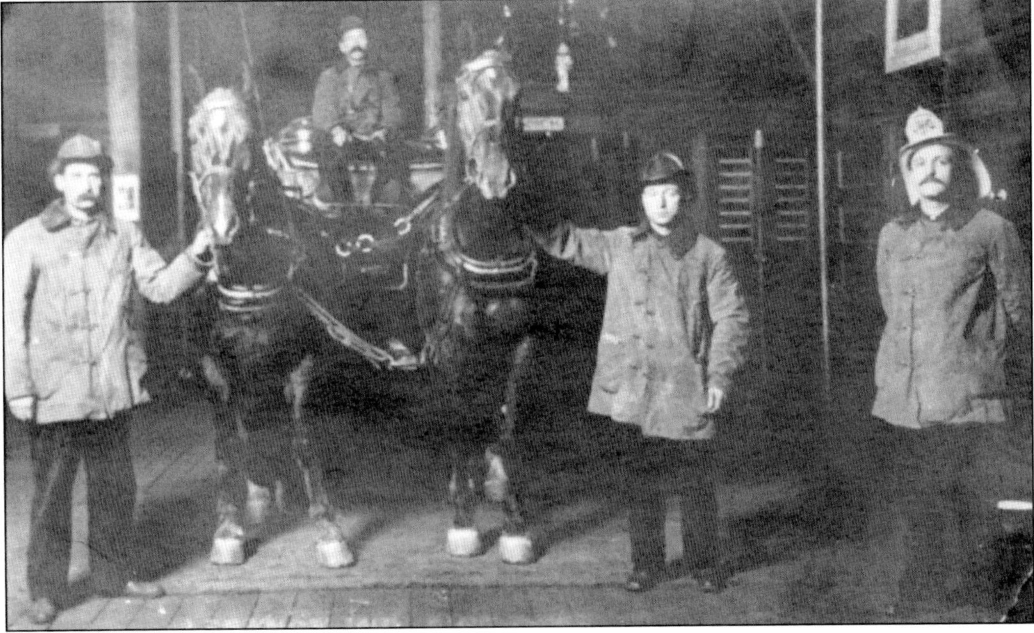

Shown in 1907 with upgraded equipment, these men previously fought fires with little more than their uniforms and buckets. The original city water lines were hollowed-out logs beneath the streets. When a fire broke out, the firemen had to dig down to the "water main," bore a hole in the log line, and scoop up water from the ground as the hole filled. Wagons were mostly used to transport buckets to the site of a fire. In 1872, Lebanon purchased its first real fire wagon capable of pulling pre-filled buckets with teams of trained horses.

The "new" city building was erected by Lebanon in 1903 and was in use until 1963. The impressive three-story building housed nearly all city offices, including barns for the fire wagons and sleeping quarters on the third floor for the firefighters. A brass pole was in place for quick access to the street level when the fire bell rang.

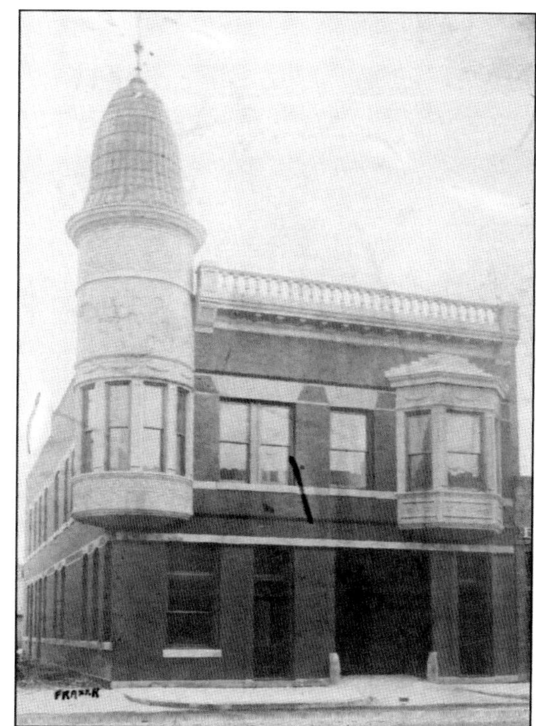

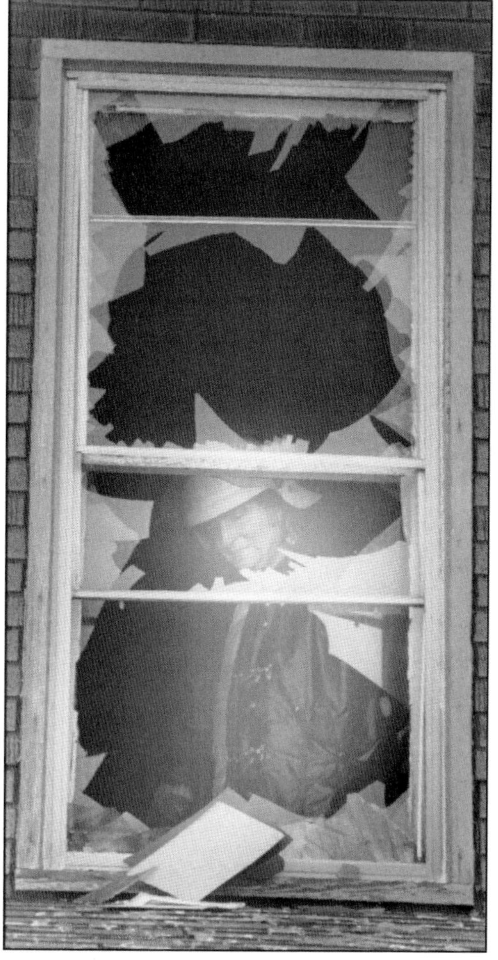

In a more modern photograph (taken in the early to mid-1970s) fireman Charlie Thompkins battles a blaze in a two-story home. Today, though fighting fires is still dangerous work, firefighters are better trained and equipped than in the early years of Boone County. (Judy Thompkins Coon.)

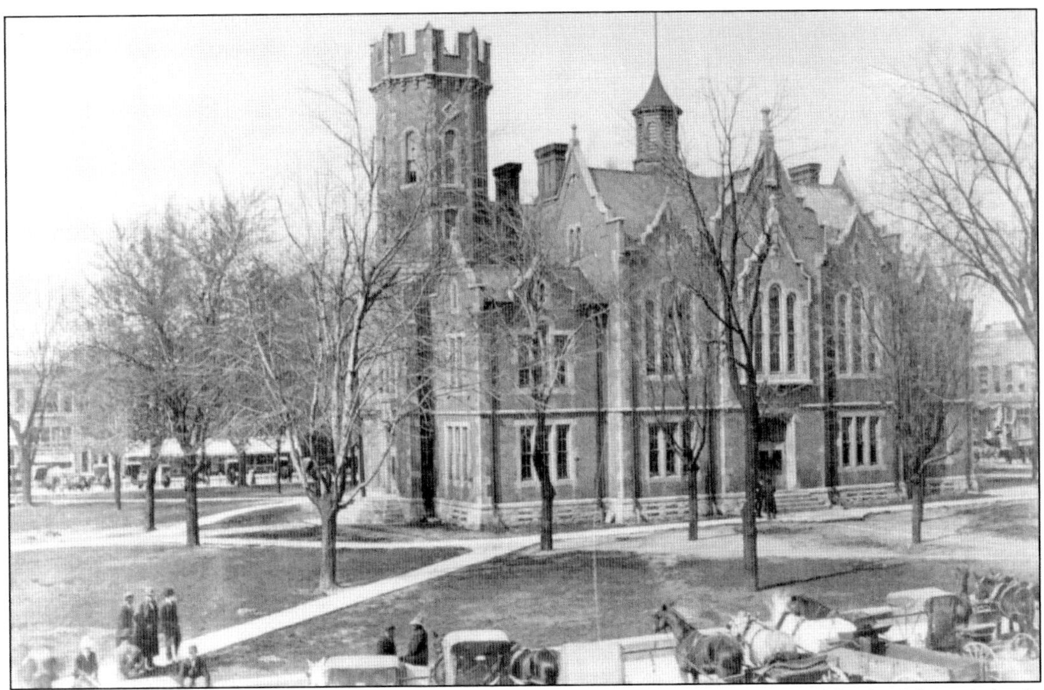

This fine brick courthouse, constructed in 1856 to replace the previous public building (which has a failing foundation), was the third of the four that have served Boone County. It is thought that a fire occurred at the off-site storage place where county records were being held during demolition and construction to build this courthouse. This version was razed in 1909 to make way for the new, more modern courthouse, which is still in use today.

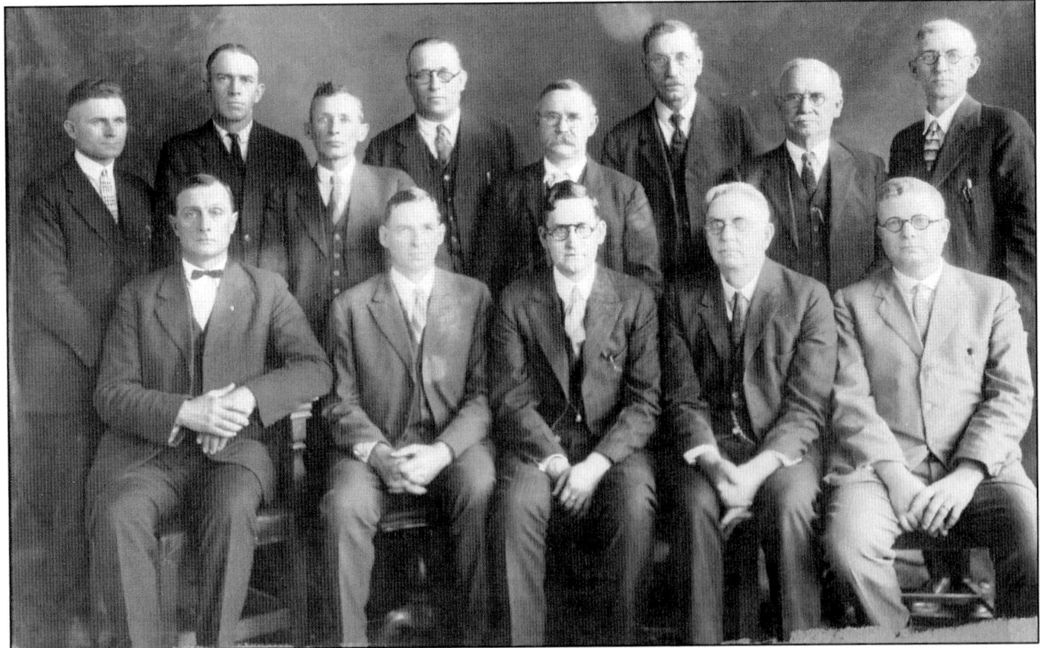

All 12 townships are represented in this 1928 photograph of the trustees. The Boone County superintendent of schools, Carmen Caplinger, is at the center of the front row.

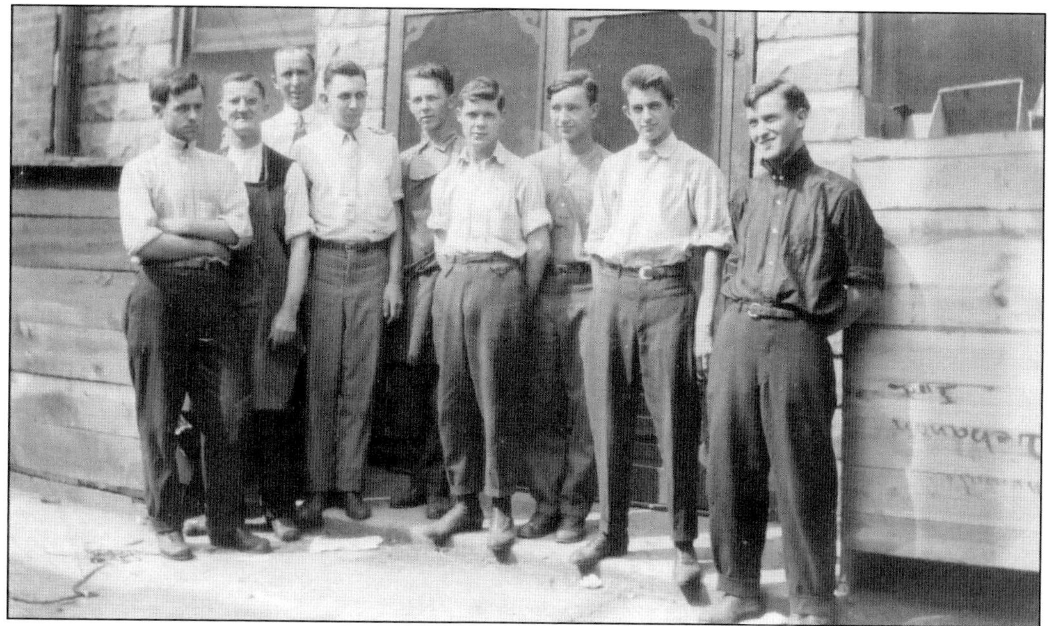

Workers at the Shumate Business Form Company pose for a photograph outside the press floor around 1914. Pictured from left to right are Russell Mills, P. Anderson, J. Walter Shumate (founder), Prentice Atkinson, Roy Atkinson, Johnnie Mullin, Bayard Shumate (son of J. Walter), A.H. Strawmeyer, and ? Sweeney.

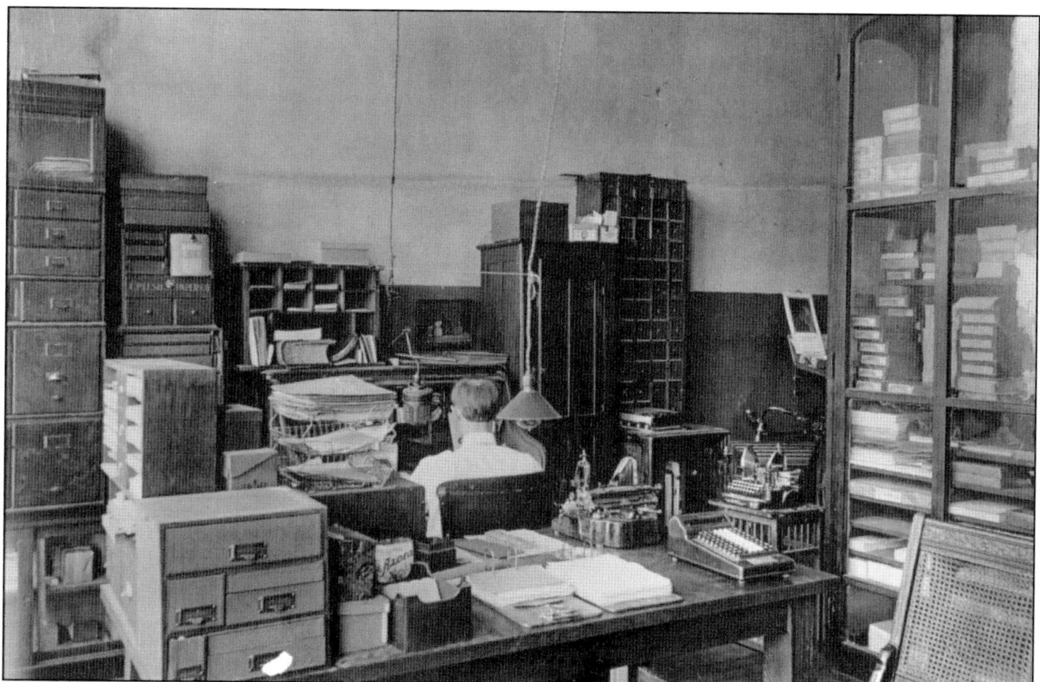

This image offers a glimpse inside the workings of Shumate in the early years. The man at the center of the photograph, fully engulfed in work, is thought to be J. Walter Shumate, who founded the business as a simple printing shop in 1900.

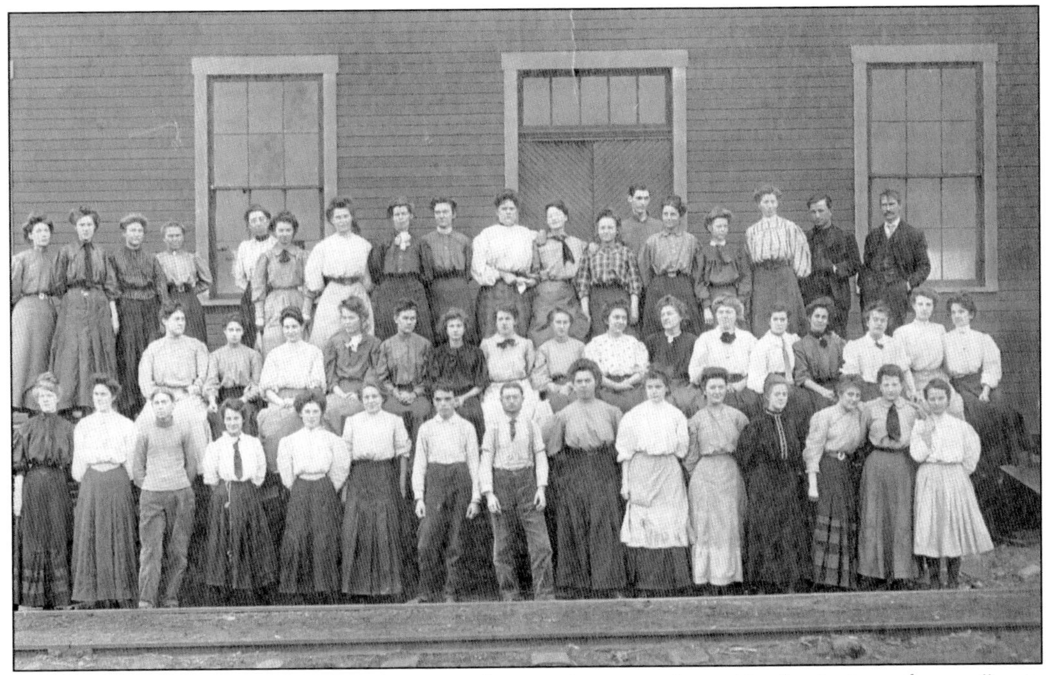

In this c. 1909 photograph, seamstresses and supervisors stand outside the "mitten factory," as it was locally known. Begun in Crawfordsville as the Gregg Glove Company, it was closed in 1909 and then sold to the Boss Glove Company from Illinois.

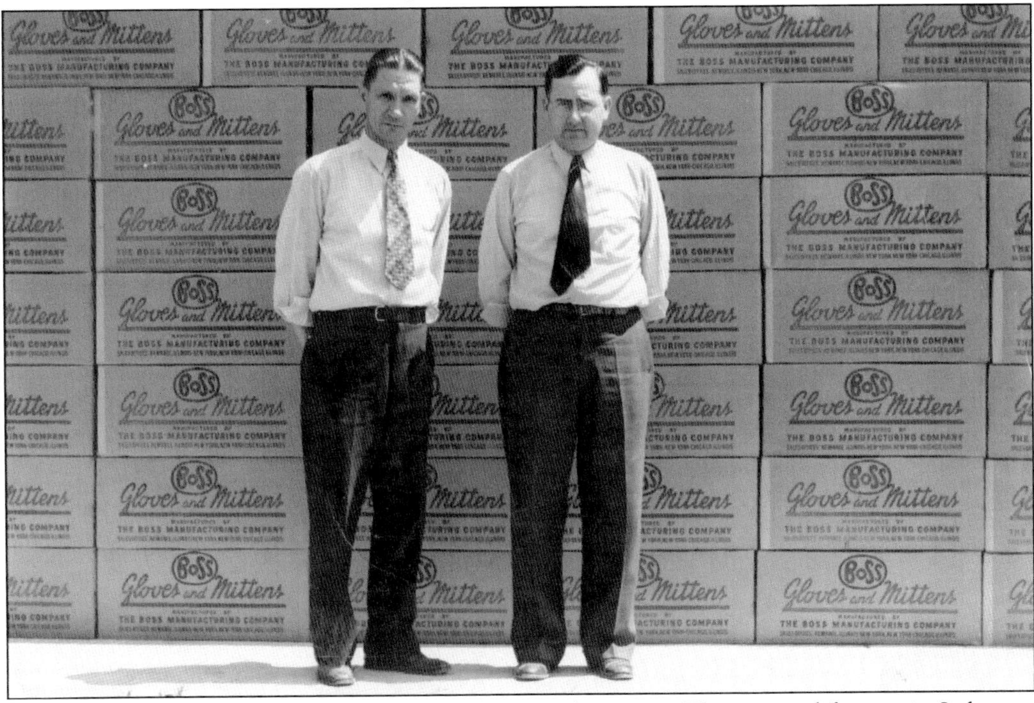

Two men stand before cases of Boss brand gloves and mittens. The original factory in Lebanon had been closed in 1909. The purchase by Boss was a welcome one, as it saved many jobs. Boss maintained full operations in Lebanon until they closed the plant in 1956.

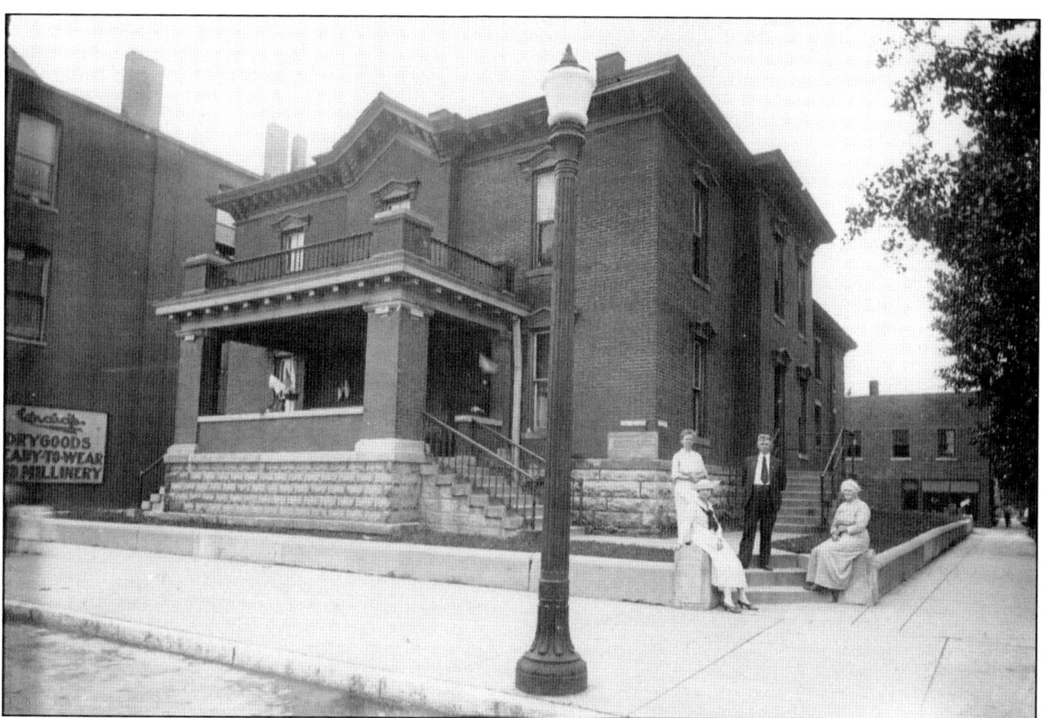

Built in 1877 and long known as the "old jail," this was actually Boone County's fourth lockup. The first two were log structures, and the third was a simple two-story brick building erected on a lot very close to where the fourth would later be located. In this c. 1918 photograph, Sheriff D.N. Lewis and his family are shown in front of the jail, where they also had living quarters.

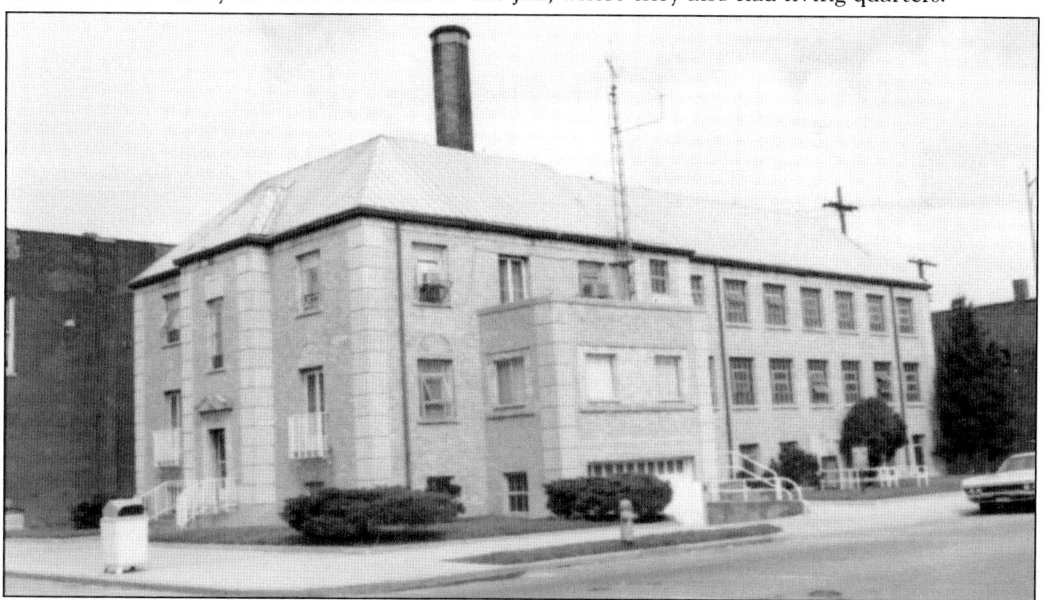

The old jail was replaced in 1939 by this new one built in part as a Works Progress Administration (WPA) or Civilian Conservation Corps (CCC) project under the Roosevelt administration. The building has been abandoned for a modern county facility and was sold at auction. The new owner is fitting the cells and common spaces to be used as a whiskey distillery with tasting rooms.

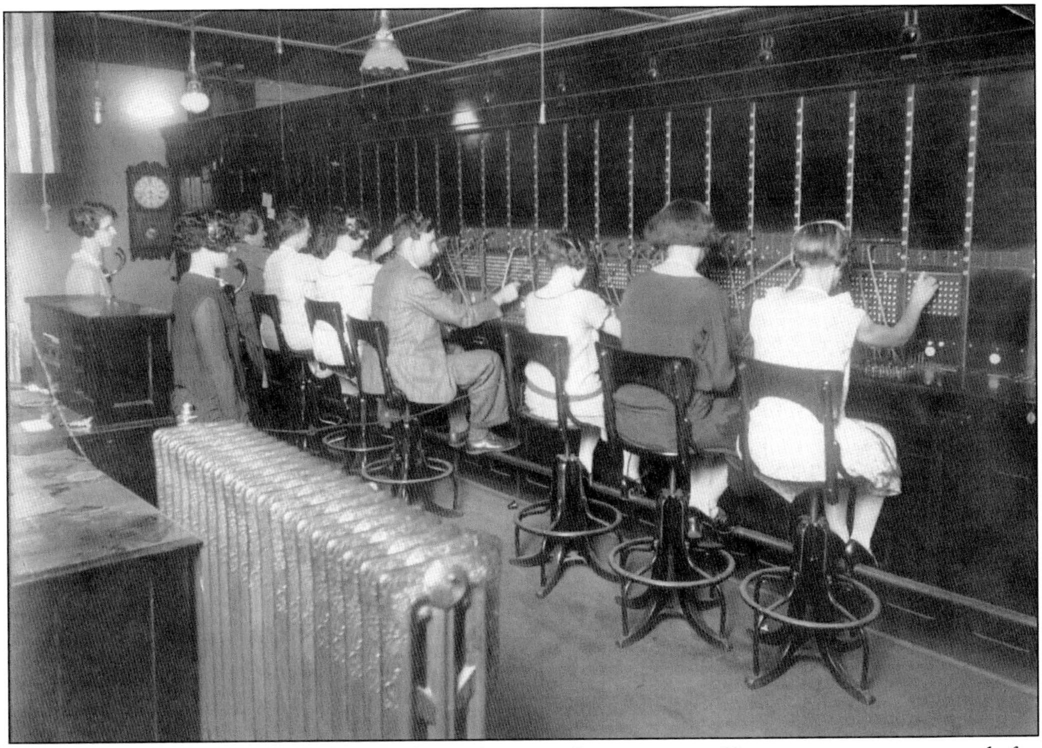

Shown here in 1928, just before making the switch to a new office, are women at work for their last shift at the old switchboards of the Lebanon Telephone Company. The back of the photograph identifies them as, from left to right, Estel Beck (standing), Mary Glendenning Hancock (standing), Alice Whitehead, Lucile Laflin, Emma Glendenning Hooton, Herman Whitehead, Roavene Youkey Clock, Fern Dillon, and Laveda Wines Davis. Alice Whitehead and her son Herman were previous switchboard operators who had been invited back for the occasion; they had worked nights together for several years until Herman's voice changed and he could no longer pass as a woman.

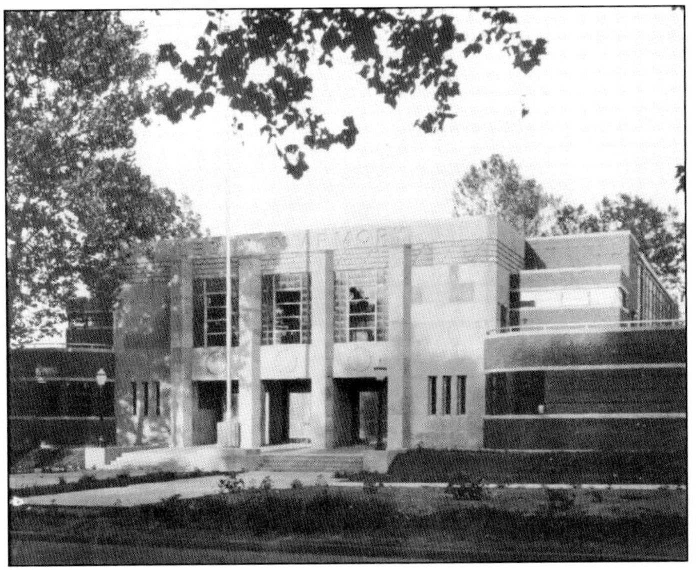

The CCC built a new armory in 1939. Considered architecturally significant, it was designed by Jacob Edwin Kopf. The building is currently under review for listing in the National Register of Historic Places.

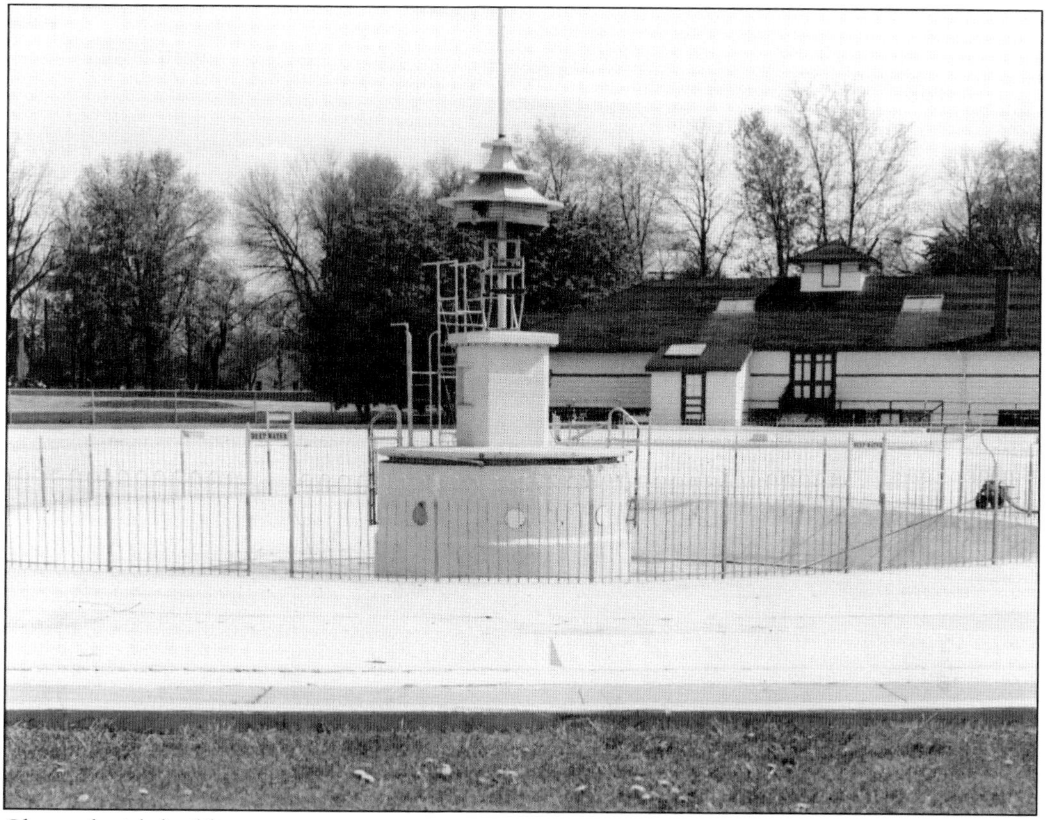

Charged with building or improvement projects that would impact citizens' daily lives, Boone County was granted CCC help with the creation of Sea Shore Pool and bathing house with lockers. The pool was open for swimming during the summer, and ice skating was allowed on the frozen pool surface into the late 1940s.

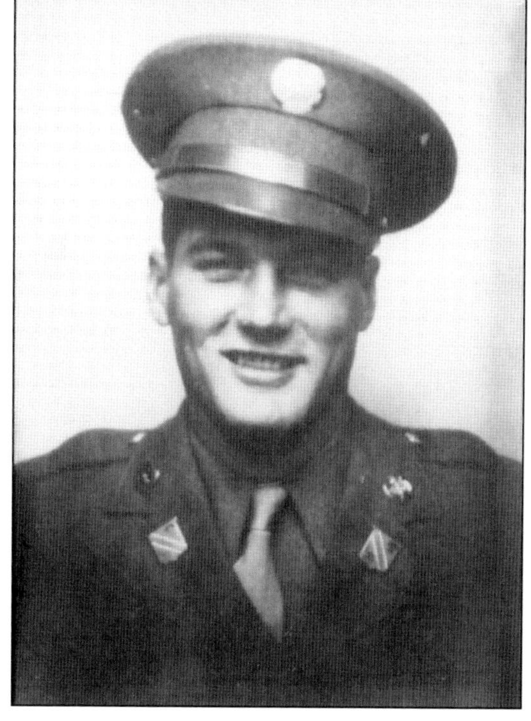

This handsome young man was one of Pres. Franklin D. Roosevelt's New Deal workers. The CCC was created for unmarried, unemployed, or discharged veterans between the ages of 18 and 35. Earl Newberry of Indianapolis signed on and was stationed at the Lebanon camp. The letters Newberry wrote to his mother (some contained a mandatory allotment check to the family equaling $25 of the $30 he earned each month) were recently found among his personal papers. (Author's collection.)

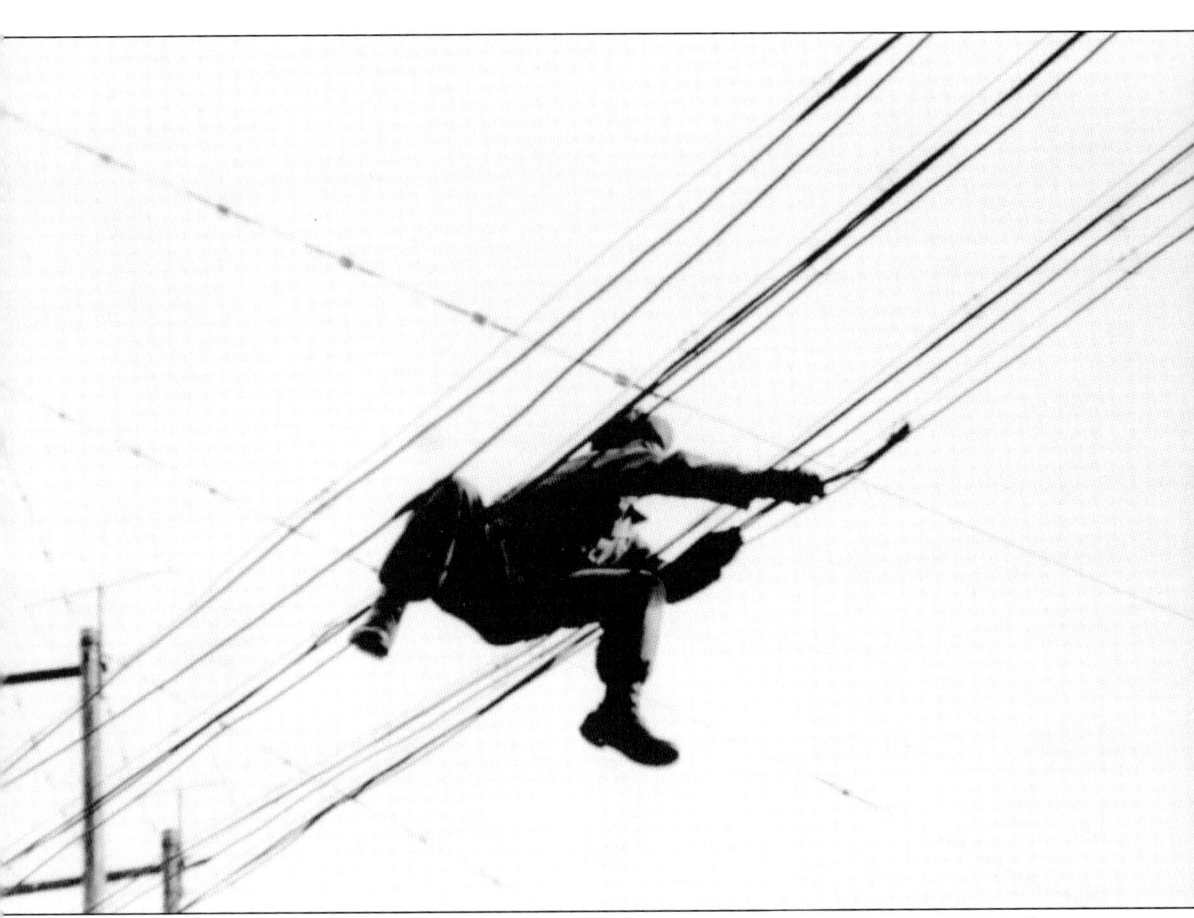

Boone was the first Indiana county with a Rural Electric Membership Corporation (known as REMC), organized in 1935 with the assistance of loans provided by Pres. Franklin Roosevelt's Rural Electrification Administration (the REA). The first poles were placed and lines run in January 1936. The original 60-mile line went live before the end of May that same year, forever changing rural life in the county.

Many improvements happened along with the REMC project, including macadamizing of several roads. This was a process invented by Scotsman John McAdam that involved binding gravel using gravel, rocks, dust, and tar. The resulting surface was much superior to the heavily rutted rock and dirt trails. Here, perplexed pigs may have heard the buzz of newly installed electrified lines next to the recently topped road. (Author's collection.)

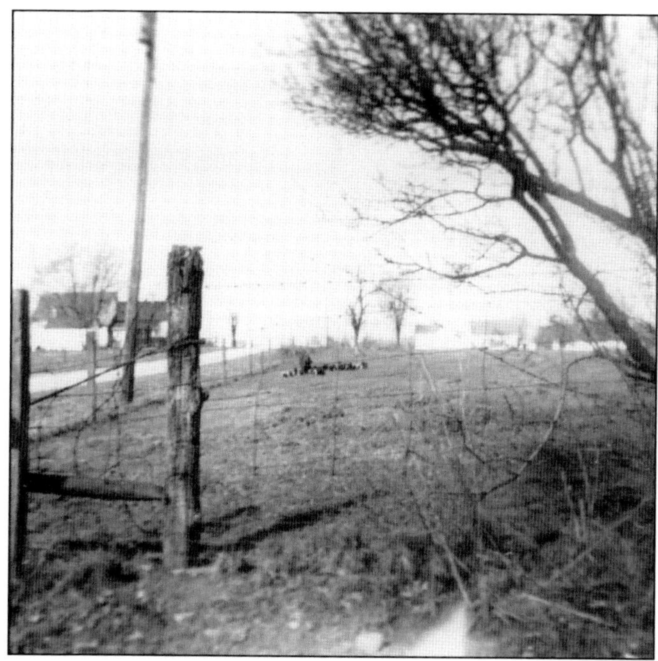

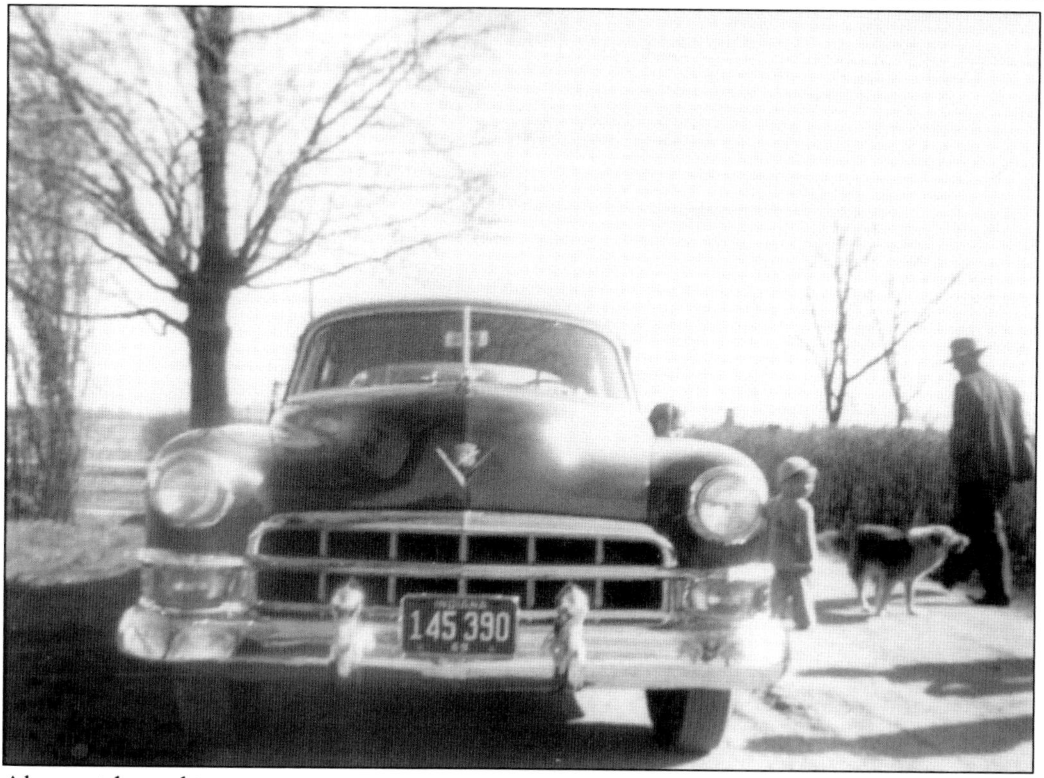

Along with road improvements came more opportunity for country folks to share visits with their city relatives. Here, big-city attorney and beloved uncle Jim Bingham braves the new roads with his flashy new car; he was greeted by his nephew Richard and the resident farm dog near Fayette. (Author's collection.)

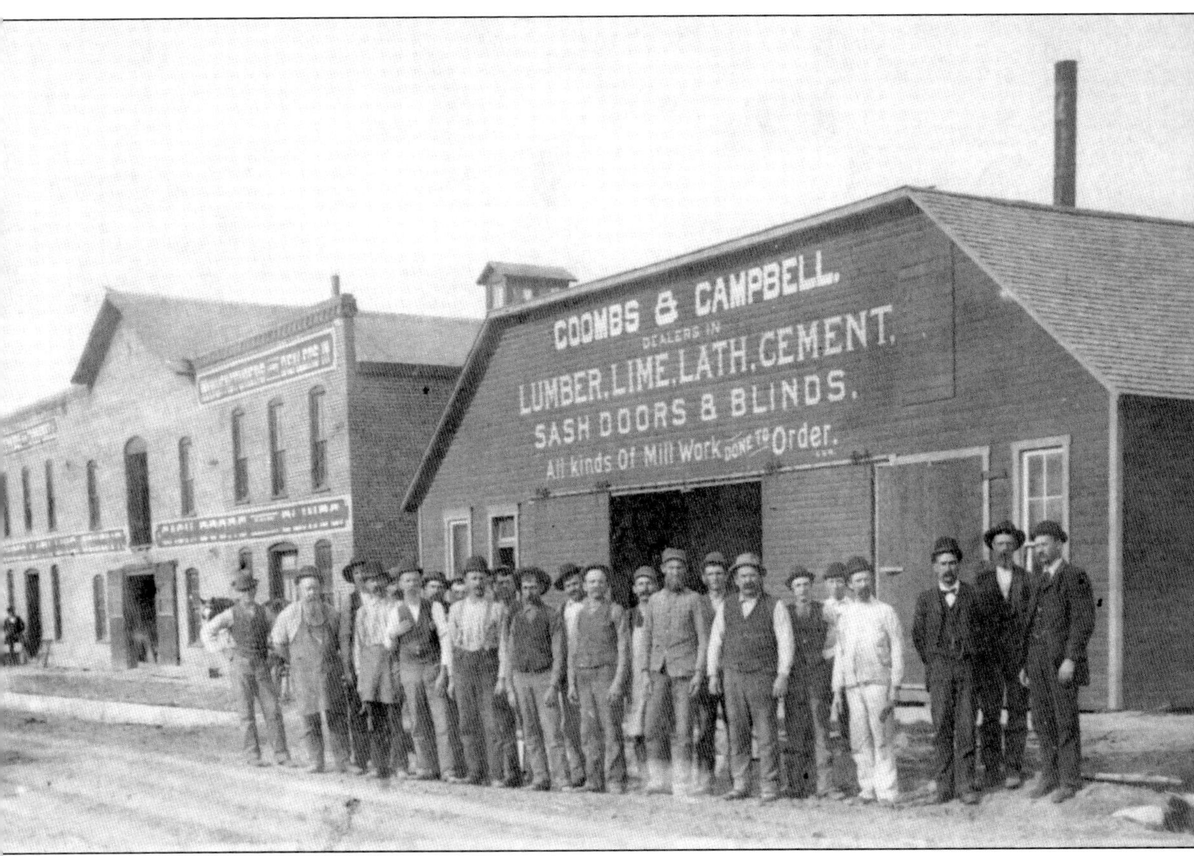

The planing mill of Combs & Campbell was a forerunner of the Campbell Smith and Richie Company. The company processed raw logs into usable lumber for building and manufacturing. Eventually, they began producing the popular Boone Cabinets, a brand of the Hoosier Cabinets that made kitchen furnishings and organized storage a reality for homes across the nation. Today, Boone Cabinets are one of the most sought-after brands in the antique Hoosier Cabinet market.

Five

Caring as a Community

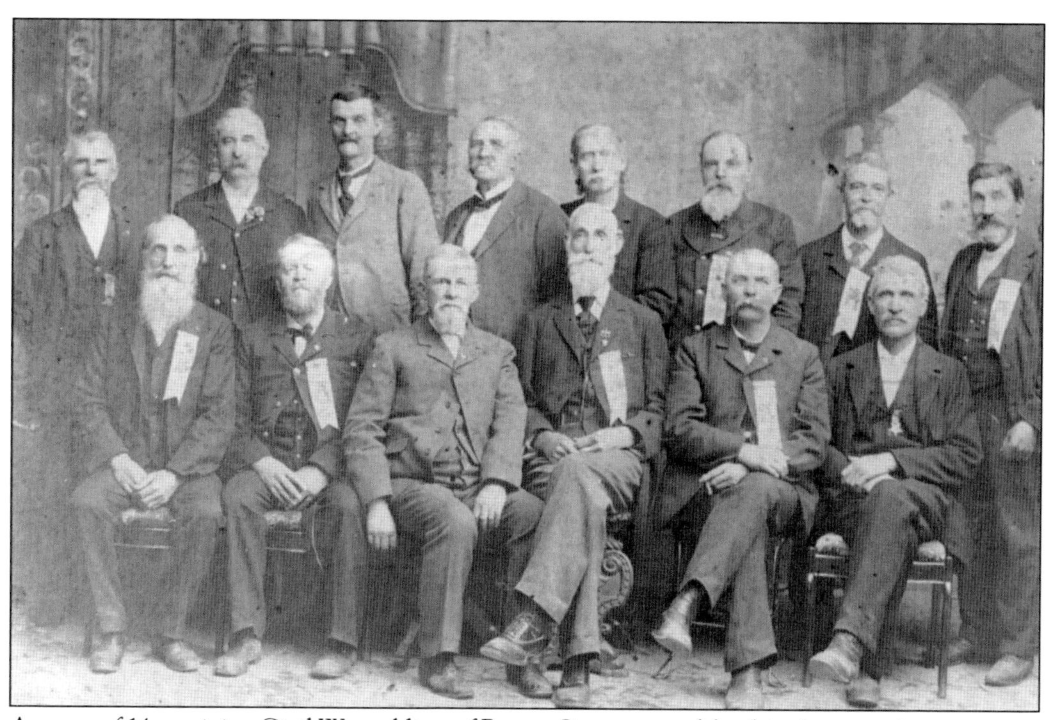

A group of 14 surviving Civil War soldiers of Boone County posed for this photograph at a reunion held around 1920. Unfortunately, they are not individually identified.

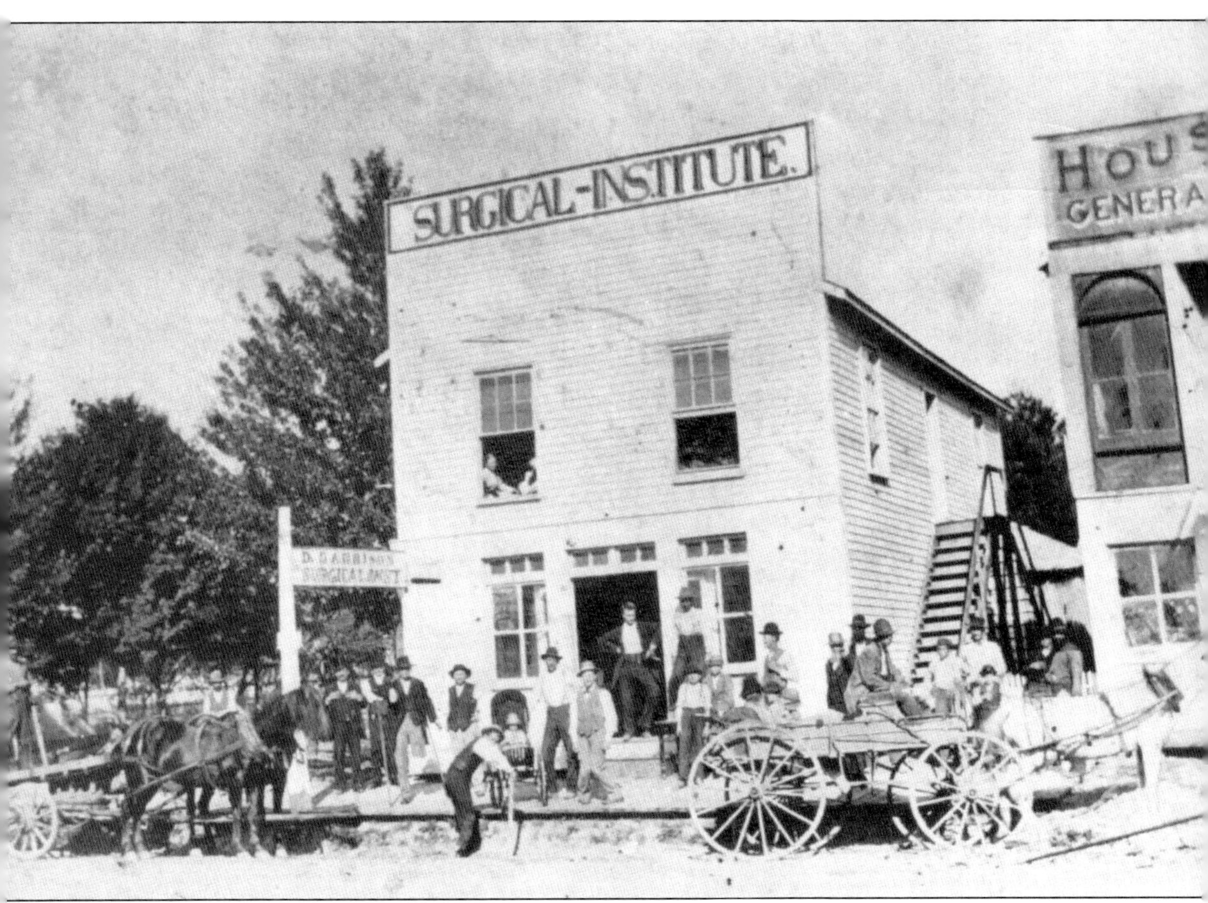

Opened in the mid-1870s, the Surgical Institute at 129 North Meridian Street in Lebanon was Boone County's first clinical medical facility. Owned and founded by J.F.L. Garrison, a battlefield assistant surgeon during the Civil War, the Surgical Institute predated antibiotics and offered only whiskey for anesthesia. Nevertheless, ill and injured people came from all corners of the county desperately seeking relief. "Doctor" Garrison closed the hospital about five years before dying of tuberculosis in 1893. His obituary noted his "extreme passion for drink." He is interred at Oak Hill, no doubt near some of his previous patients.

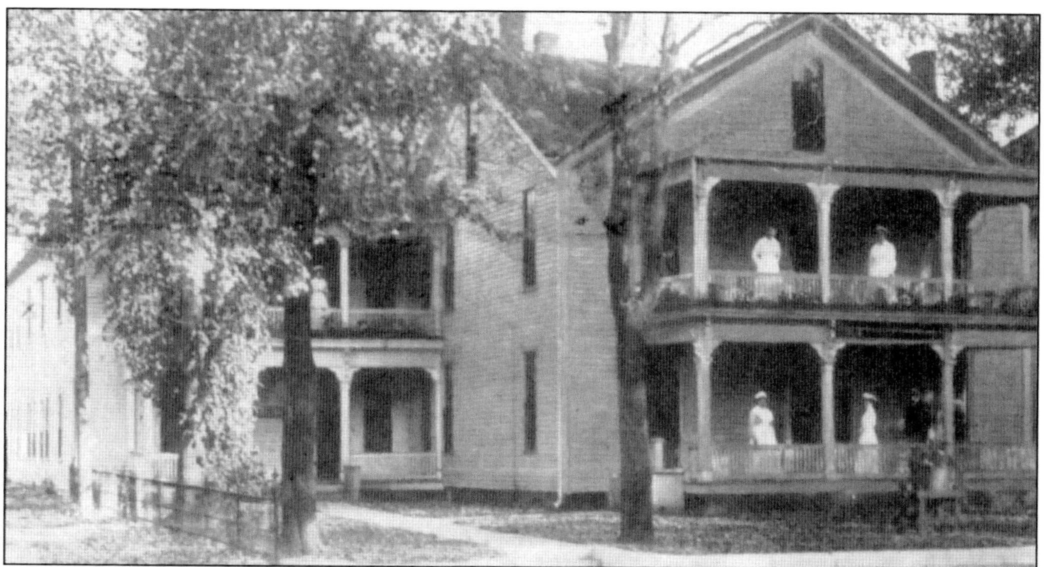

The Williams Hospital opened in 1903 at East and South Streets in Lebanon. Though rather selective in the cases admitted (they advertised care for "all cases except insane and contagious"), the facility was quite an upgrade from the previous hospital. Dr. W.H. Williams, a trained physician, opened the new facility with two patient beds. By 1915, it had expanded to 35 beds, created a three-year nursing school on-site, and adopted modern improvements such as x-ray, laboratory, and ambulance services.

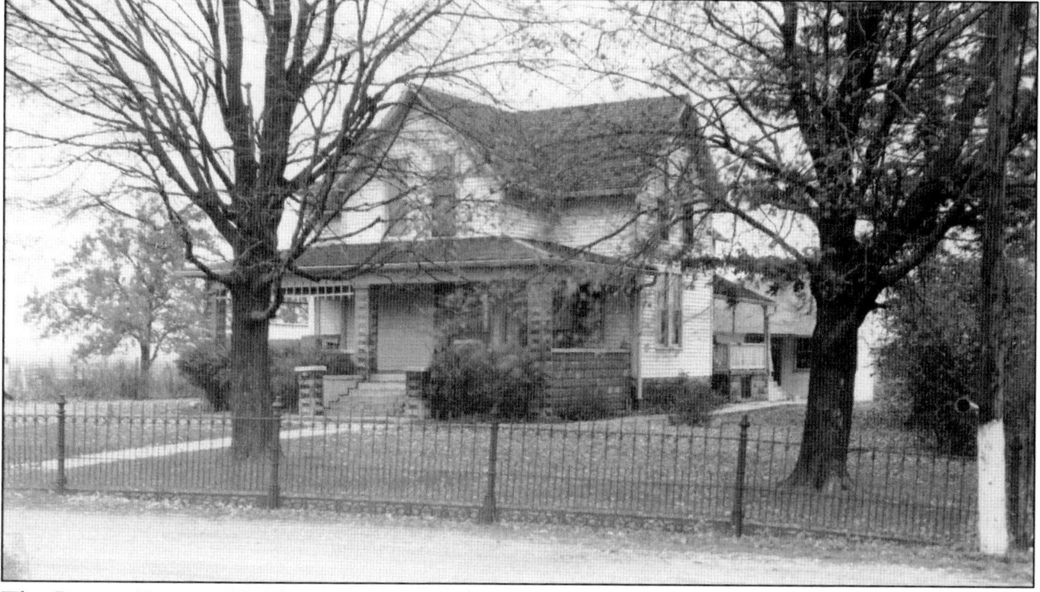

The Boone County Children's Home was founded in 1898 on a tract of land with a large home on it just south of the county infirmary. The county orphanage operated until 1938. Previous to 1898, orphans in the area were sent to live in a similar facility at nearby Westfield. Beginning in the late 1920s, after Henry Ulen transferred offices for his company to Lebanon, a check arrived each December 1 into the hands of the matron, Alice Whitehead. The accompanying note stated, "Buy gifts for the children, and respect the anonymity of the giver." Whitehead served as housemother for 19 years.

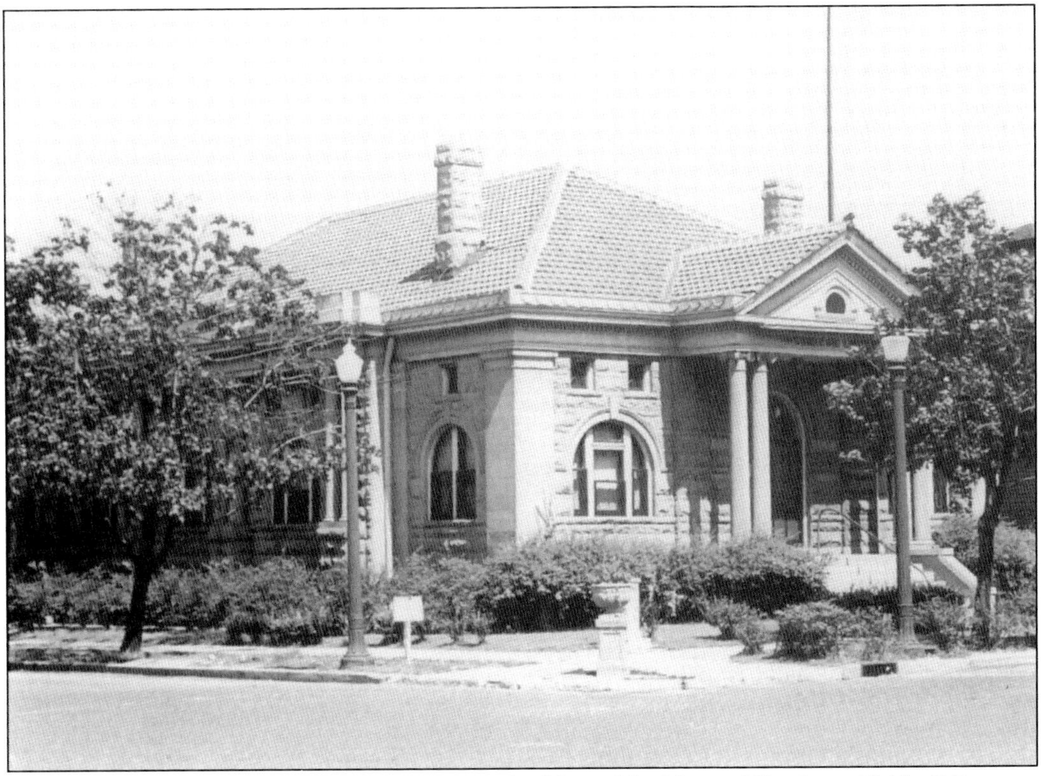

In 1904, Lebanon received a Carnegie grant to build a public library. This beautiful building was the result. Thorntown was awarded a Carnegie library in 1911. Both cities have recently expanded their libraries using complementary architectural elements.

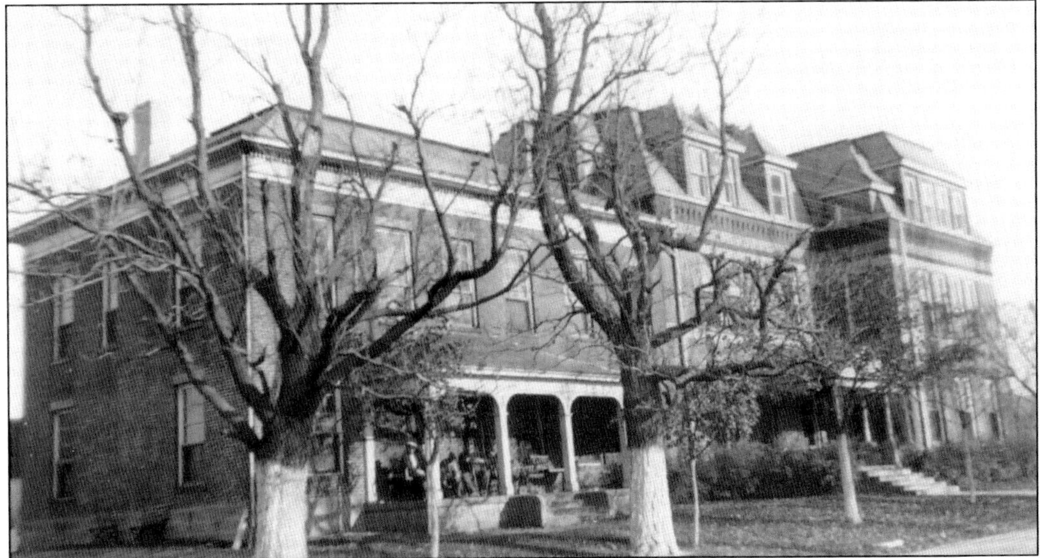

The Boone County Infirmary (later known as Mapleview Rest Home), according to the 1910 census of "paupers in almshouses," was home to 33 residents. Originally built in 1895, it was replaced with a brick structure after being destroyed by fire. The home was expanded and remodeled again in the 1940s. Currently, the buildings are vacant and set for demolition.

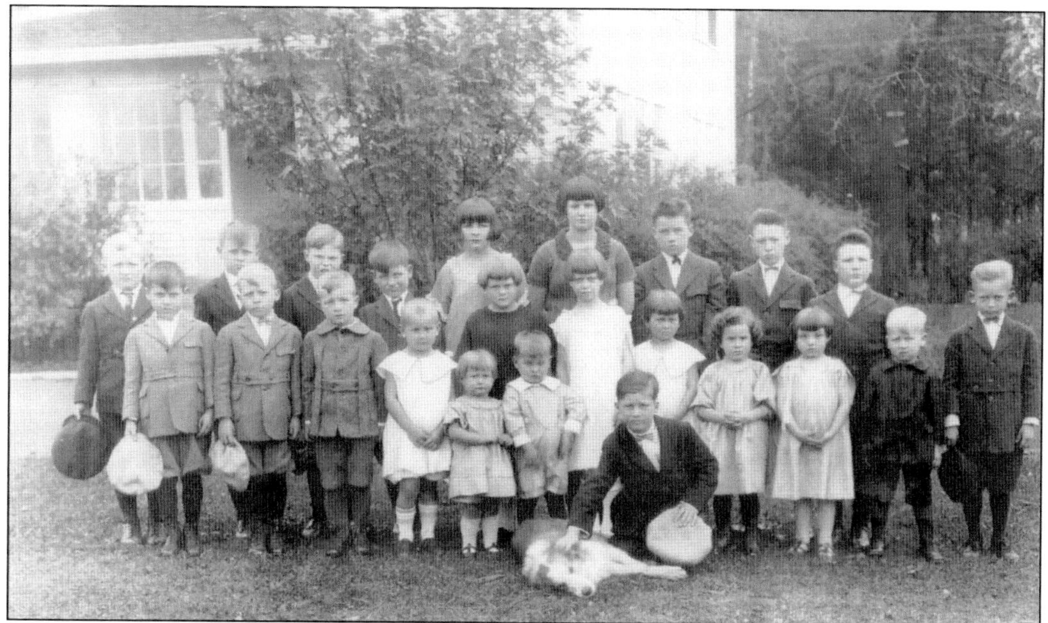

The Indiana United Methodist Children's Home was founded in Greencastle in 1915 as a ministry of Deaconess Angie Godwin. The population of children quickly outgrew that facility. Lebanon was chosen as the new site due to its central location. This 1924 photograph shows move-in day at the former Russell Ritchie home, renamed Wesley Hall. The Lebanon campus, previously used for Chautauqua meetings, included two residences on a sweeping meadow as well as wooded acreage. (Indiana United Methodist Children's Home.)

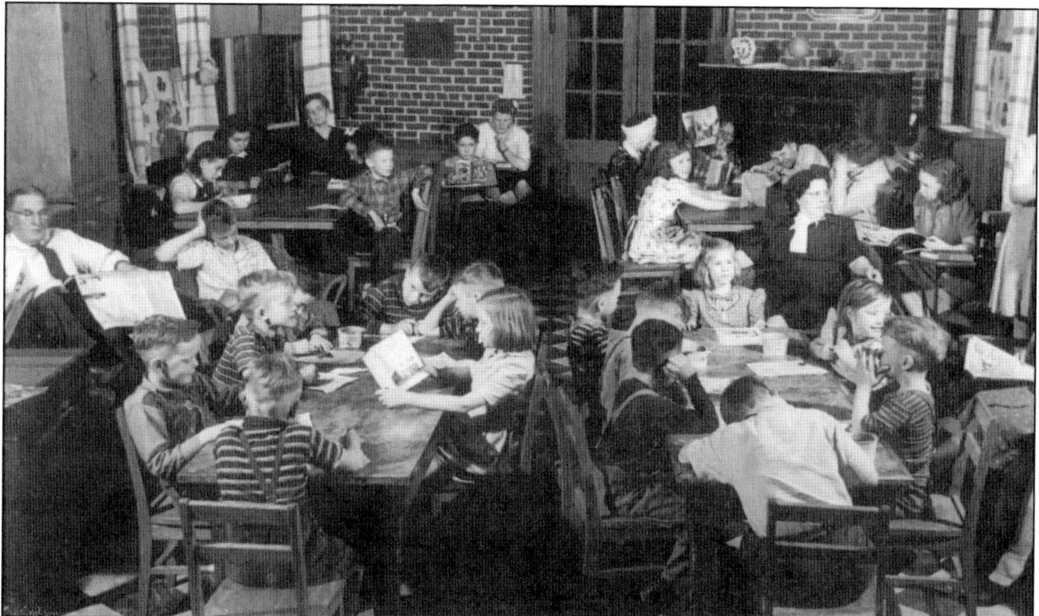

The children at the Indiana United Methodist Children's Home are shown here settled in and studying. Several staff members are on hand to supervise and provide a nurturing environment for the children. The original mission of the home was to prepare orphaned and abandoned children for placement in more permanent homes. (Indiana United Methodist Children's Home.)

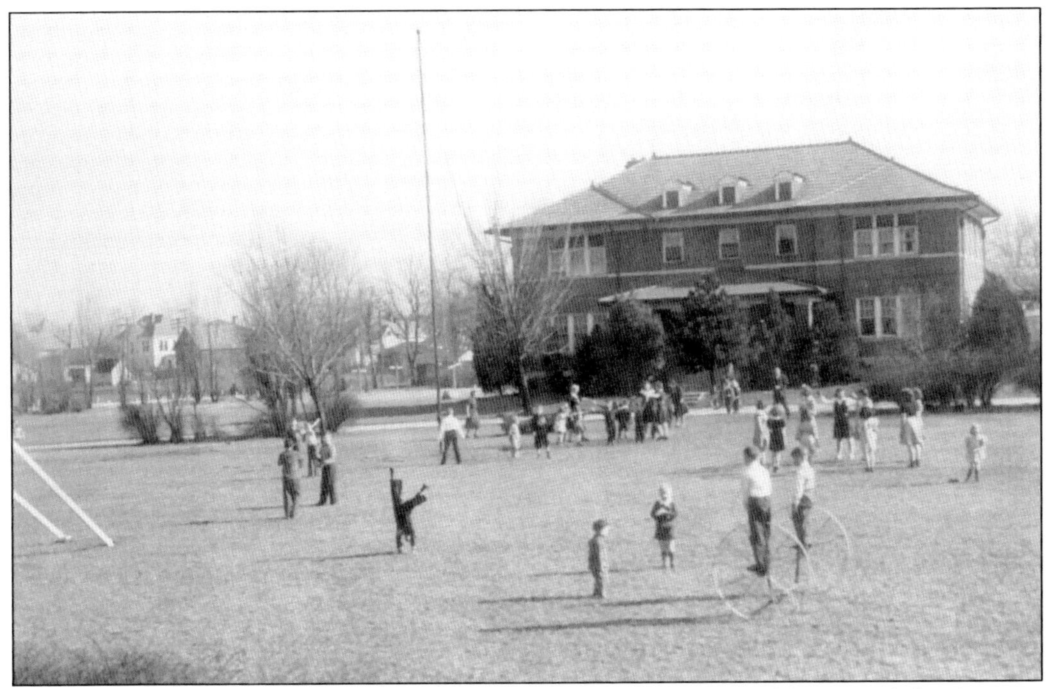

Residents of the Indiana United Methodist Children's Home make use of the grounds for playtime. A variety of outdoor activities were provided to keep the children healthy and of "congenial attitude." (Indiana United Methodist Children's Home.)

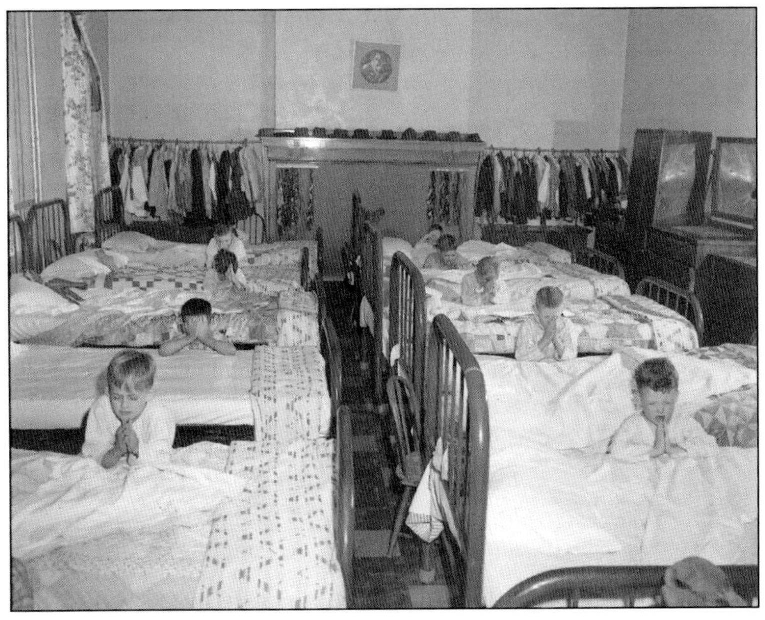

In the boy's dormitory, residents say a bedtime prayer. The home is still operating in Lebanon. The focus of service has changed to meet the needs of today's clients, who are less likely to be orphaned children and more likely to be adolescents removed from neglectful or abusive situations. Efforts are now focused on behavioral issues and trauma recovery. (Indiana United Methodist Children's Home.)

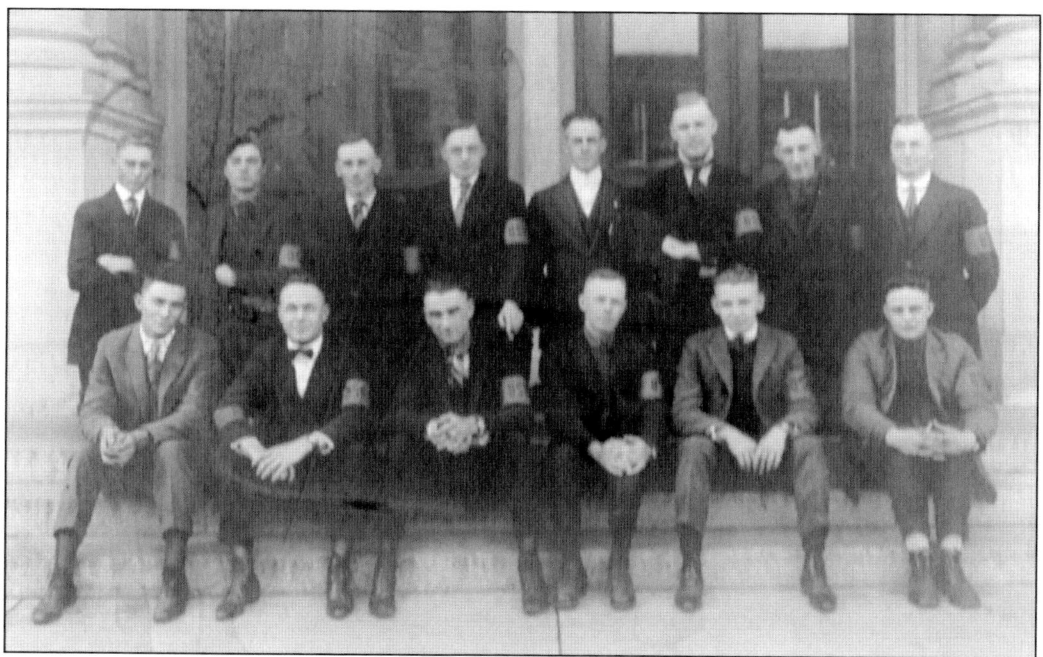

This group of 14 young men posed on the courthouse steps for this photograph before leaving the county seat. They were the original Boone volunteers to the US Army during World War I. The young men are unidentified, and it is not known how many of them returned after service.

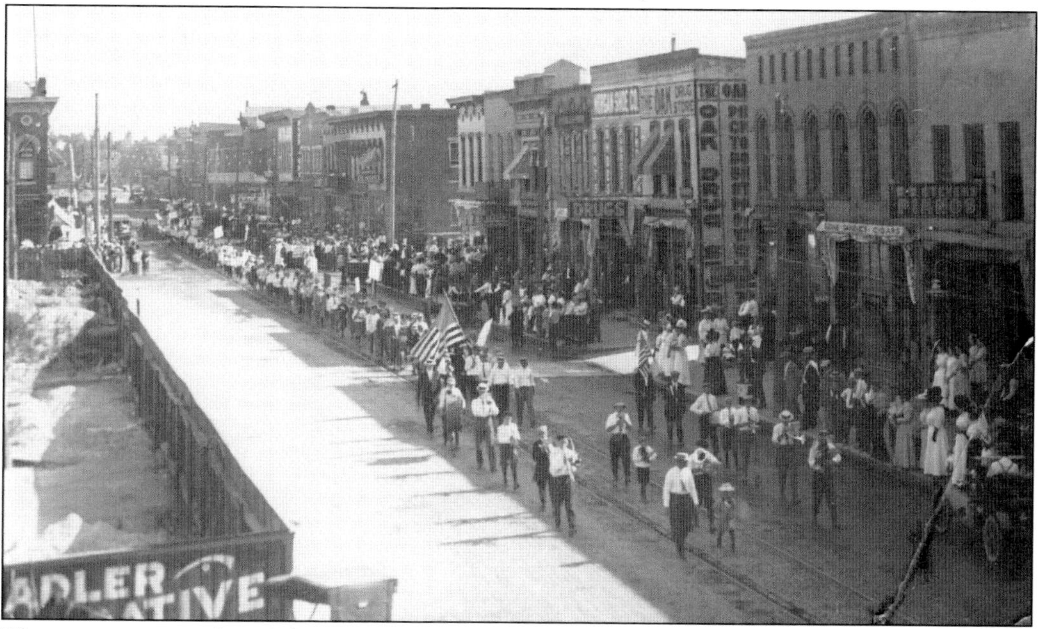

This street scene is from July 24, 1911, when the Dry Day Parade was held in Lebanon. The pubs and taverns, having previously been shut down from 1907 to 1908, were all voted closed again for two years. No doubt some of the townspeople had heard the preaching of Henry Ward Beecher at nearby Trader's Point, or perhaps read his sister's (Harriet Beecher Stowe) novel, *Uncle Tom's Cabin*, and were inspired to act against the evils of drink and the ills it caused against society. Taverns eventually reopened for business until Prohibition became law in 1920.

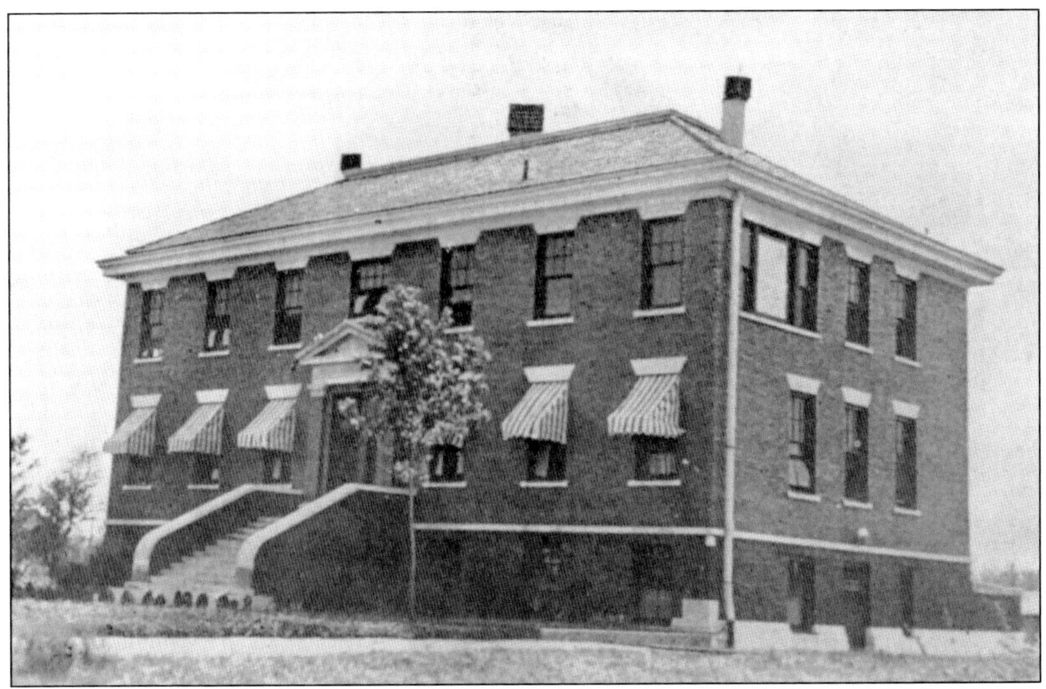

In 1915, successful Clinton Township farmers Flavius and Mary Witham gave the kingly sum of $15,000 toward the founding of a county-owned hospital to serve Boone citizens. The idea of a non-private hospital was hotly debated as being financially irresponsible by some, and of moral and Christian necessity by others. The following year, ground was broken on the Witham Memorial Hospital.

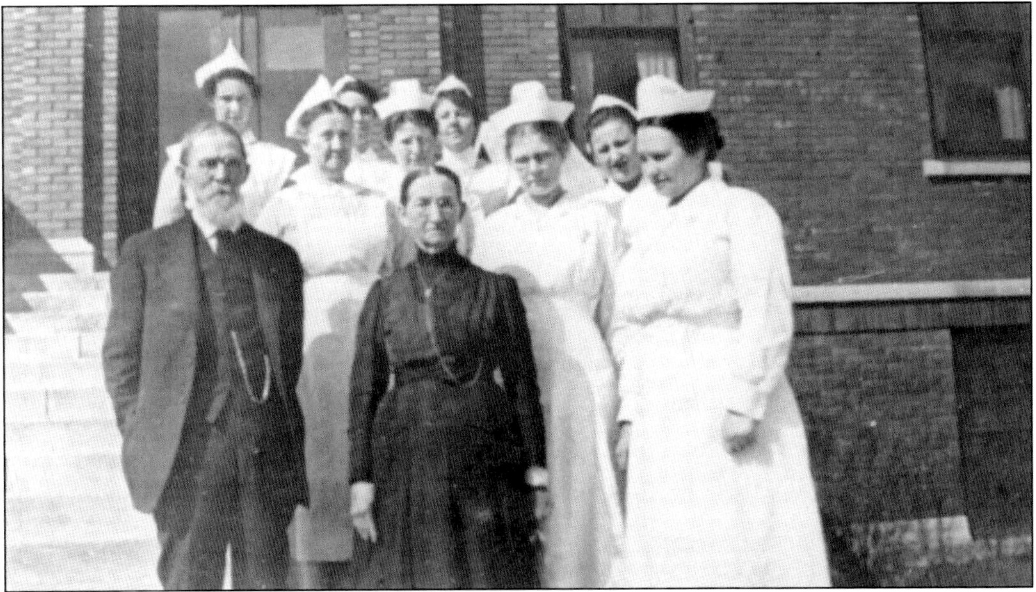

Shortly after completion of the Witham Memorial Hospital in 1917, the Withams posed with nursing staff. Today, Witham continues to grow, serving the people of Boone and surrounding counties at many locations with exceptional staff and facilities. They celebrate 100 years in 2017.

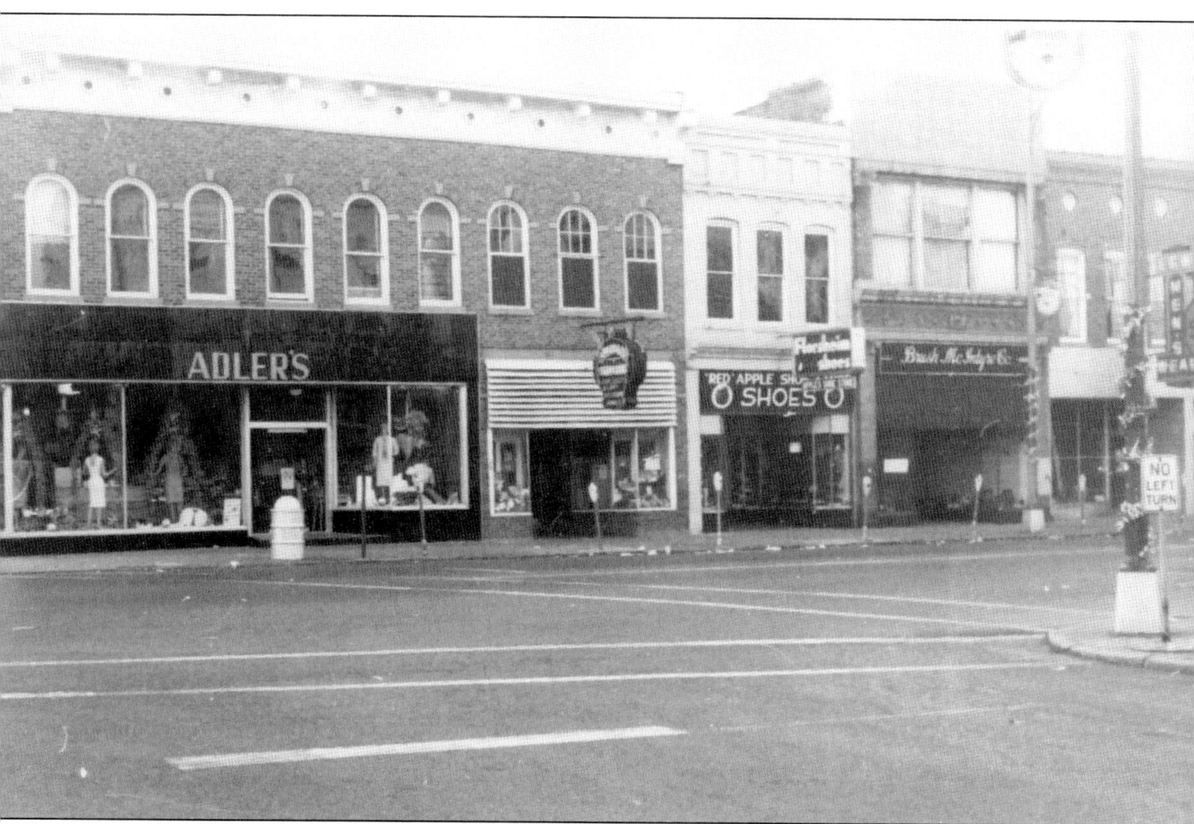

Adler's, the Sugar Bowl, and Apple's Shoe Store were longtime fixtures on the courthouse square in Lebanon. All three proprietors were known for their generosity. However, Rudell "Red" Apple was quietly one of the county's largest philanthropists. He aided many of the local poor by giving away shoes and needed cash to families. Tuffy Hedges, the second owner of the White Cabin Restaurant, was another quiet hero to those in need; he was known for opening on holidays and giving a free hamburger to any down-on-his-luck neighbor or family in need.

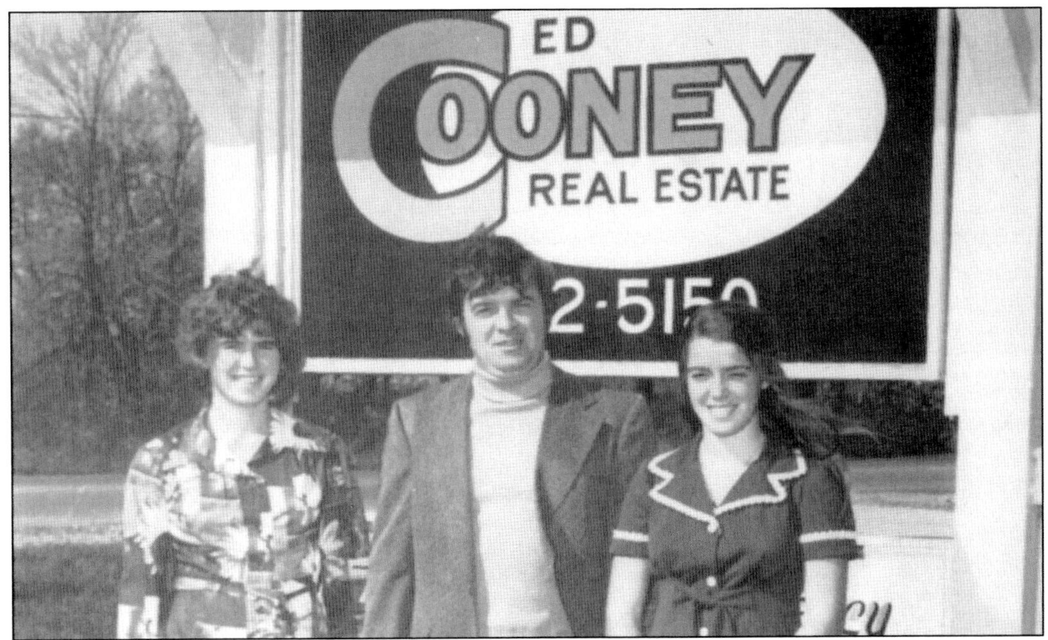

Ed Cooney poses here with his daughters Michelle (left) and Lisa. Ed could always be counted on as a community booster, offering baseball team sponsorships or helping out any child in need.

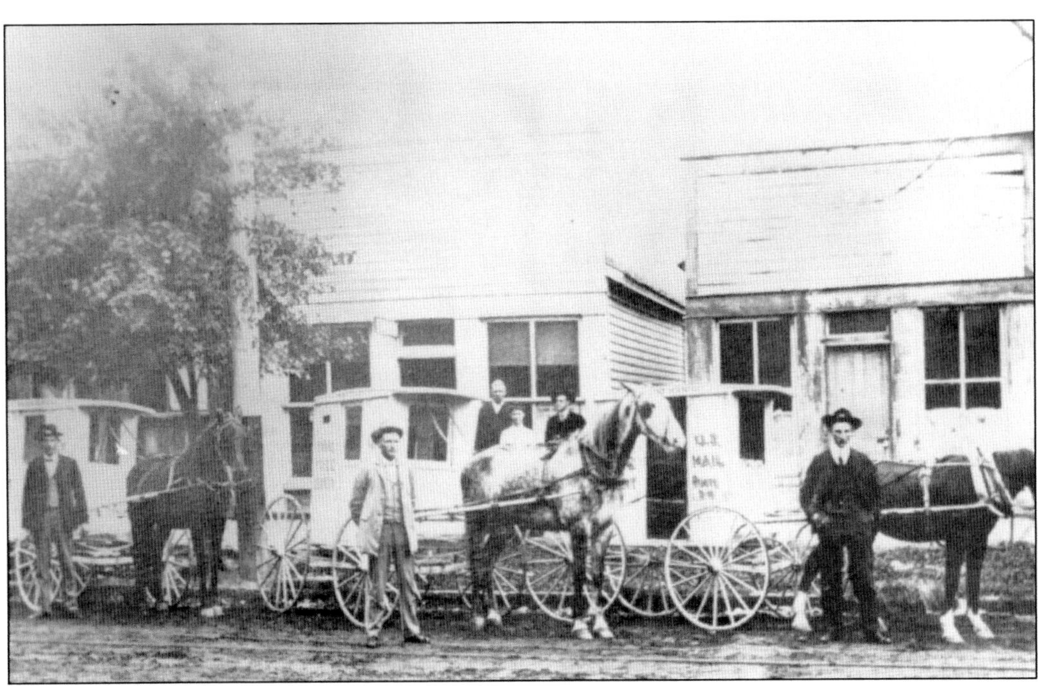

To serve the rural community, Lebanon's new post office served as a hub of home delivery for previously underserved areas. Here, postal workers show off their fleet of vehicles.

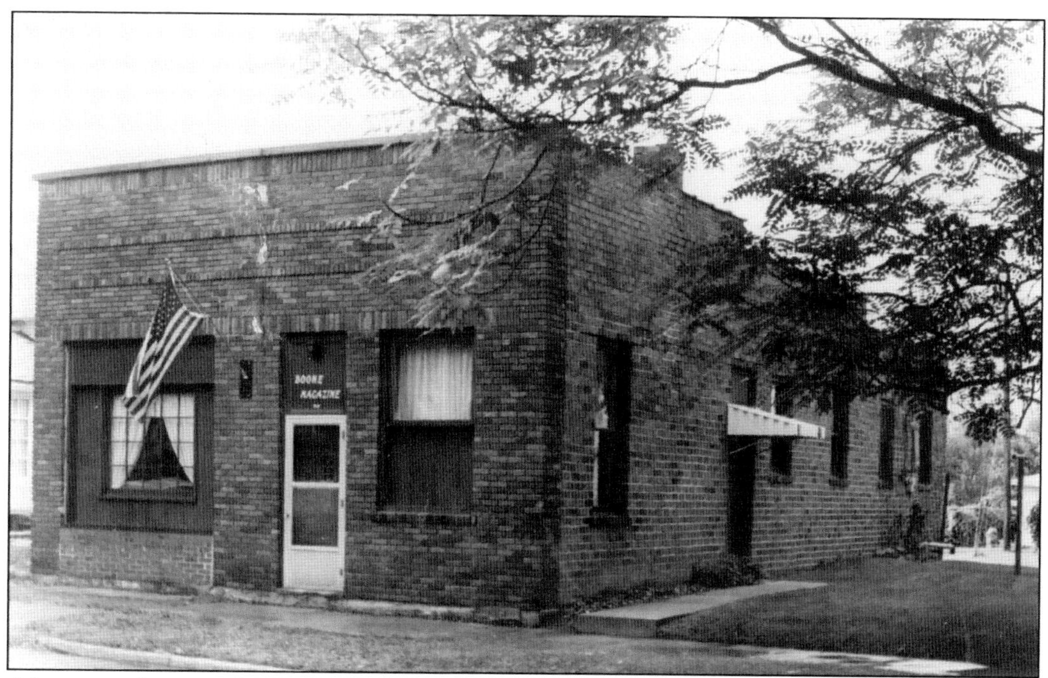

After several successful years, *Boone Magazine* moved offices from Zionsville to Lebanon. The sturdy brick building was used as warehousing for pump organs and pianos sold by the W.W. Stevens Music Store when built in 1921. The old-time stories reported in "Your County Magazine" may have incited much of the enthusiasm for the 1976 bicentennial events.

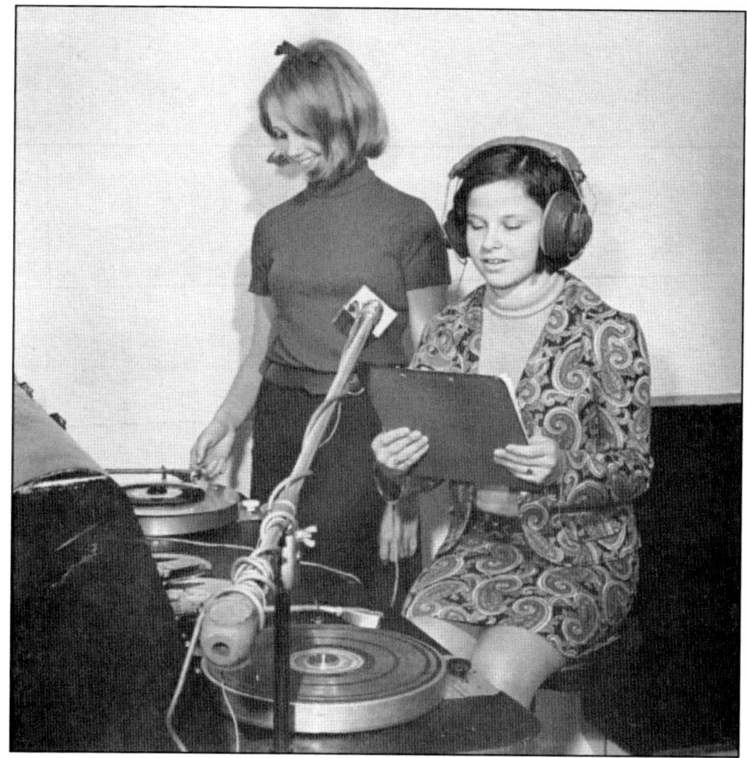

In 1967, Warren Wright came to Lebanon and established radio station WNON. Daily farm, local, and regional news was reported between musical offerings. Of special interest to families were the sports scores and weather-related closings and announcements. A popular daily broadcast originated from Cowan's Cubbard, the cafe inside Akerman's Drug Store. The show kept everyone up to speed on county news and events. Here, a pair of high school students spin a record for listeners.

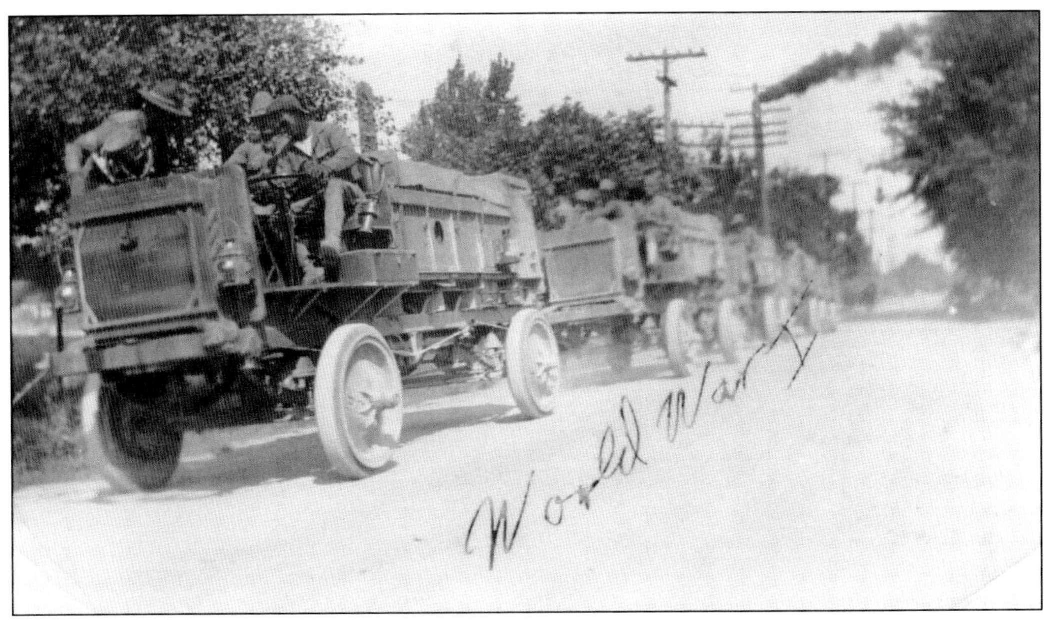

One afternoon during World War I, the Army trucks pictured above were driven into Boone County and along the Indianapolis Road (Old 52). Done as a part of the government's efforts to keep spirits high at home and to promote the latest set of newsreels coming to the local moving-picture show, the convoy made quite an impression. Below, three military airplanes touched down for a quick visit during wartime, likely promoting war bonds and a lift to war-weary spirits.

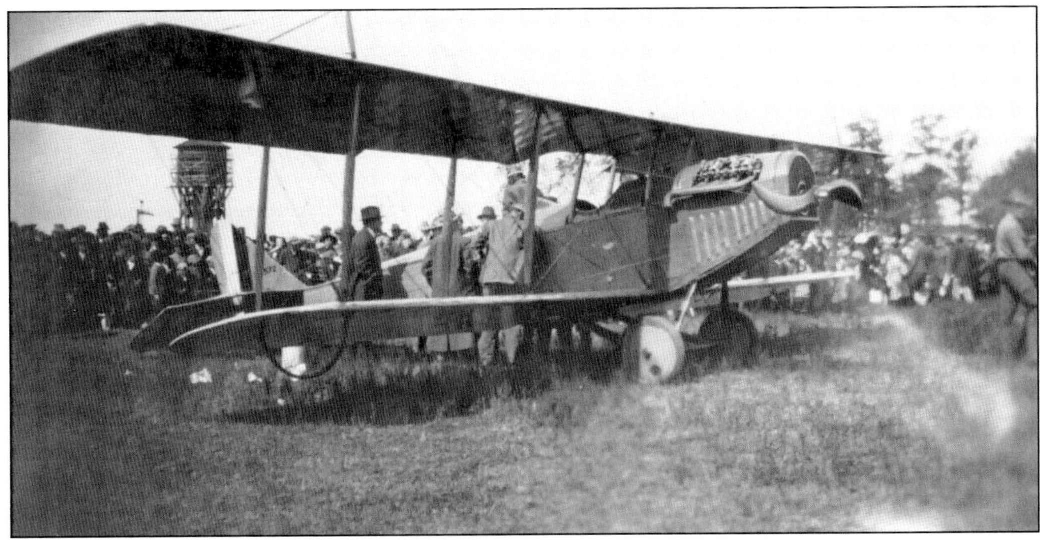

Six

Farming the Land, Dodging the Weather

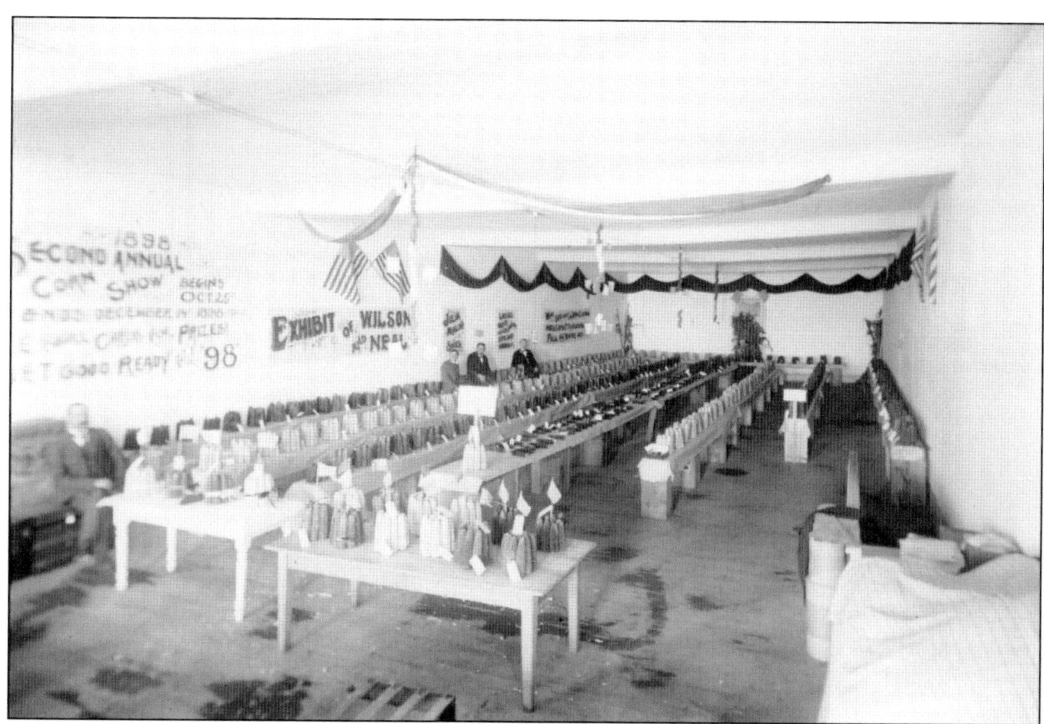

Once cleared, the soil in Indiana was a perfect match for corn. In 1897, the first Corn Fair and Exhibition was held in Boone County. Tents were set up at the old fairgrounds, the current site of Lebanon's Memorial Park. Farmers from all around exhibited and competed for awards for prizes including best ears. This photograph shows an expo tent from 1898.

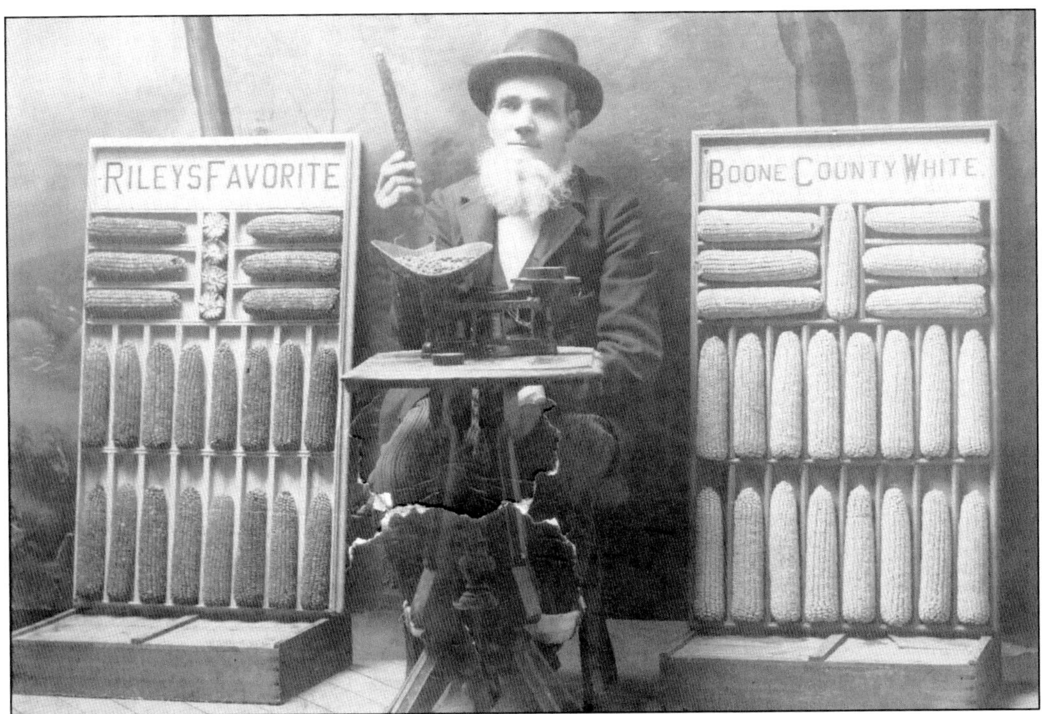

Farmer James Riley proudly shows off a lengthy cob from one of his selectively bred ears. The scales were used to measure the yield produced by each grower's entry. (Thorntown History Museum.)

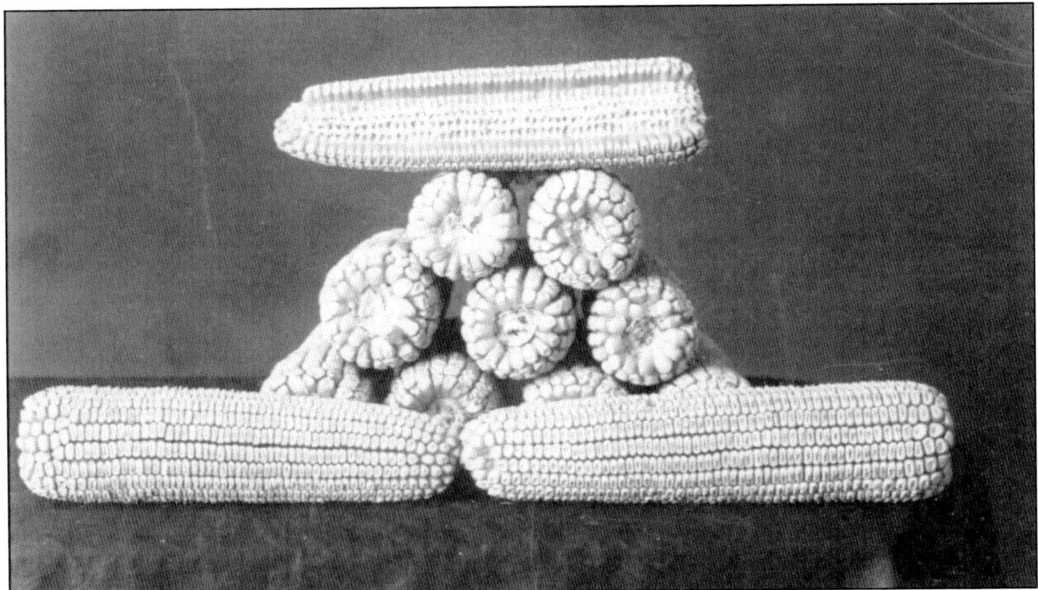
This is a close-up of a farmer's sample ears on display for judging. This variety is labeled Boone White. In 1918, the first winner of a 4-H prize was a young man from Zionsville named Dwight Bender, who won for the Poland China pig he raised. He also went on to win prizes in corn-growing. Unfortunately, when Bender enrolled at Indiana University, he soon fell ill. He died around his 20th birthday at the Albuquerque hospital his mother had rushed him to, known for its treatment of consumption (tuberculosis).

Weather was always on a farmer's mind, whether his primary trade was in field crops, tree-lined orchards, or livestock. This scene near Terhune shows the devastation caused by a late winter ice storm. The heavy ice coating destroyed trees and made travel impossible. (Author's collection.)

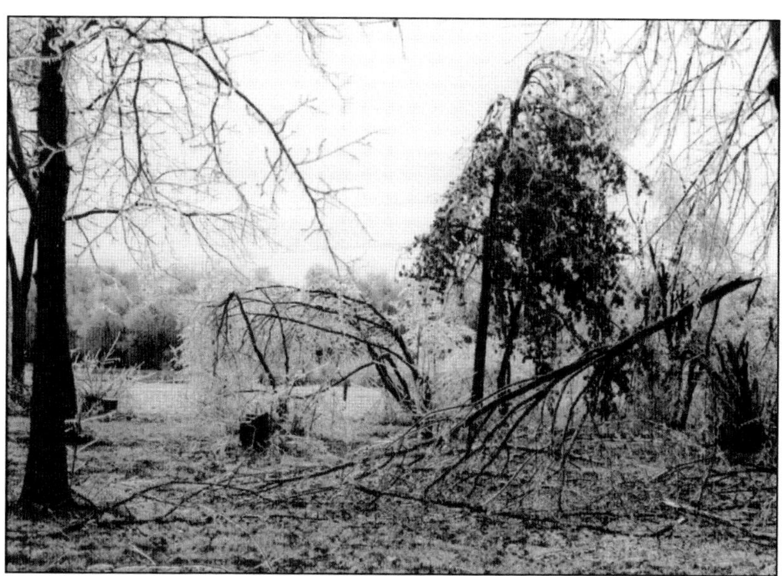

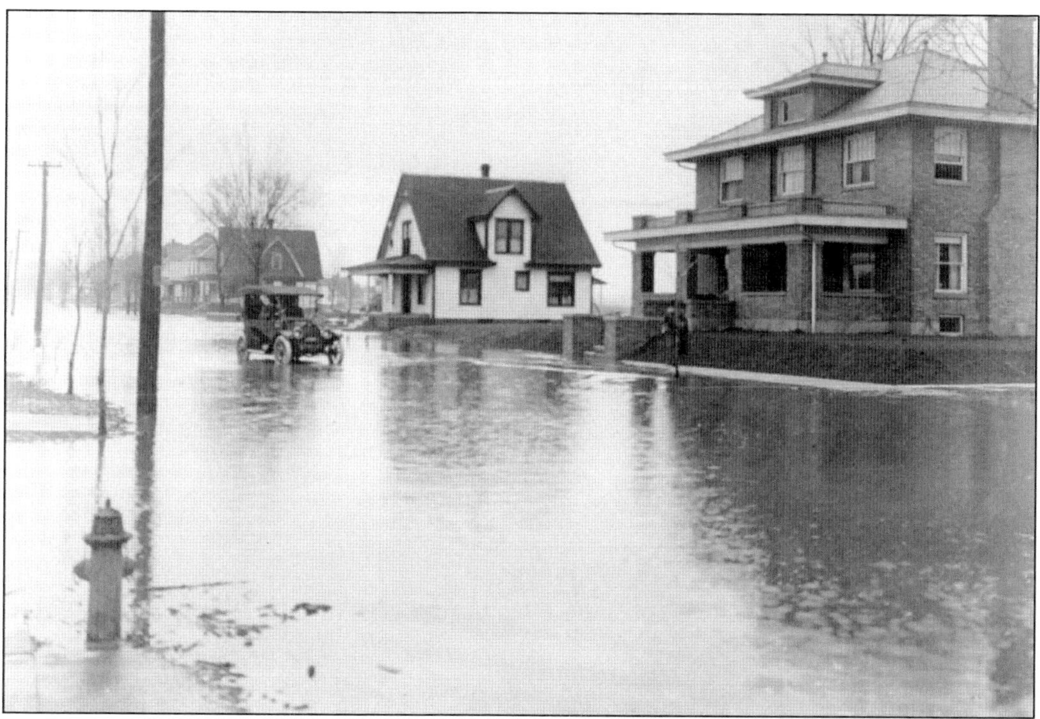

The Great Flood and Cyclone of 1913 did not wash Boone from the map as it did nearby West Indianapolis, Peru, and many other places in the Midwest. However, it certainly left its mark. On Easter Sunday, March 23, a monster storm was born. Tearing a path from Nebraska to Ohio over the next three days, it succeeded in destroying entire towns and leaving more than 250 people dead. The US Army Signal Corps had outlawed the use of the term "tornado" in 1882, calling the word "panic producing." Nineteen of these unnamed "weather events" touched down in three days. The ban on the word tornado was officially lifted in 1952.

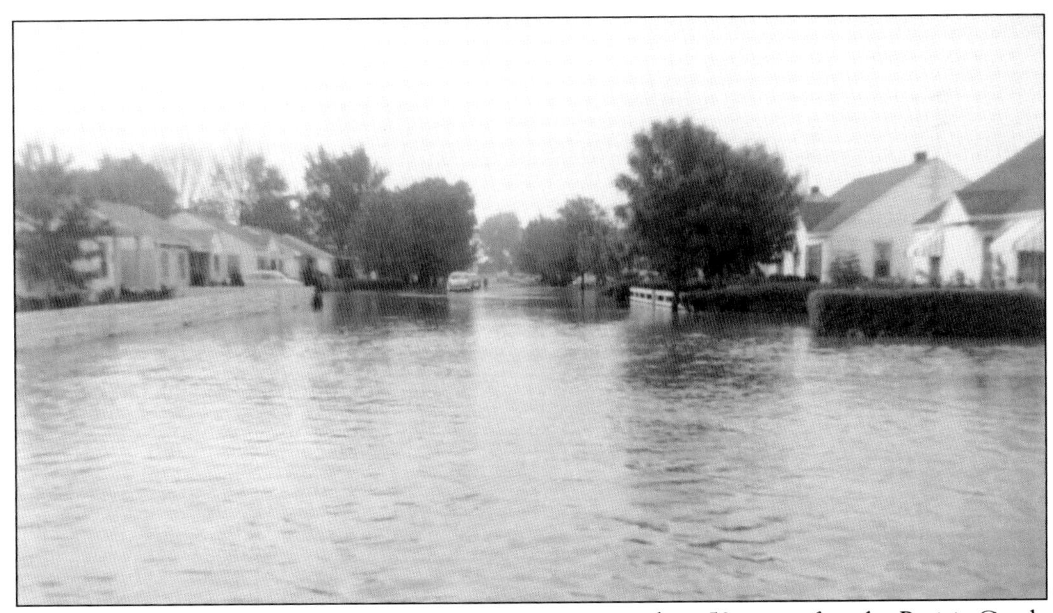

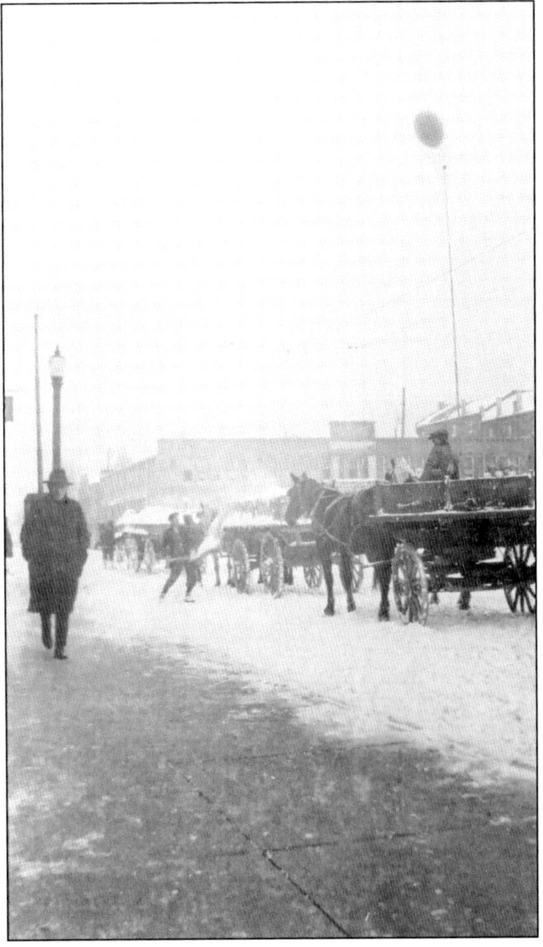

More than 50 years after the Prairie Creek dredging project, Mother Nature proved she could still cripple civilization with water. In 1957, this flood set the National Guard into action rescuing people from their homes. The waters were said to be high enough that they entered homes, causing many to set their expensive, newly acquired televisions and other cherished belongings on top of dining tables and sofas in hopes of saving them. Once again, nearby West Indianapolis was underwater, which became the impetus for the Eagle Creek Reservoir project.

In 1912, a large snowstorm dumped several inches of snow on Boone County, making even the courthouse square impassable. Teams of horses were brought in to pull large wagons. Men shoveled snow into the wagons, which were then driven out to the countryside and dumped. The storm paralyzed commerce for days. Merchants were not amused.

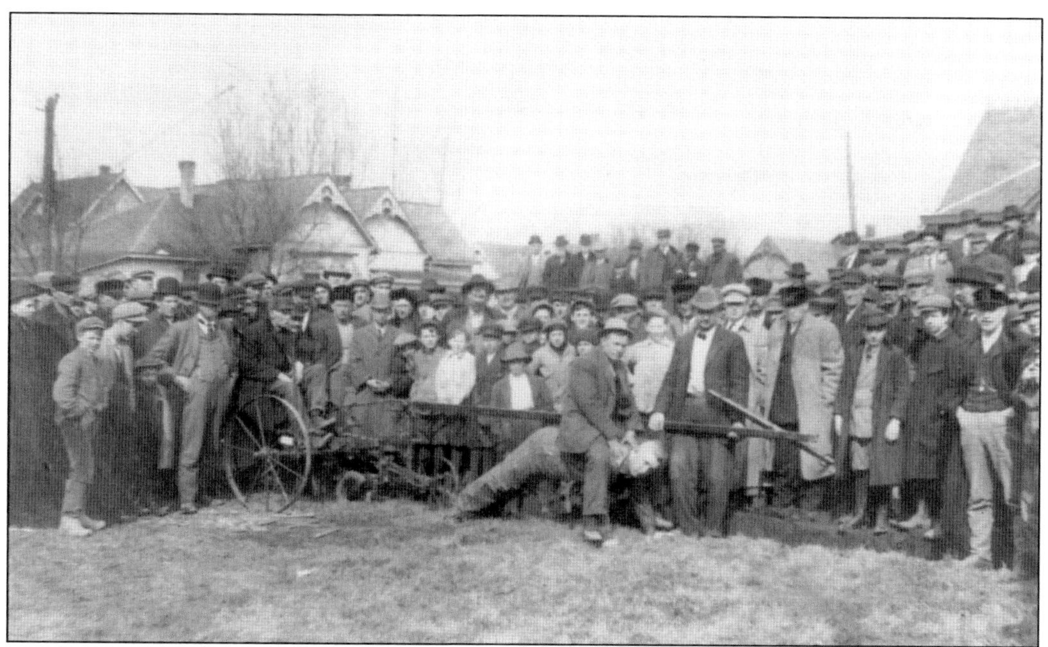

From the beginning, Boone settlers made their way by farming in some manner. Here, Hooton Hardware shows the ease of pulling their latest plow as two unidentified men stand in for a farmer and his mule to show how improved labors could be with the utilization of the newest implements.

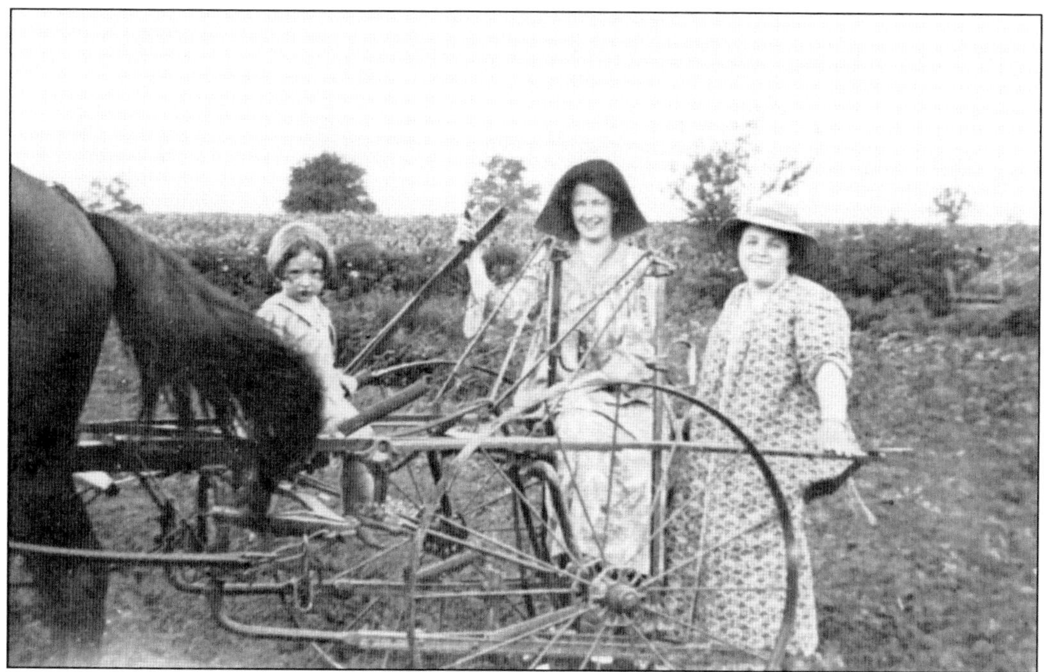

The women using this corn cultivator are demonstrating that advances in implements made the work of a farmer light enough for all to help. The young girl was likely just along for the ride.

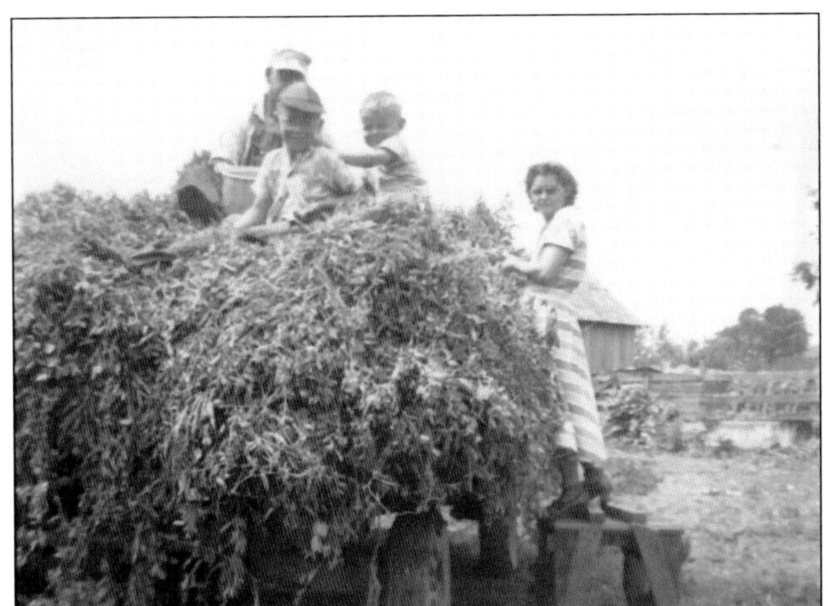

Most farmers in Boone County raised corn, feed grasses, and livestock. However, a few acres were usually set aside for "tender" crops such as melons, tomatoes, or table beans. Here, a Perry Township family works to harvest and load a wagon of peas. (Miller family.)

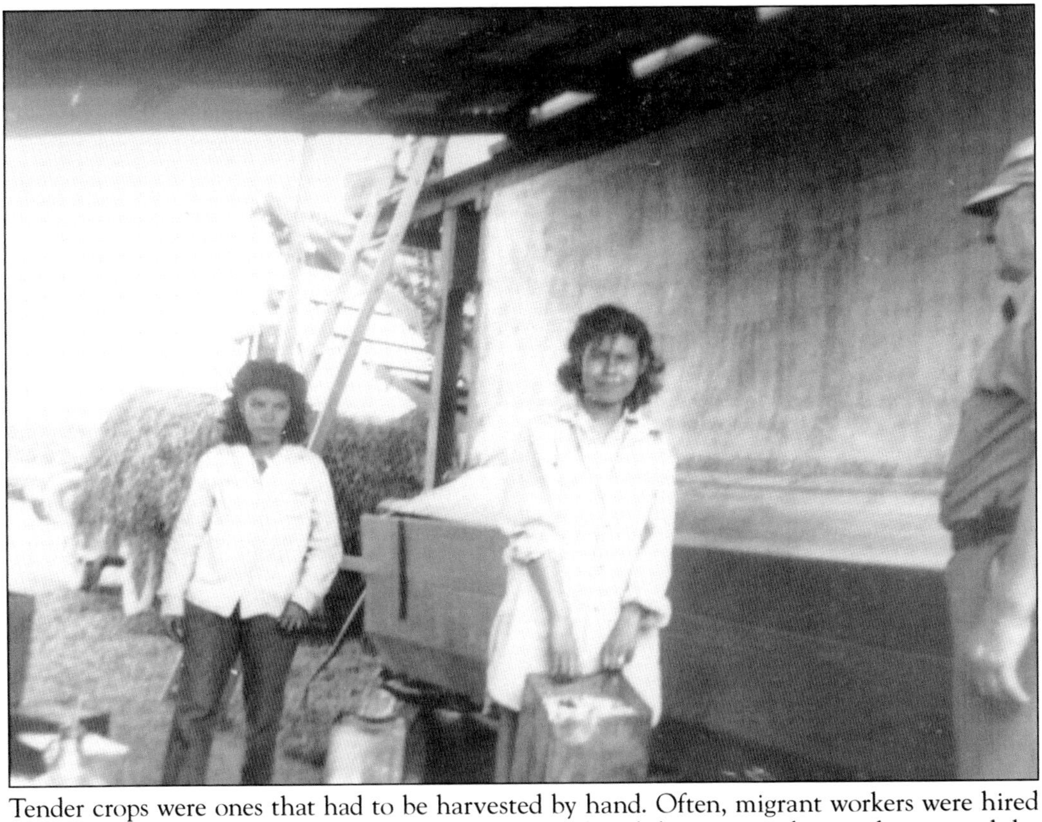

Tender crops were ones that had to be harvested by hand. Often, migrant workers were hired to help pick these time-sensitive crops. Many farmers hired the same workers each year, and the families became friends as they worked side by side for several days each summer or fall. Here, Rafaela and her sister Maria, longtime seasonal workers on the George Everett farm, help with the pea harvest around 1949. (Miller family.)

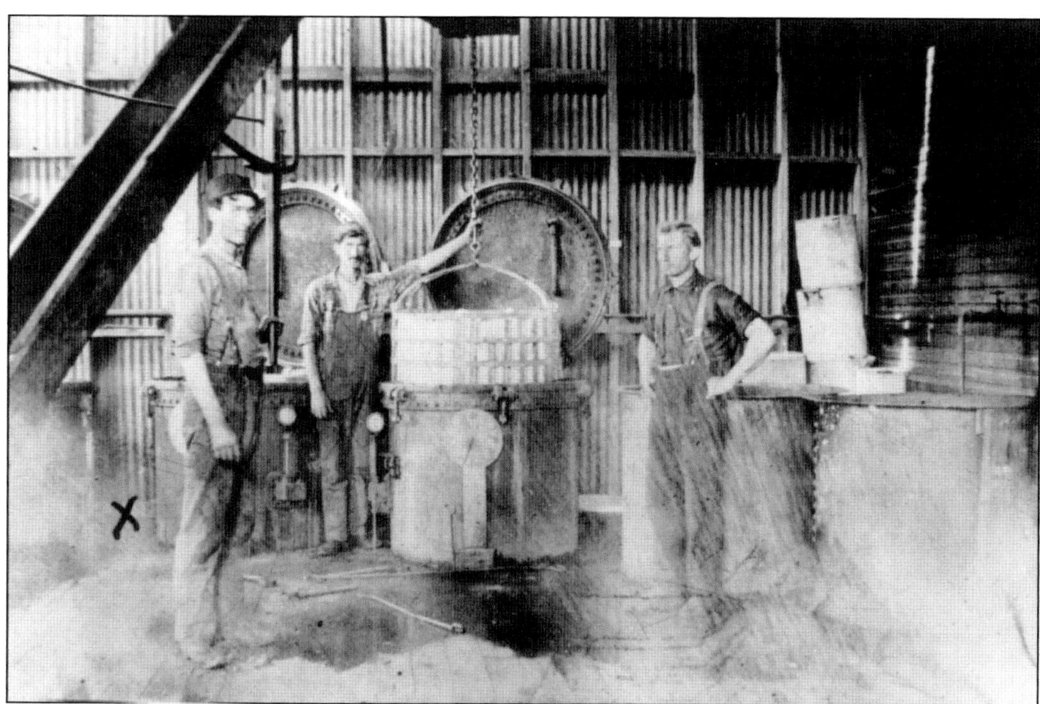

Some tender crops, like tomatoes, ended up at the canning factory. Shown here around its opening in 1890, the factory canned all sorts of food items. Originally known as the Lebanon (and then American) Canning Company, it was finally bought by the Ladoga Company. The smell of ketchup being canned and labeled for the Brooks brand by the Ladoga plant was said to be wide reaching. Many in town recall the late-summer smell up until the plant's closing around 1950.

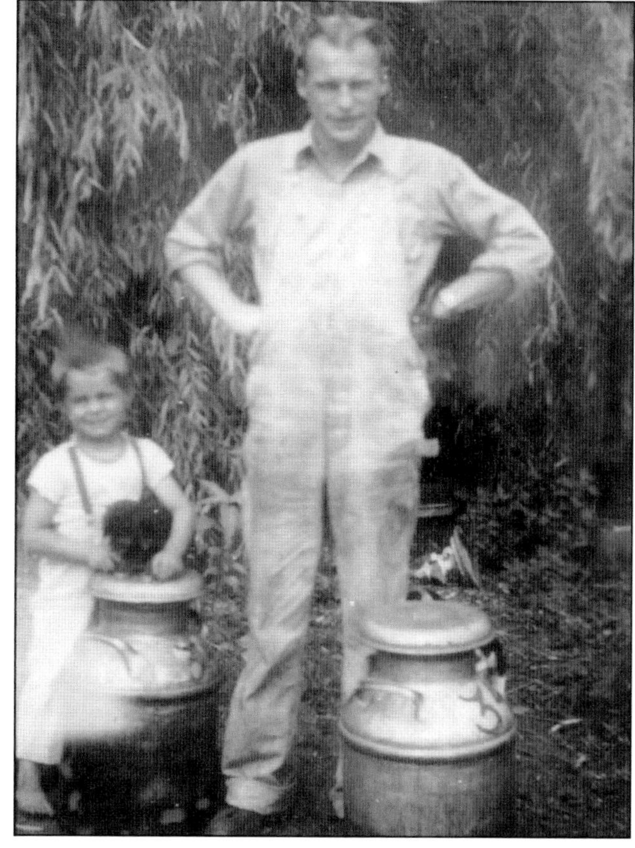

In rural Boone County, milk hauler Charles "the Dutchman" Hatewan was a constant visitor. On his daily route, he traded empty cans for filled ones headed back to the Condensed Milk plant for processing. (Miller family.)

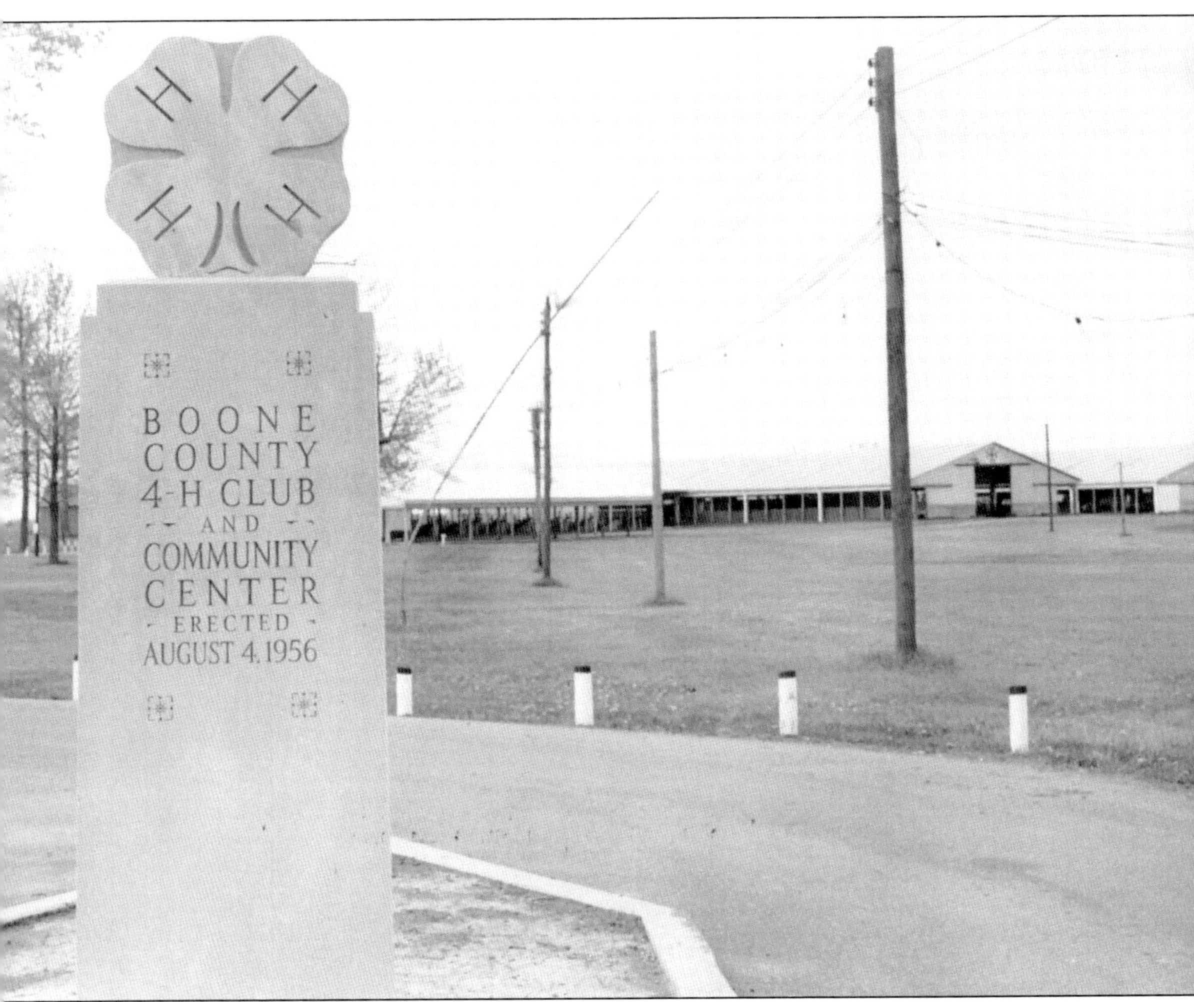

In the 1940s, a group of concerned citizens gathered to brainstorm a better way to serve the thriving membership of the county's 4-H. For years, the project displays and livestock shows were separated into various venues and held on different days. The livestock and animal showmanship judging was held on the site of the old fairgrounds, which by then were serving as Memorial Park in Lebanon. Girls' projects, such as sewing and baking, were at times displayed at Lebanon High School. Finally, in 1953, the county commissioners granted a lease to the organization for the land vacated by the defunct CCC as the new 4-H fairgrounds. The annual event eventually grew from a three-day exhibition to a week-long expo.

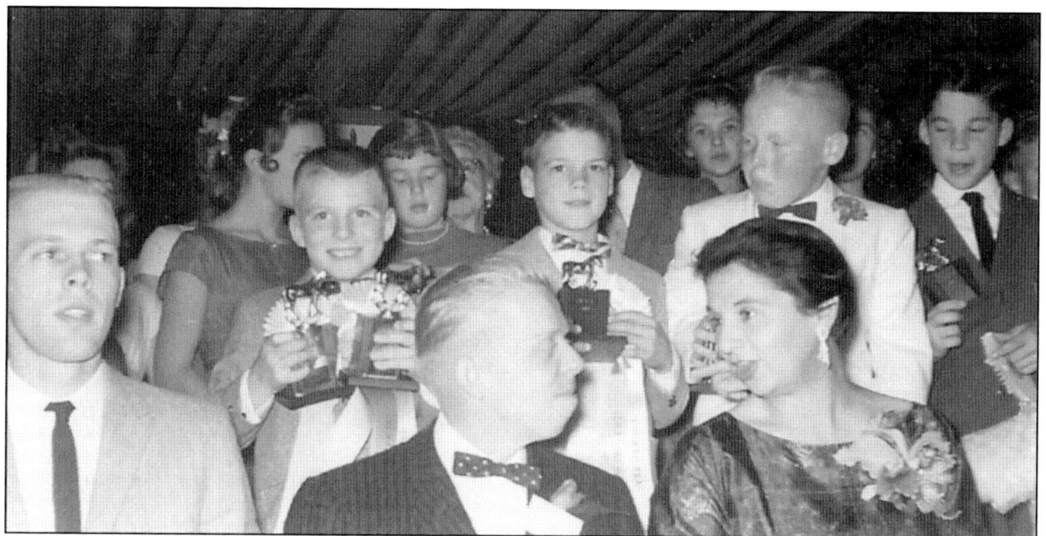

These proud 4-H boys and their parents show off livestock trophies at the county fair awards ceremony around 1950. The ceremonies were always quite the community event, requiring Sunday clothes and freshly washed faces. (Ruth Everett.)

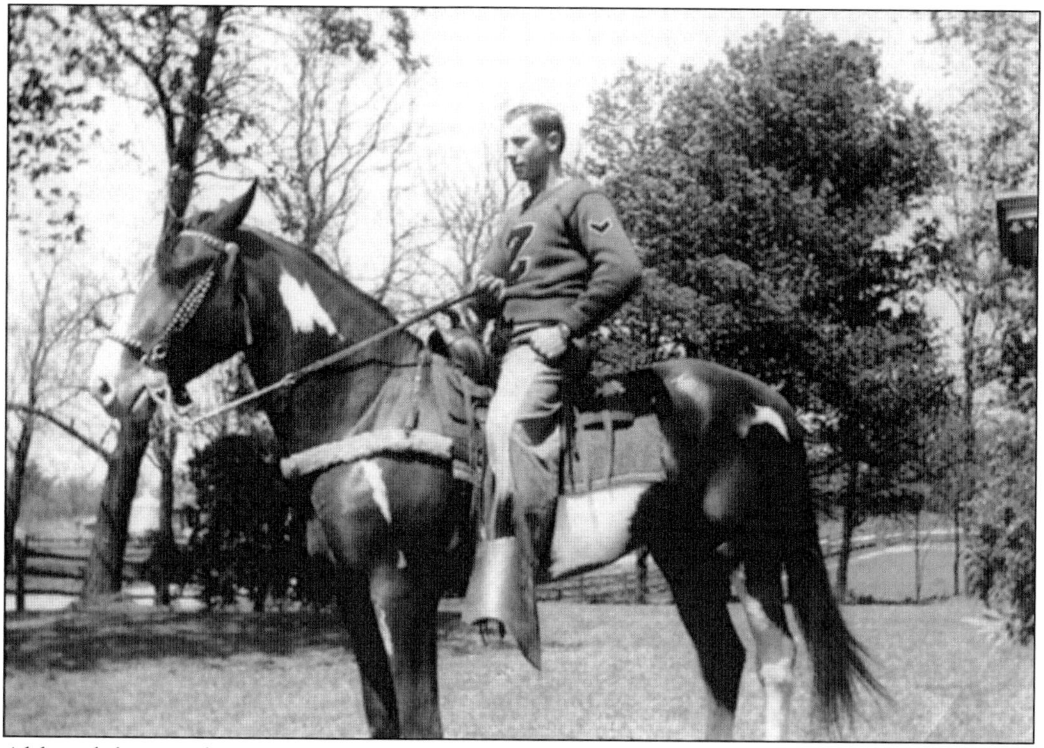

Although hogs and corn were by far Boone County's most prolific agricultural products, a steady trade exists to this day in horses of all variety and uses. Percherons, Belgians, and other draft horses and mules were raised for work, pulling, and general transport. Later, horses were bred for sporting. Jumpers and barrel racing became more popular as machinery allowed farmers and their families more leisure time. Here, Leon Schooler sports his Zionsville High School sweater as he poses on his jumper. (Ruth Everett.)

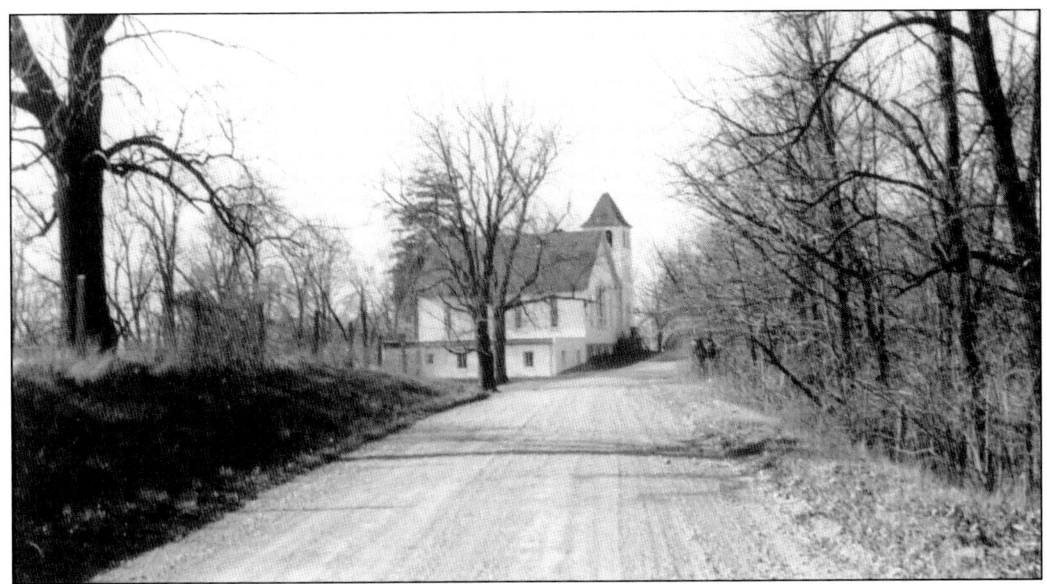

The far southeastern corner of Boone County, which is neatly severed across the middle by Interstate 865, is an area known for many beautiful horses. The Boone portion of Trader's Point and the town of North Salem were mostly razed to grade the area to drain into the Eagle Creek Reservoir after the devastating flood of 1957. The Salem United Methodist Church (built in 1885) and cemetery are now within the protected area of the Traders Point Hunt Rural Historic District.

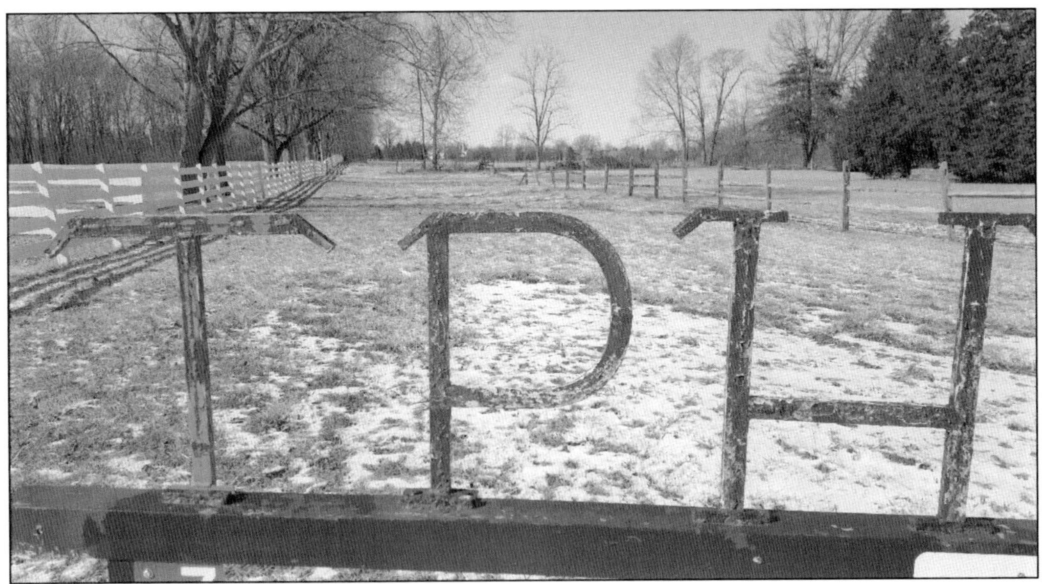

The tradition of fox hunting has reigned here since 1934. Traders Point Hunt Club has always been politically correct, hosting only drag (fox-less) hunts from its inception. Emphasis is placed on horsemanship and the specialized training of the hounds. In 1975, polo was brought to Boone County from South Africa on a farm near Whitestown, which the new owners named Rancho Allegre. After this Polo Ranch was vacated, another, Hickory Hall Polo Club, revived the sport in 2002 on land near Zionsville owned by the Chandler family. (Author's collection.)

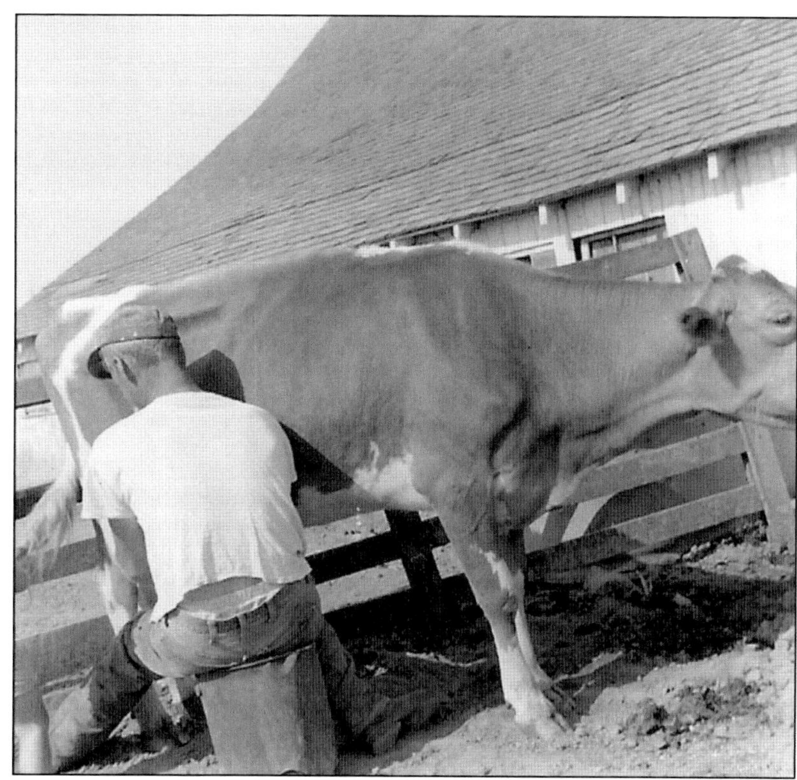

Hand-milking continued for farmers who did not have large herds. Most farms kept a cow or two for breeding and sales of spring calves—and to keep the farmhouse icebox stocked for thirsty and hungry children. (Ruth Everett collection.)

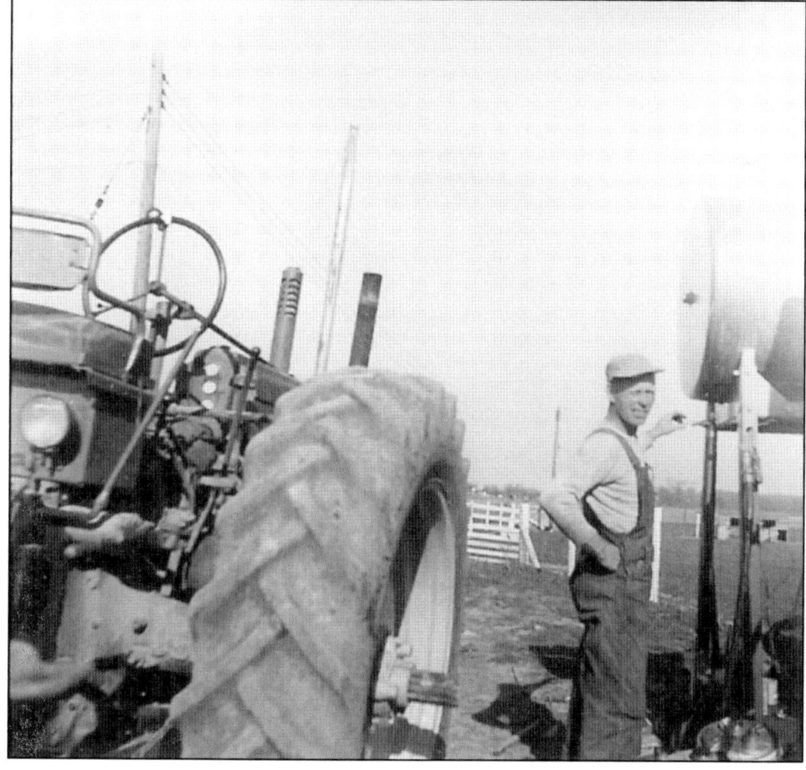

With the popularity and cost-effectiveness of tractors, farmers kept gas tanks on site for convenience. This one was a simple gravity-fed tank that could be moved close to fields being worked to save time. (Ruth Everett collection.)

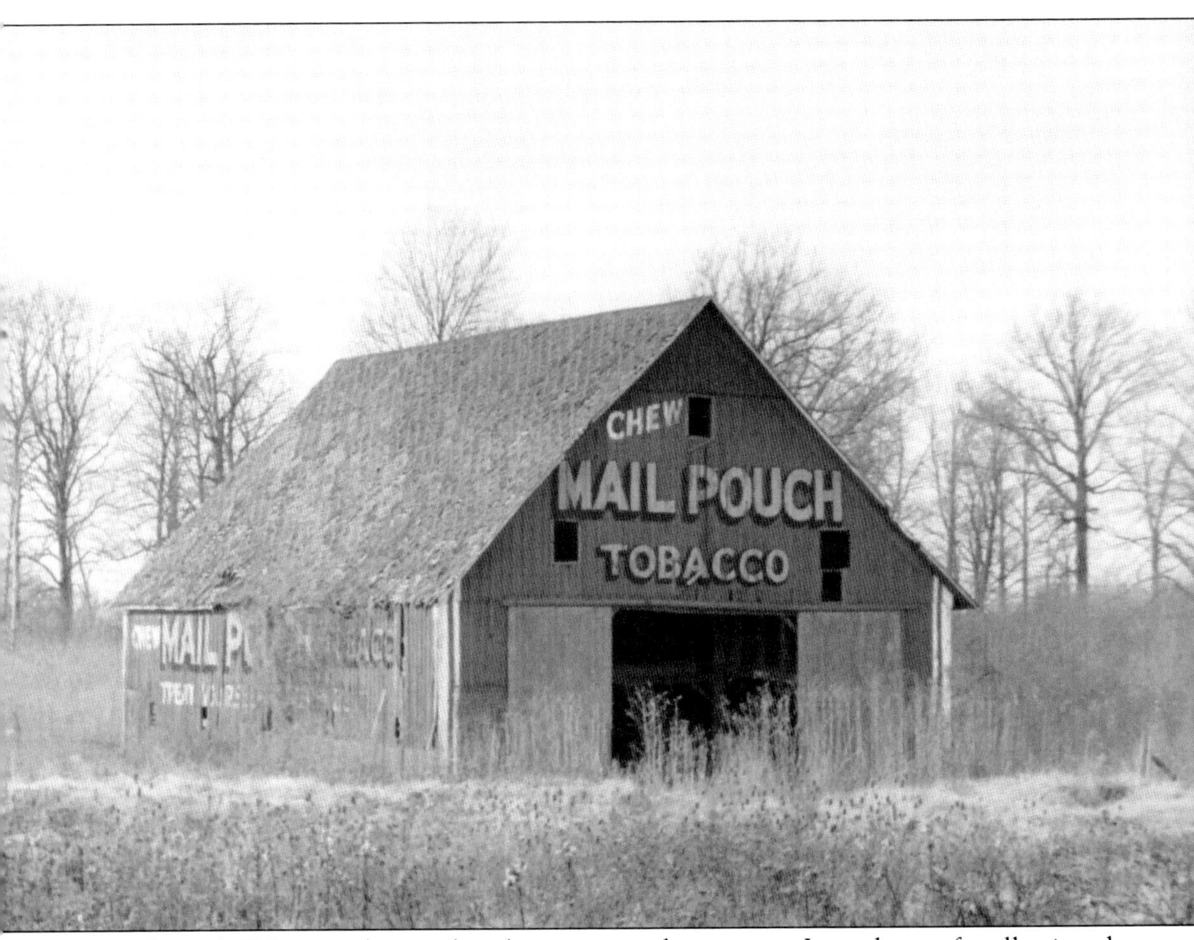

Mail Pouch Tobacco advertised on barns across the country. In exchange for allowing the advertisements to be displayed on their buildings, farmers received around $20 per year and a freshly painted barn every few years. In 1974, the barns and their art were put under protection by the federal government as symbols of the country's agricultural heritage.

Seven

School, Sports, and Stuff to Do

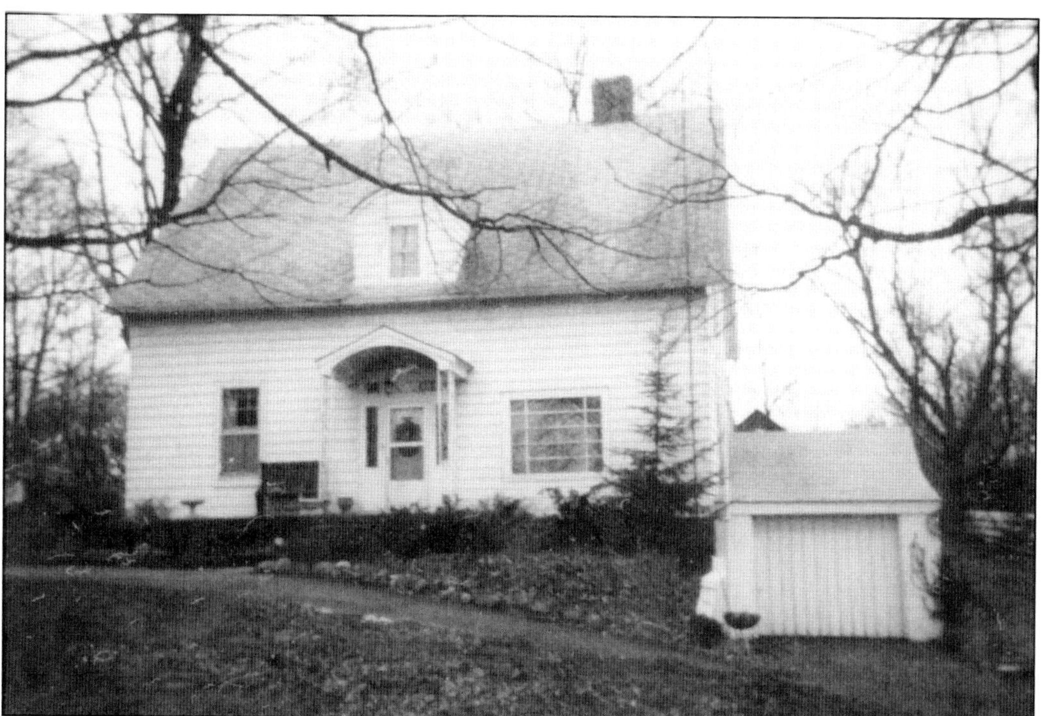

Built in the mid-1860s by Irish immigrant George Ryan, this house originally had a second-story porch used by the Ryan family for community band practices. Ryan sponsored and conducted a band, made up of local boys living in Mechanicsburg, that traveled to area performances in a special moon-shaped and brightly painted wagon outfitted with seats like modern bleachers, according to Boone County historian Ralph Stark.

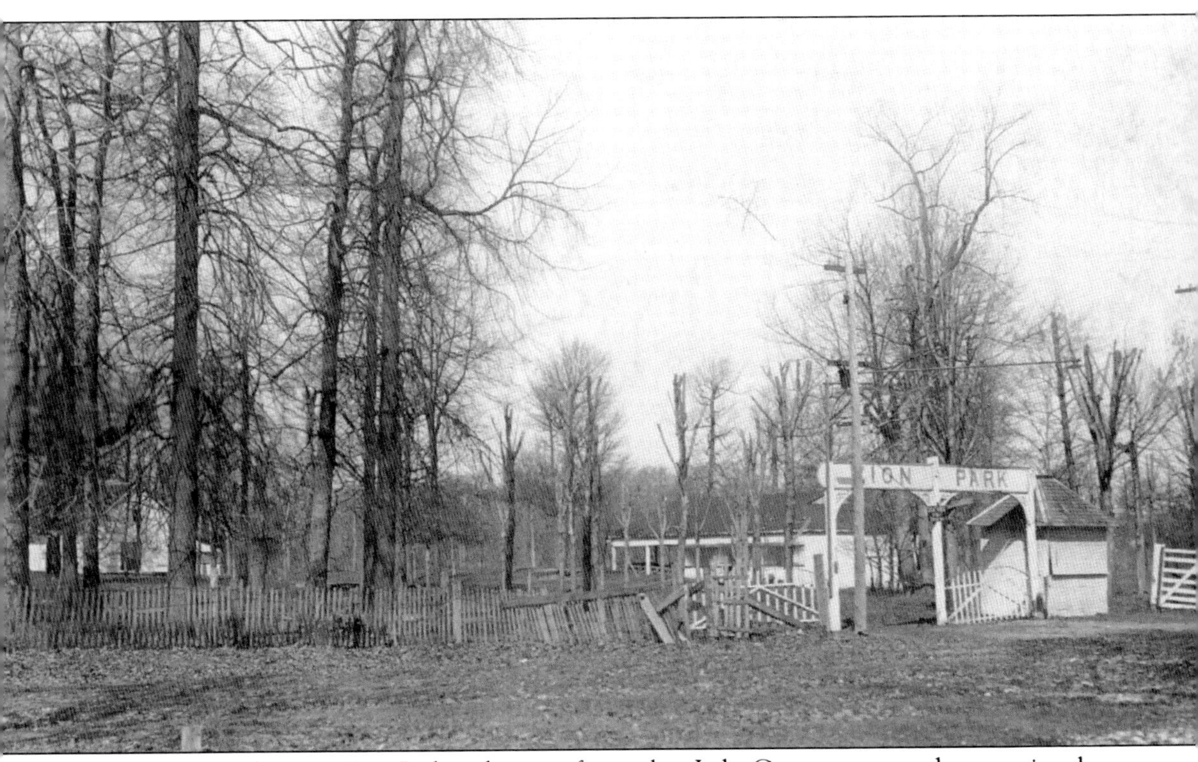

Zionsville was home to Zion Park and—most famously—Lake Como, a manmade recreational area offering entertainments in the Chautauqua tradition for 16 days each summer. Other amusements and events were held year-round, making the park quite popular. After the 1913 spring flood, most of the dam wall built to create Lake Como was destroyed. By the time the dam was replaced, automobiles, picture shows, and the outbreak of World War I caused attendance at Zion Park to fall off. The park was in sporadic use until it was finally closed around 1917. In 1928 it was purchased by Fred Gersh, who built a large house at the center of the former attraction, naming it Parkway Gardens; Gersh used the space to curate species of dahlias. In 1933, he won the Gold Medal from the American Dahlia Society at Chicago. Gersh named his champion bloom Zion's Pride. Eagle Township purchased Parkway Gardens in 1946.

Many Boone County farm wives grew dahlias but also had a particular fondness for peonies. The mounding bushes flourished, fuss-free, at nearly every home. Even residents of Zionsville, known across the state as "Dahlia City," grew long rows of peonies in fencerows beside tiger lilies and rambling roses. (Miller family.)

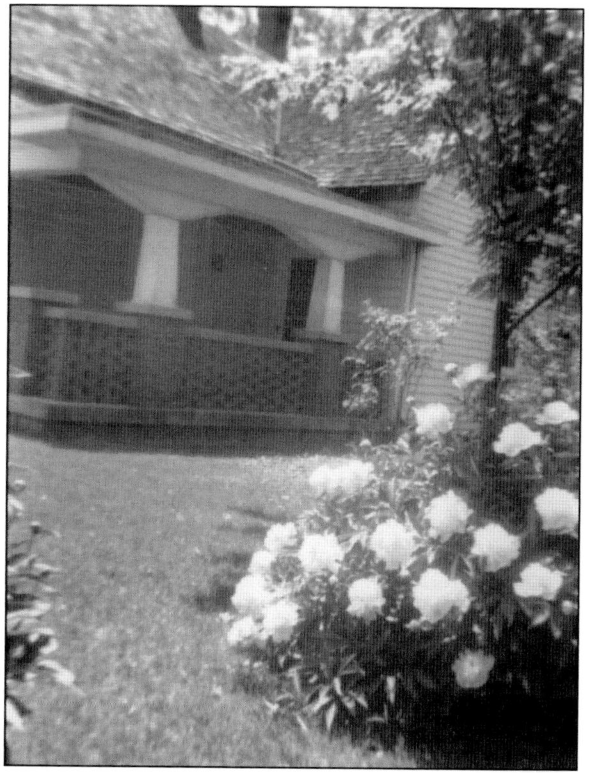

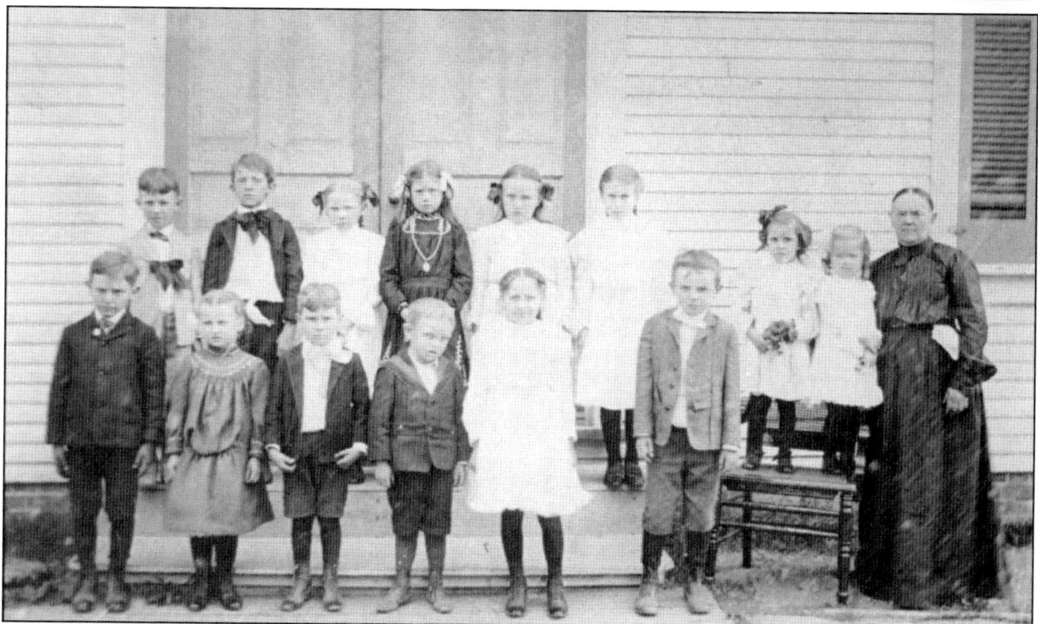

This 1903 Sunday school class posed for a photograph outside the Salem Methodist Church. From left to right are (first row) Hershel Marsh, Tressie McClaine, Earl Marsh, Walter Klingler, Buena Marsh, and Merrill Pavey; (second row) Myron Crane, Omar Green, Minnie Wilson, Muriel Sanders, Amanda Klingler, and Osa Hill. The two tots standing on the chair are Ruby Green and Mary Hill. Teacher Hethy Pavey is at far right.

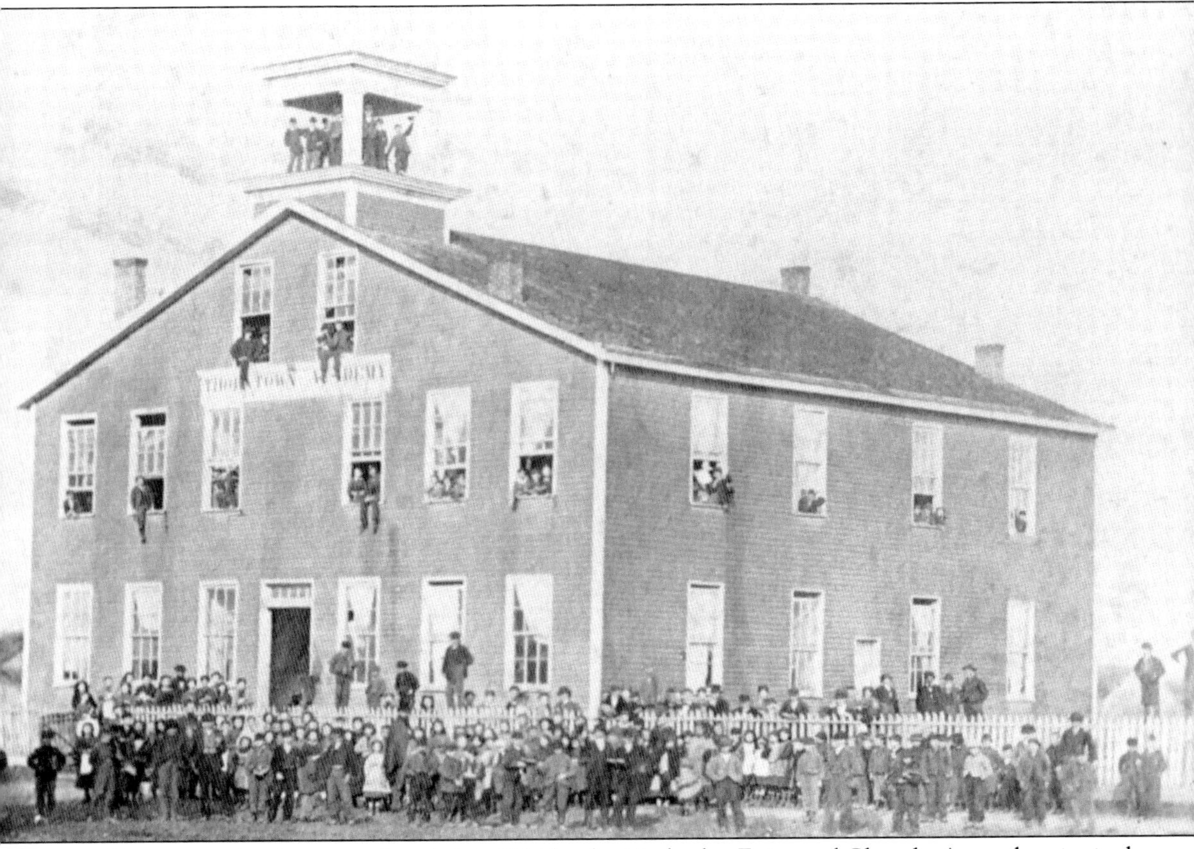

Thorntown Academy was founded in 1854 by the Methodist Episcopal Church. An early principal of the academy, Charles N. Sims, went on to be chancellor of Syracuse University. By 1861, there were 342 students enrolled in primary through intermediate grades and high school. With only seven seniors that year, during the outbreak of the Civil War, the school barely had a graduating class. Twenty-five young men left the academy that spring to enlist in the Union army after Fort Sumter was fired upon. (Thorntown History Museum.)

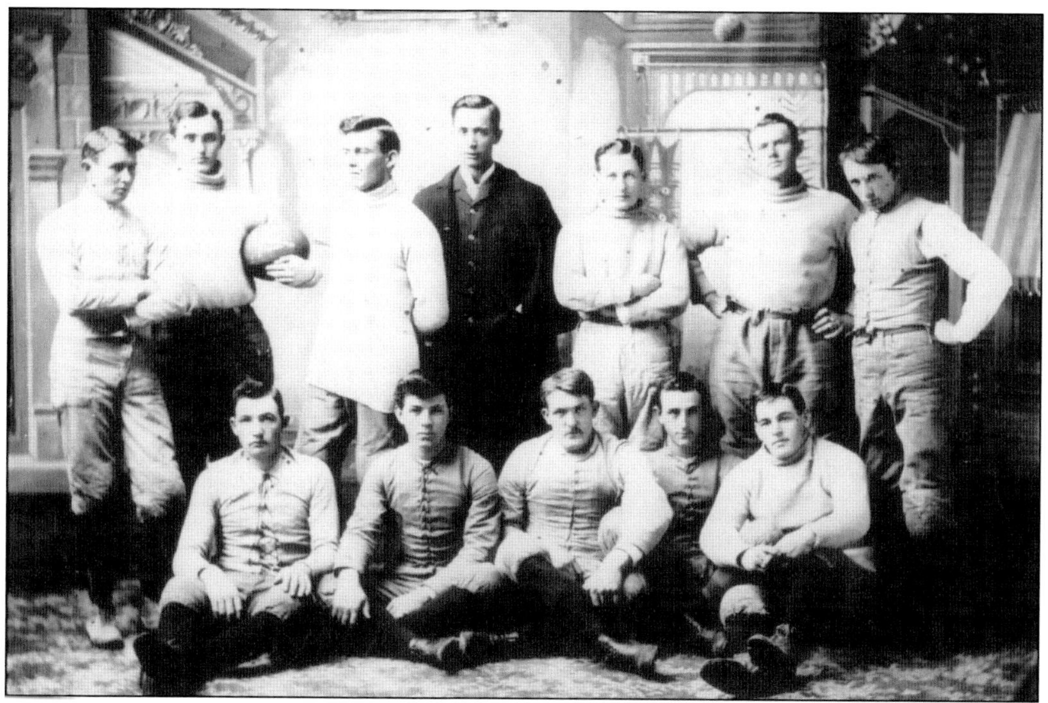

Schoolwork, chores, sports, clubs, church, and social obligations kept the youth of Boone County in constant motion. The county got its first football team in 1892 when Lebanon High School formed a team.

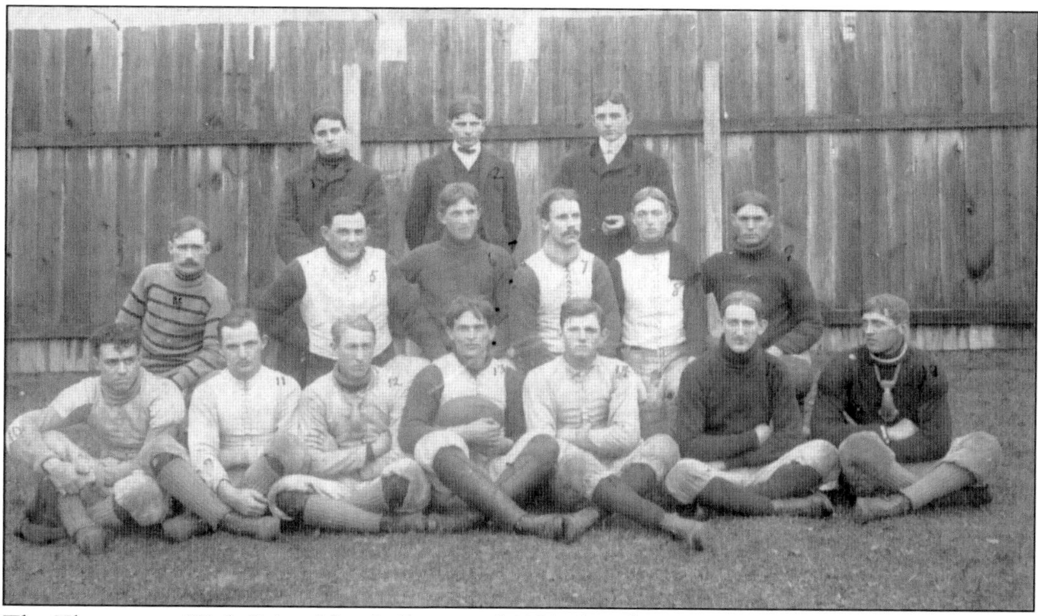

The Thorntown High School football team of 1903 played seven games, winning four—not bad for the Kewaskees. In 1974, Thorntown High School was part of the consolidation that made up the Western Boone County School District (the Stars).

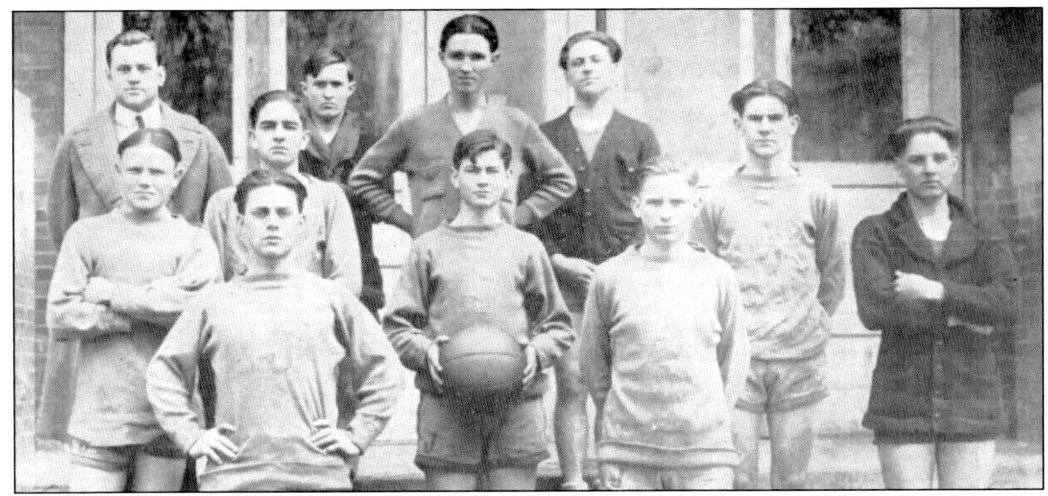

The undisputed "Sport of Kings" in Boone County is basketball. When sanctioned tournaments started with the 1910–1911 quest to crown a championship team, Boone County was at the epicenter of what came to be known as the cradle of high school basketball. This photograph shows the 1914 Jamestown Little Giants squad. (Tri-Area Library History Vault.)

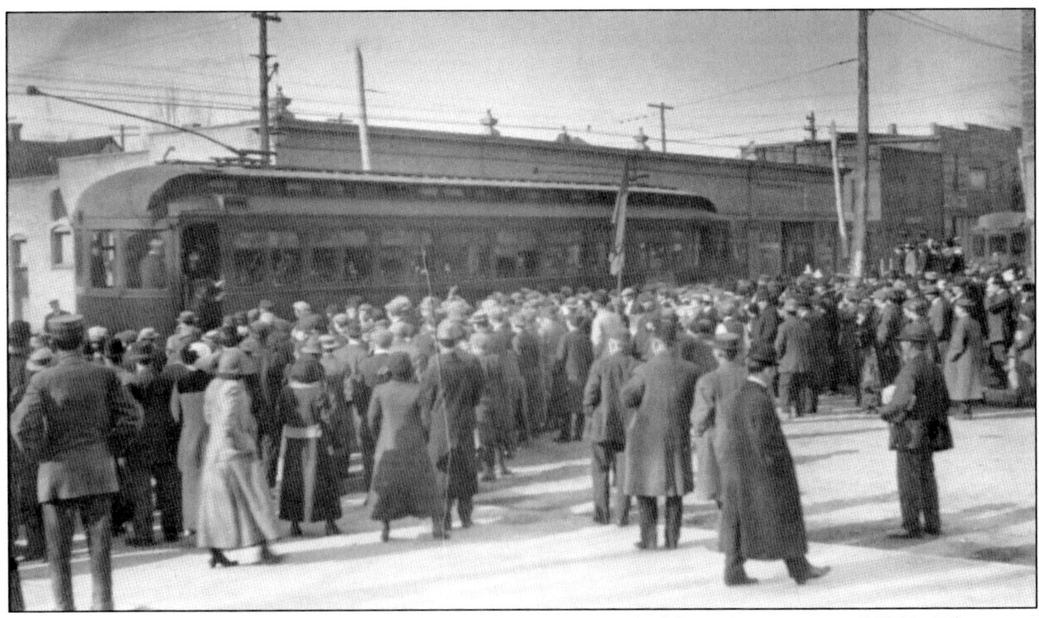

The first state basketball championship tournament was held in the spring of 1911. The next year, the Lebanon High School Tigers won, defeating their opponents 51–11. The city went wild for its homegrown heroes. A huge crowd gathered at the interurban stop to welcome the team as they arrived.

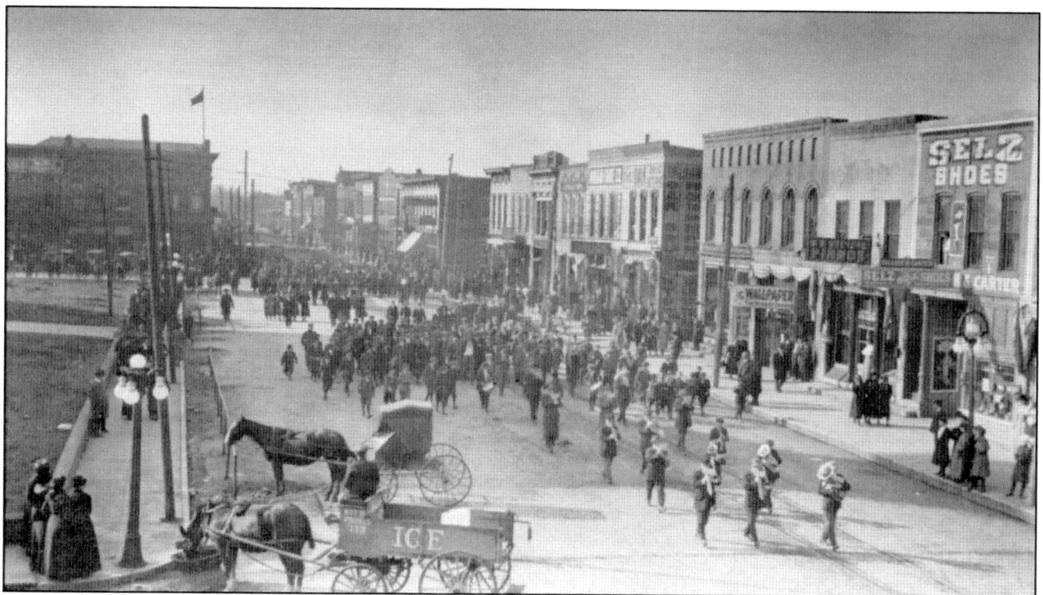

The 1912 state champions, fresh off the train after winning the tournament in Bloomington, Indiana, were greeted by hundreds of people. A parade was organized to escort the team to Lebanon High School, where a large celebration was held. Lebanon went on to win again in the 1917 and 1918 championships.

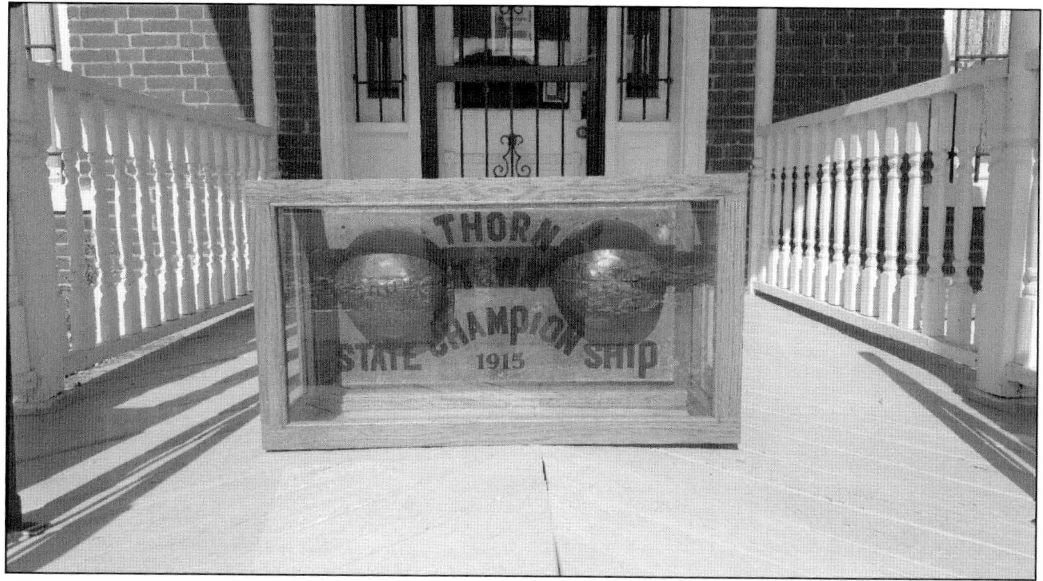

Thorntown brought home the state championship title in 1915. As the team was greeted with hysteria equal to that of the Lebanon fans, the trophy was somehow snatched. Thorntown coach Chet Hill took matters into his own hands, knowing there was no championship win without a tangible trophy. Coach Hill cleverly sawed the winning ball in half and enclosed it in a large glass box, along with a commemorative plaque. This may be the state's most unique trophy. At about three feet long and a little over a foot high and wide, the custom-made piece would be awfully hard to steal. (Author's collection.)

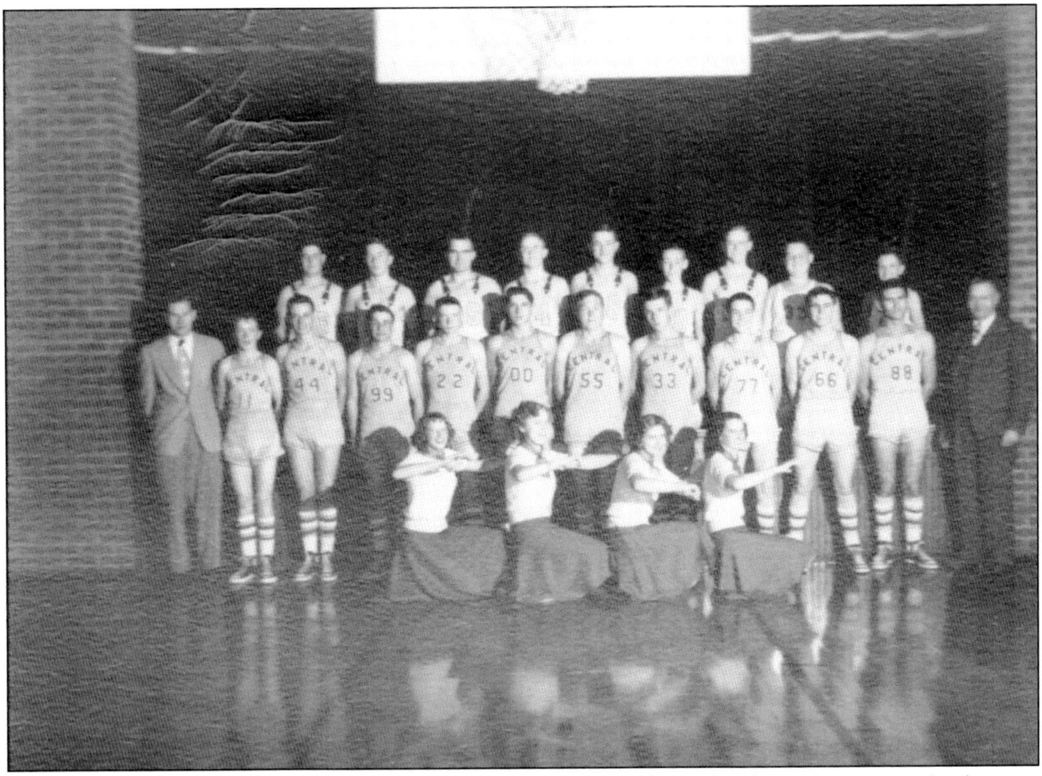

Other schools in the county had unusual nicknames, too. There were the Dover Devils, Pinnell Purple Dragons, and Wells Rockets. Perry Central's teams were called the Midgets. As several old-timers in the area have conveyed, the tiny school was once written up in a national publication for its unique team nickname. No one seems to know how or why the moniker came to Perry Central. Pictured is a 1940s Midget squad. (Miller family.)

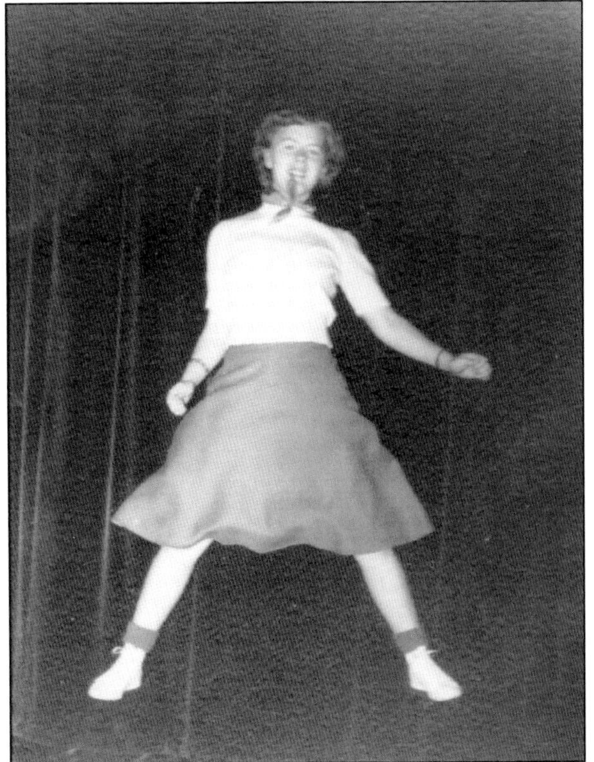

Perhaps school enrollment played a part in the Midget nickname. The class of 1952 had five boys and three girls. With such a limited student body, in order to have a team, all boys had to play basketball and all girls were recruited for the Yell Team (cheerleading). This cheerleader shows off a peppy jump in her Midget's Yell uniform around 1950. (Miller family.)

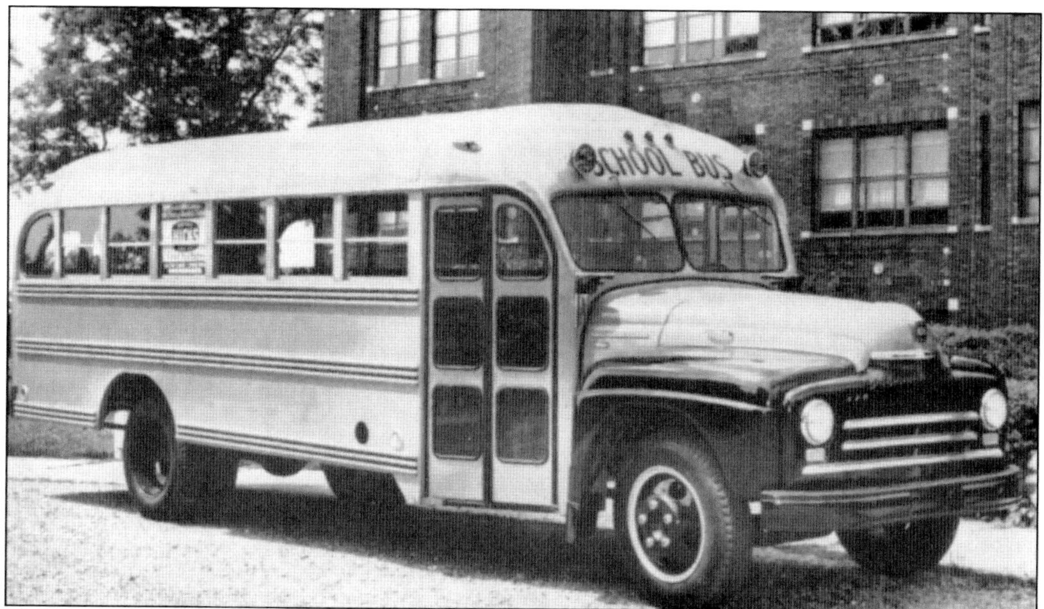

Children around the country were fortunate to ride school buses designed and built in Boone County. Earl Hicks, mechanic and inventor, received an honorary degree from Columbia University for his advances in the field of engineering. Hicks, who patented several safety features still used on school buses today, was always concerned with the safety of children. One of his simplest inventions was the familiar stop arm used to alert motorists that children are actively boarding or exiting from buses. (Miller family.)

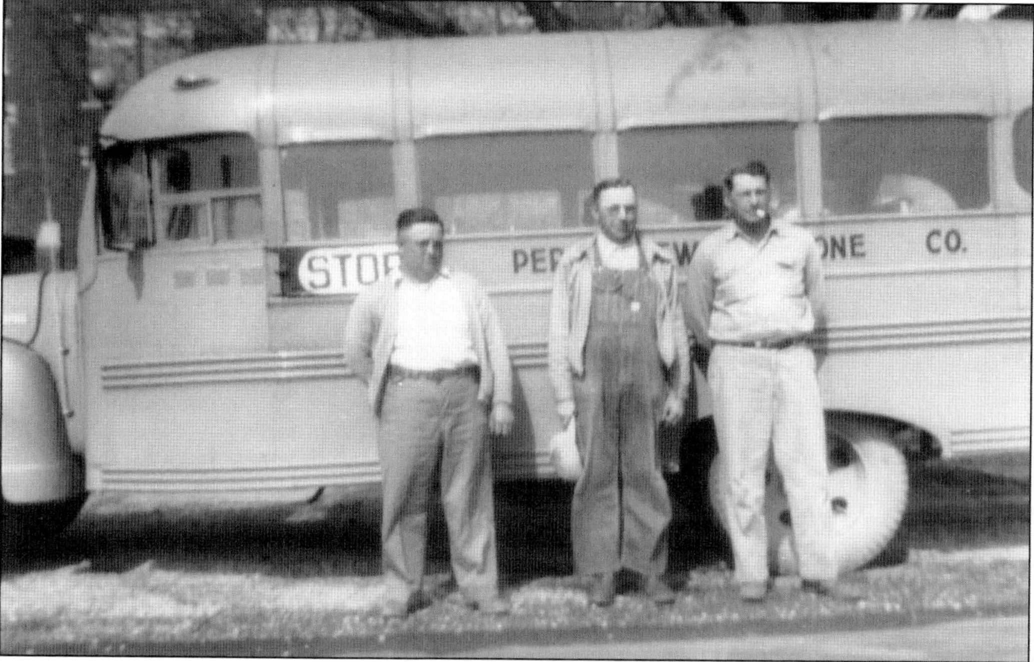

School bus drivers in the early years were often area farmers who were accustomed to driving large equipment. This group of drivers relaxes before school is dismissed and their afternoon route begins. (Miller family.)

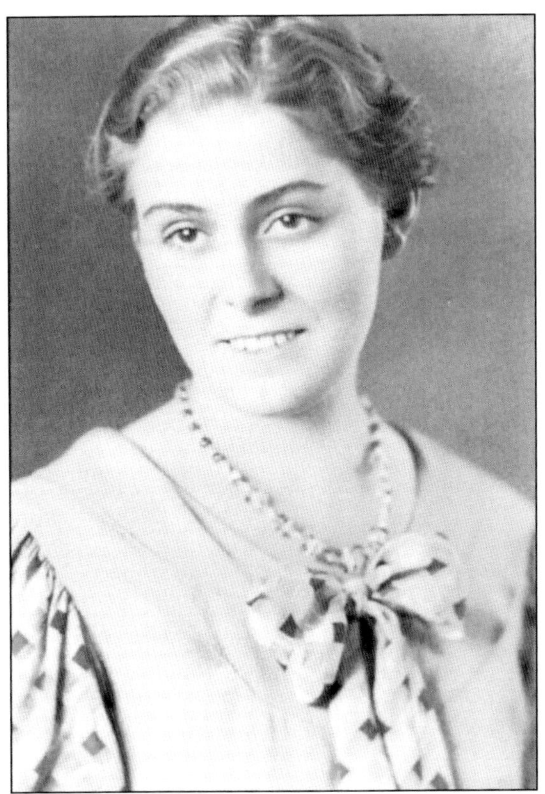

Local girl Hazel Everett graduated from Perry Central School. She went on to receive a two-year degree in teaching at Indiana Normal School, then a master's degree at Ball State University. Returning home, she taught house-bound children across Boone County and spent time on staff at both Central and Stokes Elementary Schools before retiring at her family home within a mile of Perry Central. (Miller family.)

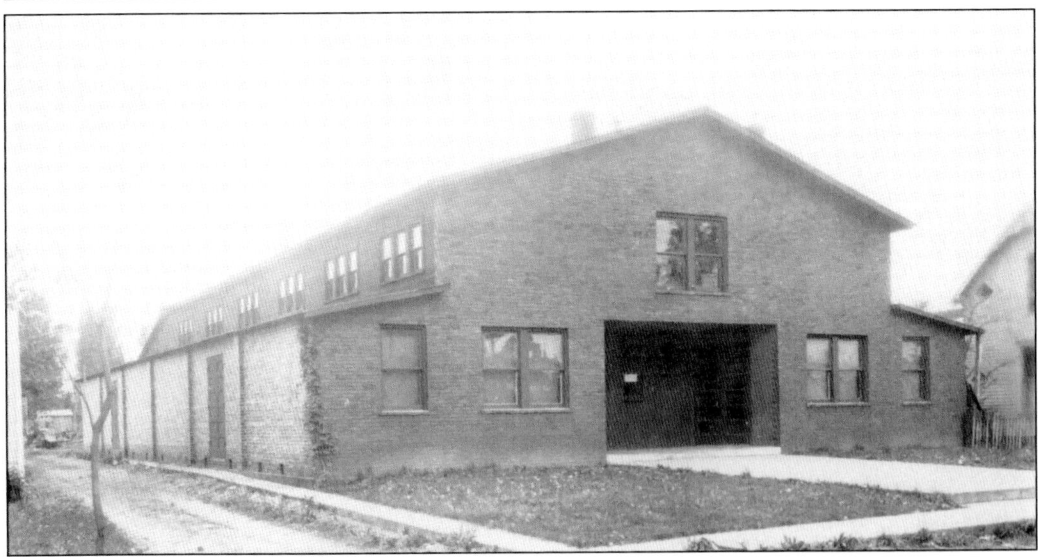

The Advance Community Center was the social hub of town. In addition to hosting meetings and dances, the building also served as the home court for the Advance High School Osceolans basketball team. The quarters were close for basketball. Only five rows of bleachers lined the wall, and the end walls were nearly flush with the out-of-bounds lines. Adding to the risk, the building was heated by a potbellied stove in each corner. This remained the basketball gym until Advance and Jamestown schools were consolidated into Granville Wells during the 1950s. (Tri-Area History Vault.)

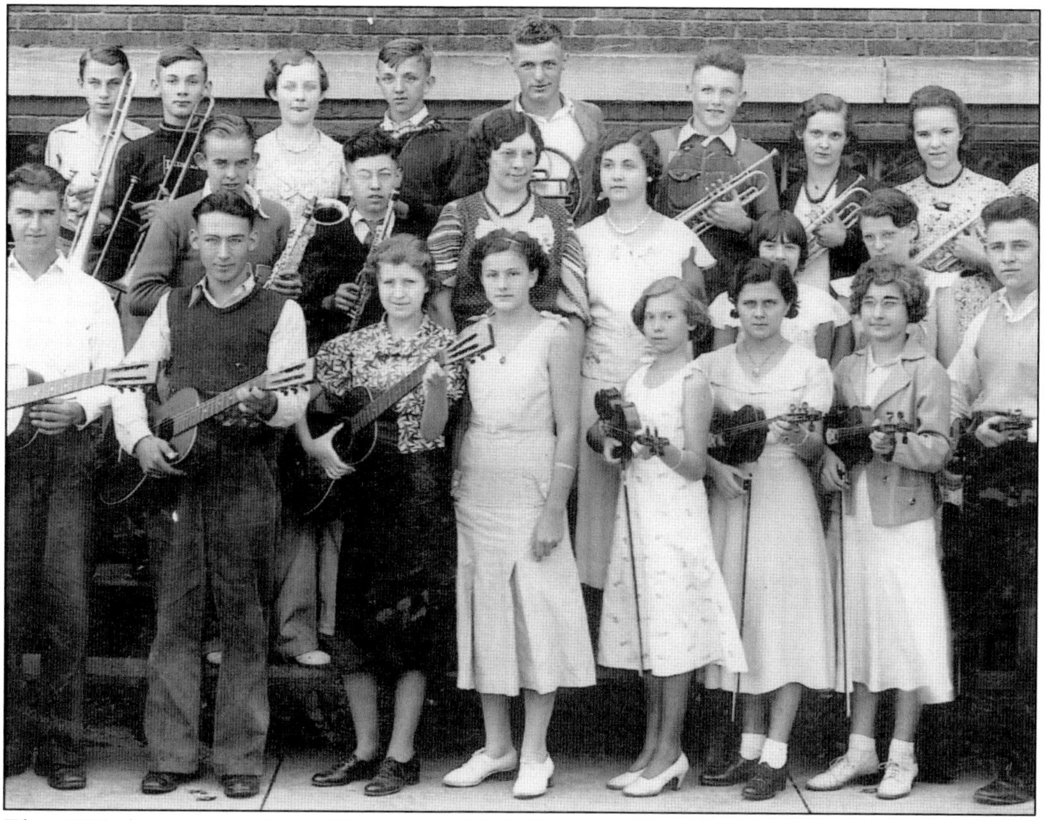

This 1935 photograph is from Whitestown High School. The orchestra was popular at basketball games all around the area. Whitestown, named after local businessman Albert S. White, was one of the small schools consolidated during the 1960s into the Lebanon school system. (Thorntown Museum Archives.)

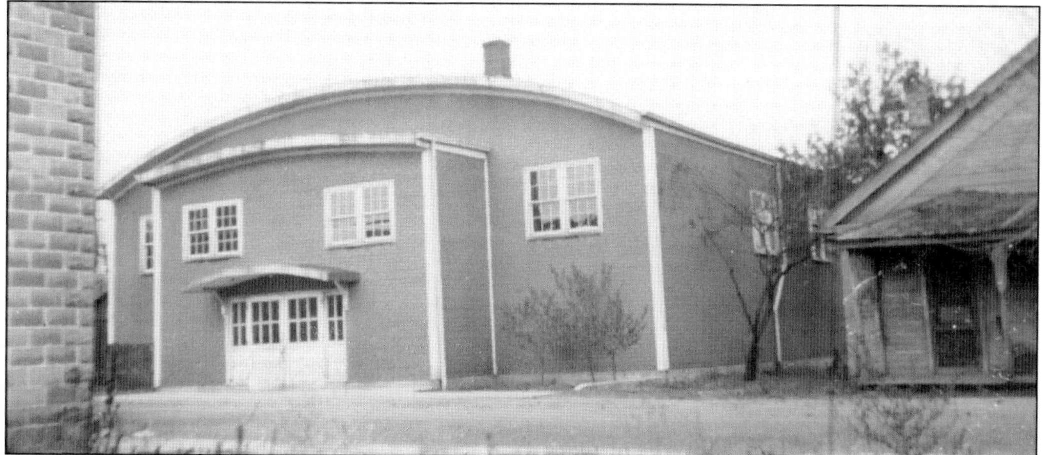

In Whitestown, the old Community Building was converted into a roller rink. The fun there was fast and dangerous. The floor was slippery and a bit uneven, adding to the excitement. Before walking home or hitching a ride with friends, kids often made their way up the street to Frank's Foodliner, where Frank and Peggy Coahran stocked a good amount of ice-cold Grape Nehi, Mason's Root Beer, and bubblegum cigars—perfect refreshments for parched and exhausted skaters.

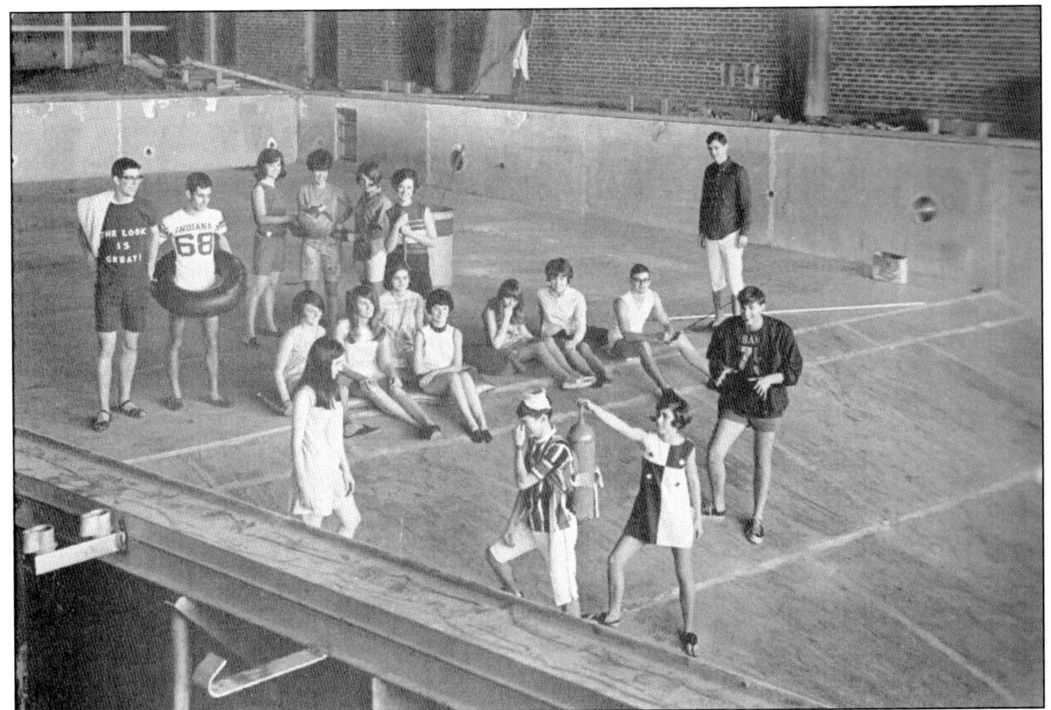

In the 1960s, many small rural schools were consolidated into the new, modern Lebanon High School. Here, students clown for the camera in 1967 as they anticipate the activities to come in the new pool, which was still under construction

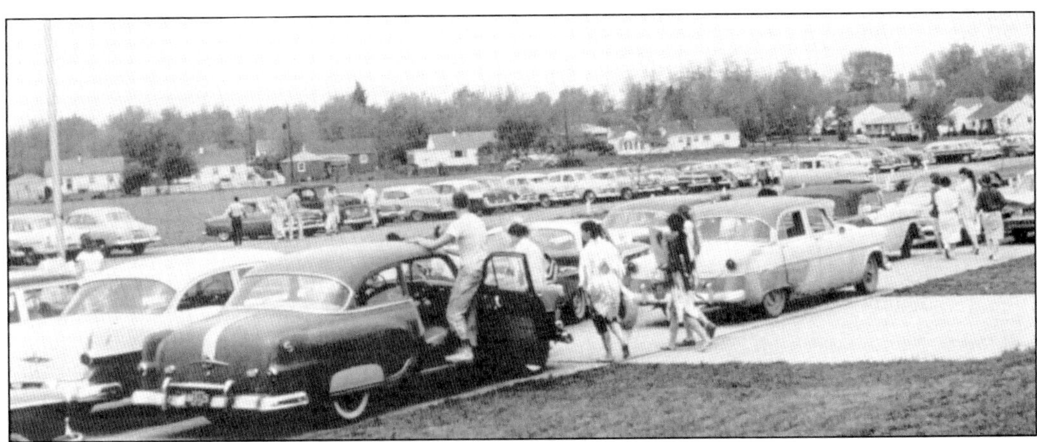

This photograph shows a last day of school at the new Lebanon High School. The view toward the parking lot—and the enthusiasm expressed at the beginning of another summer—seems unchanged from then to the present.

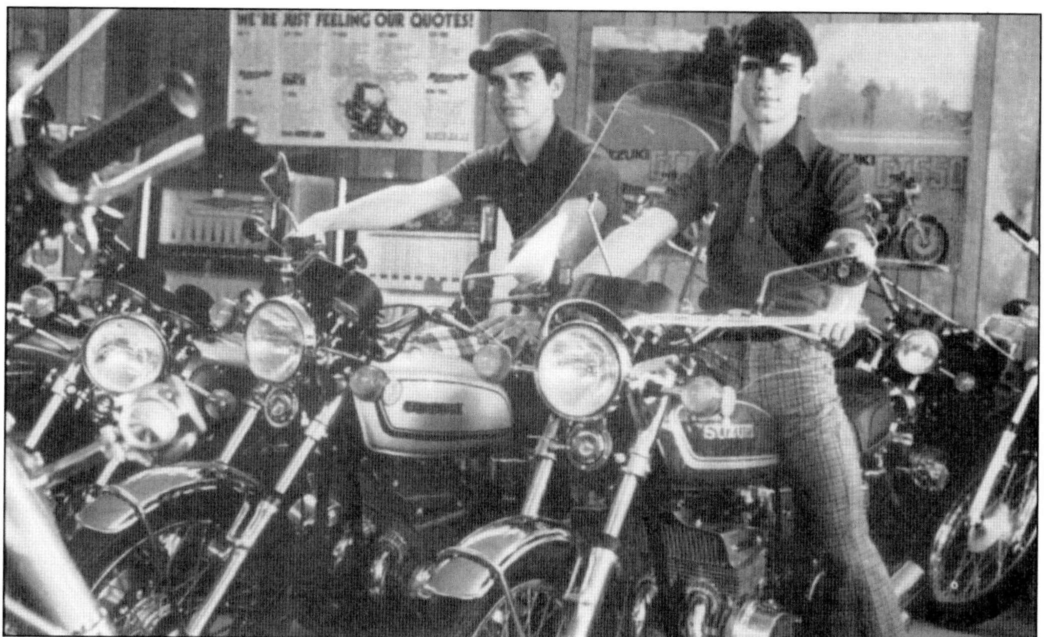

Otis D. (O.D.) Scott, originally from Jamestown, opened Scott's Cycle Sales and advertised in all the high school yearbooks. A marketing innovator, Scott featured graduating students in his ads. Here, the White twins, Ralph and Ray, demonstrate what wonderful gifts Scott's had for grads.

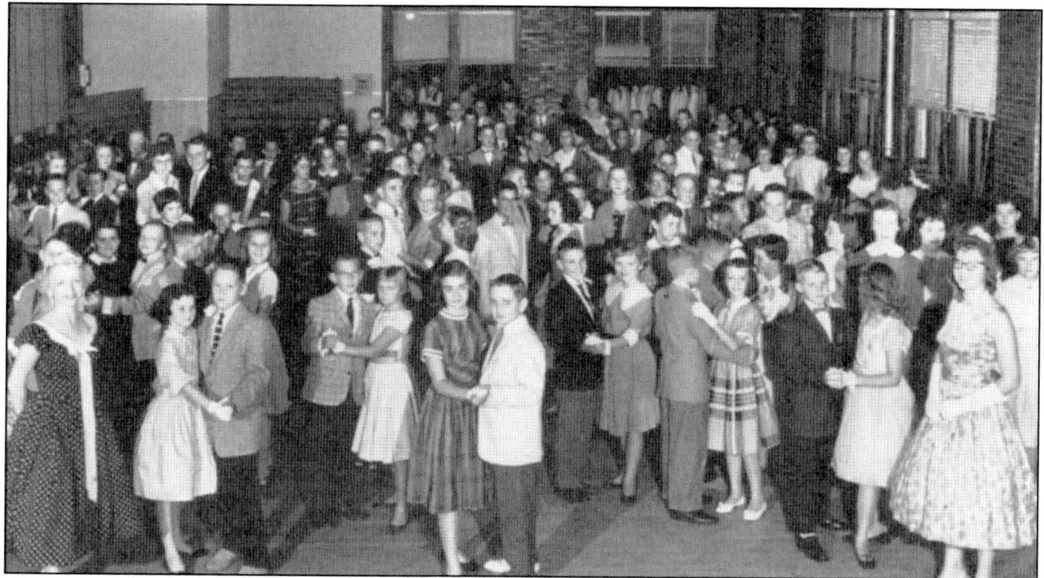

Young people could prepare for formals and other social events at Alexander's School of Dance. The weekly sessions were an event in their own right. Many went to Lebanon's Montgomery Ward shoe department to be fitted for dancing shoes. The store was equipped with a widely advertised x-ray machine to show customers the position of their foot inside a pair of shoes. The popular gizmo, called a fluoroscope, was removed from the store when they were outlawed for use in shoe-fitting around 1950.

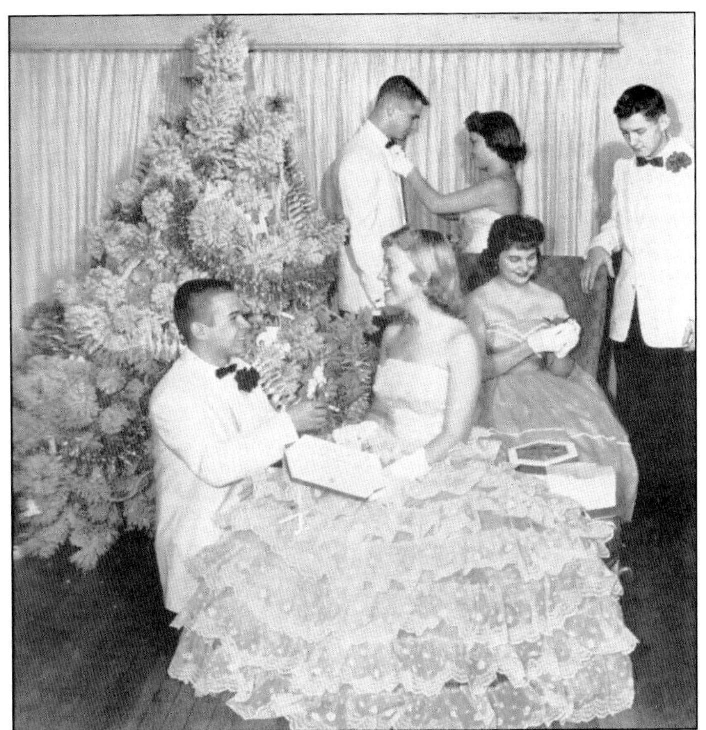

Couples pin on corsages and boutonnieres from Tauer's Floral Shop in preparation for a winter formal. Paul Tauer was a florist and one-time mayor of Lebanon. His son Paul Jr. was a history and social studies teacher in the schools for many years.

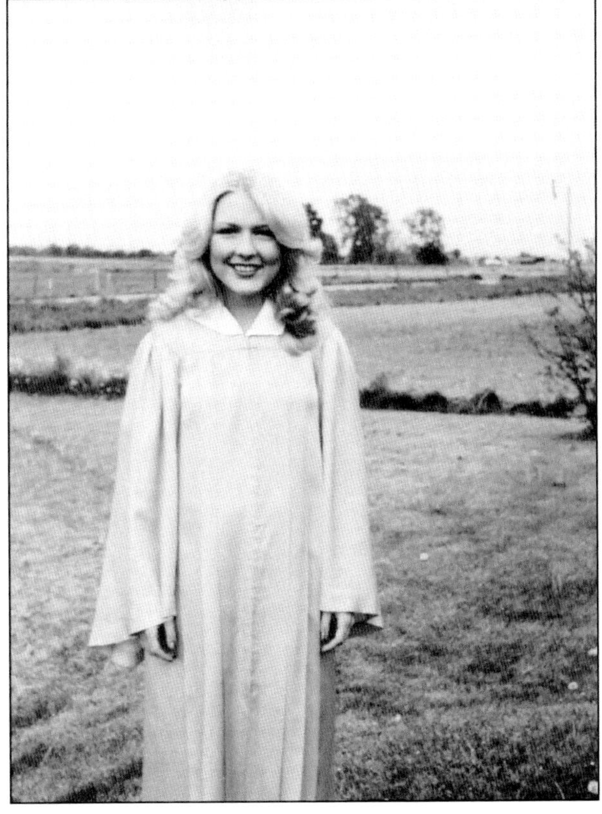

Vic Combs spent a 50-year career in education, with the majority of those years in Lebanon schools. Robert "Bob" McFrye, a retired brigadier general, gave four decades of his life to education in Lebanon. In this 1979 photograph, the author prepares to receive her diploma, no doubt with sighs of relief expressed by all parties. (Author's collection.)

Eight

Something to Celebrate in Boone

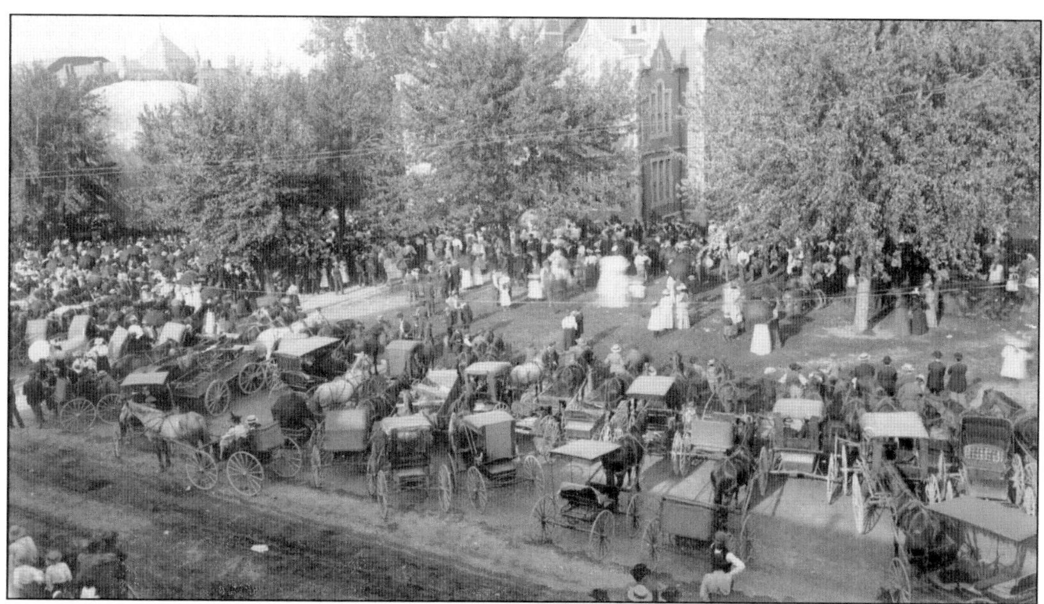

In 1890, this Merchant's Day Parade and Celebration was a huge success. The crowd size was estimated at 7,000 for the day's festivities. To the left, among the trees, a hot-air balloon is being inflated. The old courthouse is partially visible behind the trees.

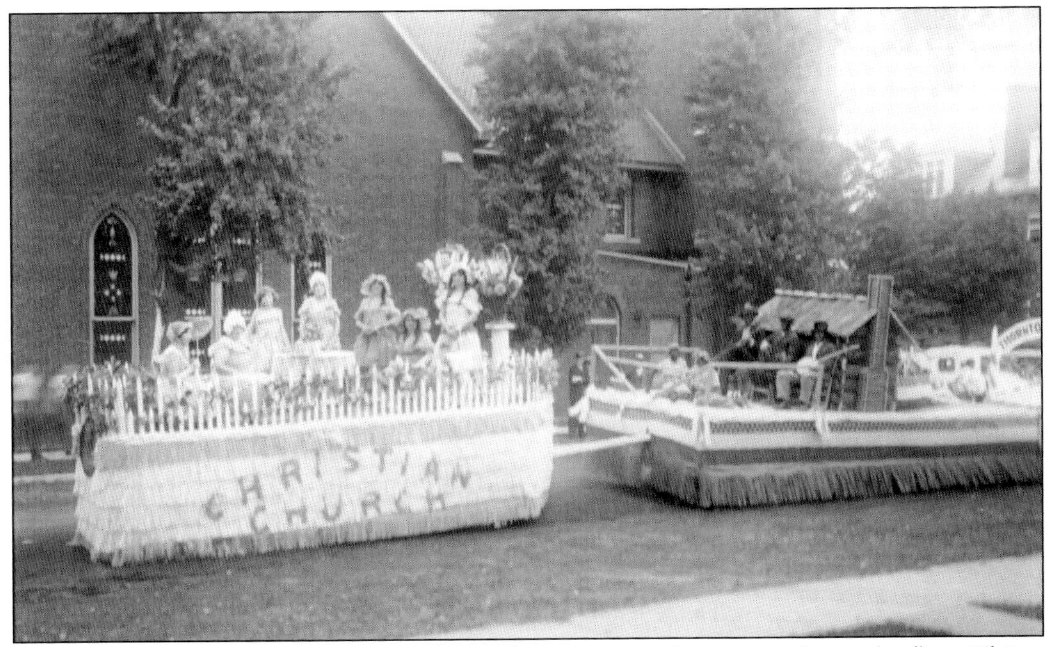

Here, a church adds its own festive touch to a farm wagon making a parade-worthy float. This is believed to have been a community picnic day in Thorntown. (Thorntown Museum Collection.)

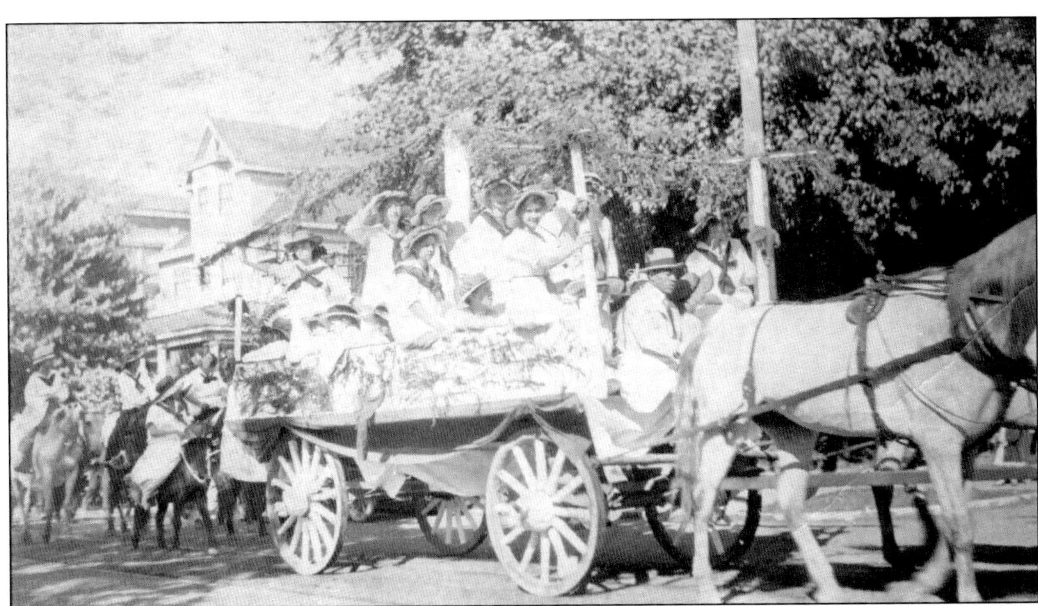

Horses were often used to pull floats in parades. The gentle driver teams were accustomed to heavy loads and lots of distraction. Often, teams pulled steam-powered calliopes without startling.

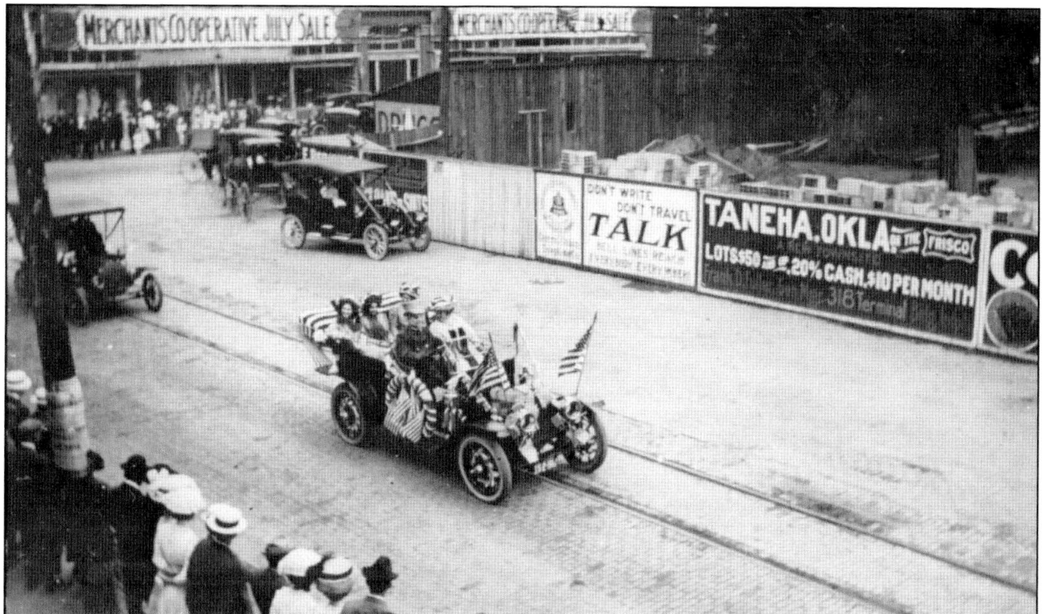

The car of the Coombs family won the decorating contest for patriotism in the 1910 Fourth of July parade. Construction barricades for the new courthouse are visible in the background; the project was about halfway to completion at the time.

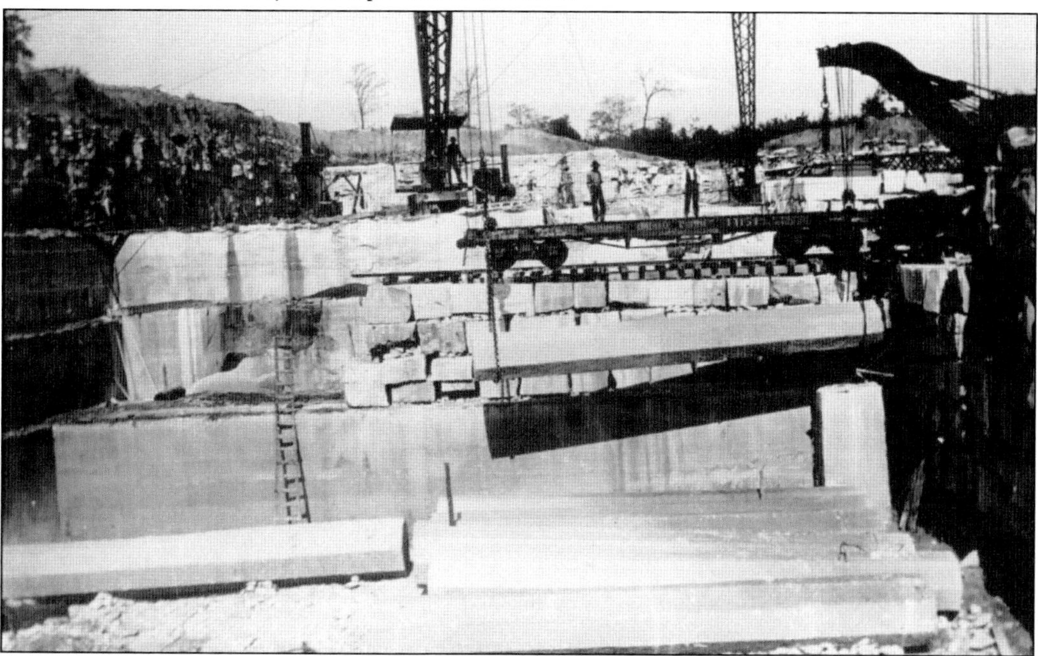

Building the current courthouse was a Herculean effort. As shown in this 1909 photograph of stone pieces, constructing the building was like playing a precision game of blocks. Part of the necessary perfection was in the central placement to make the building straddle the second prime meridian after it was discovered that this major line of measurement runs through the exact center of the courthouse square. No other public building in the world is known to lie on a prime meridian.

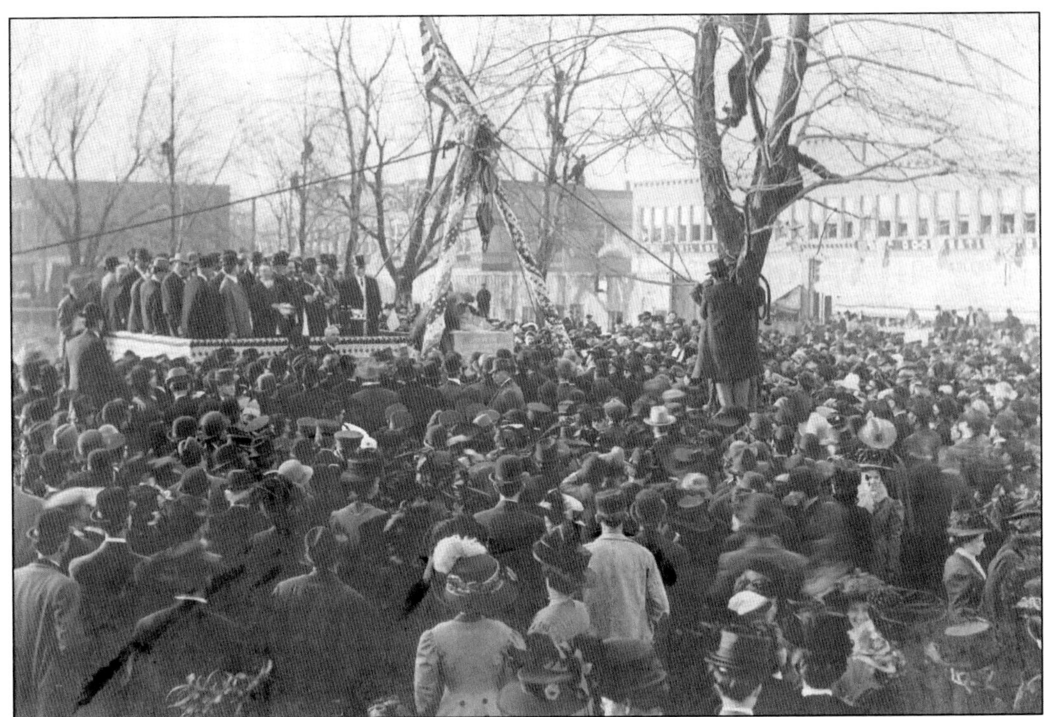

This photograph taken on November 30, 1909, shows the great excitement over the laying of the courthouse cornerstone. Note the adult man who has climbed a tree in order to get a better view.

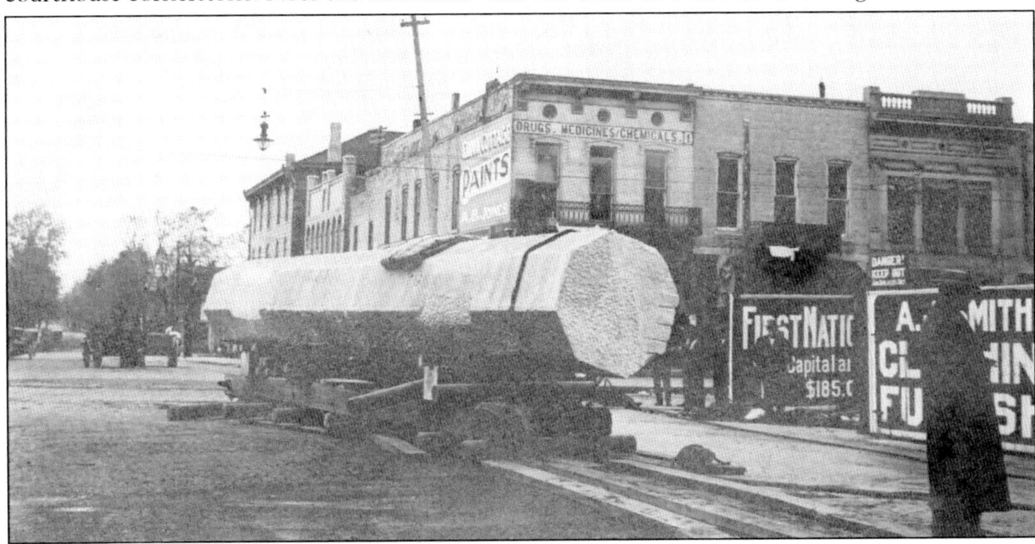

A brass line and compass figure are inscribed into the marble floor, marking the precise location of the second prime meridian. Even with such bragging rights inside, the towering limestone columns outside steal the show. Eight of these—supposedly the world's largest limestone monoliths—were brought up from Hoadly Quarry in Stinesville, Indiana, by train. For stability during shipping, they were cut and delivered as octagons. Each one of the nearly 36-foot-tall, 48-inch-base (tapered to 40-inch-wide tops) cylinders took skilled masons six weeks to hone by hand into the perfectly smooth pieces standing today. Four of the 30-ton columns are at the front of both the north and south entrances of the courthouse.

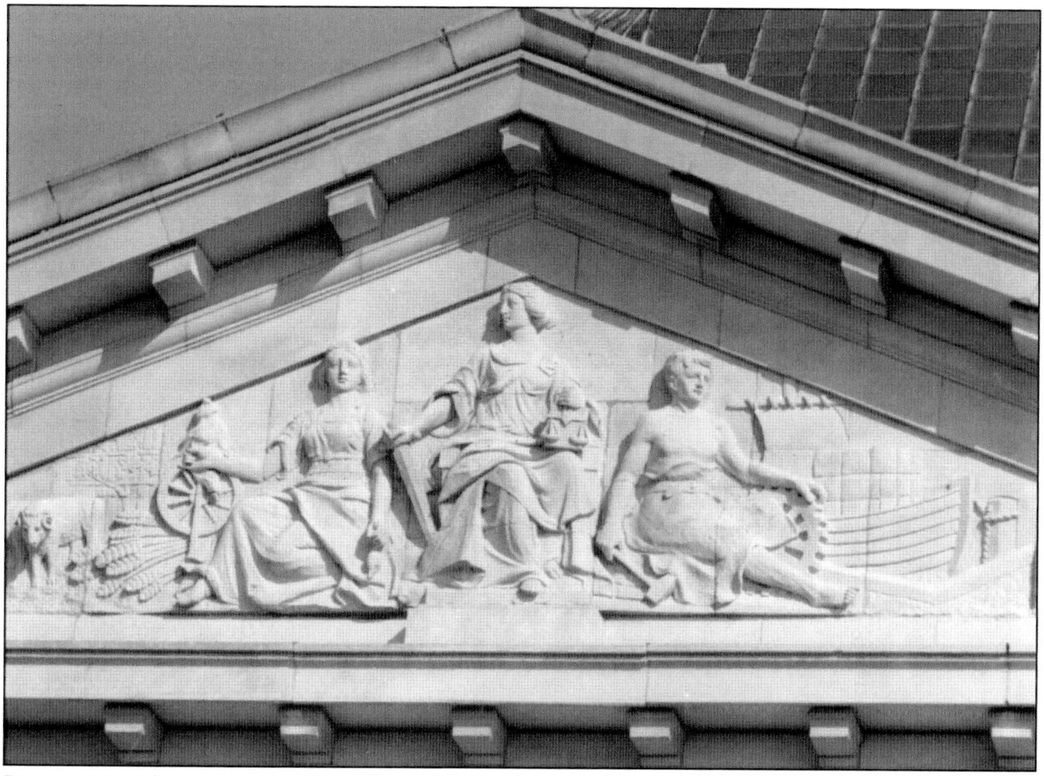

Progress on the new centerpiece was fast and steady. Shown here are the carved pediment decorations reflecting the values of the inhabitants of Boone County. The classical images indicate agriculture, justice, and industry. All these elements are a showcase of architect Joseph T. Hutton's neoclassical native limestone vision.

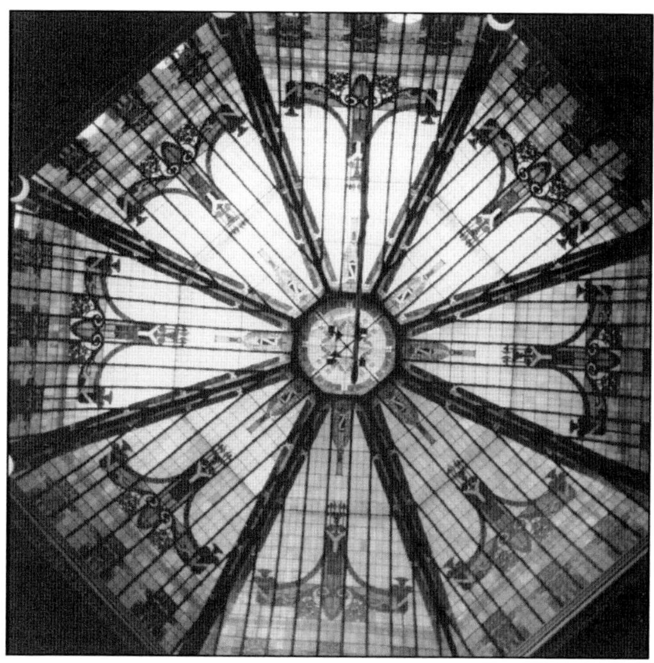

The stained-glass rotunda is the second largest in Indiana, surpassed only by the installation at West Baden Hotel. At its peak, the dome rises four stories above the floor and is 52 feet in diameter. This element, along with the impressive columns, became integral in earning the Boone County Courthouse a place in the National Register of Historic Places in 1986.

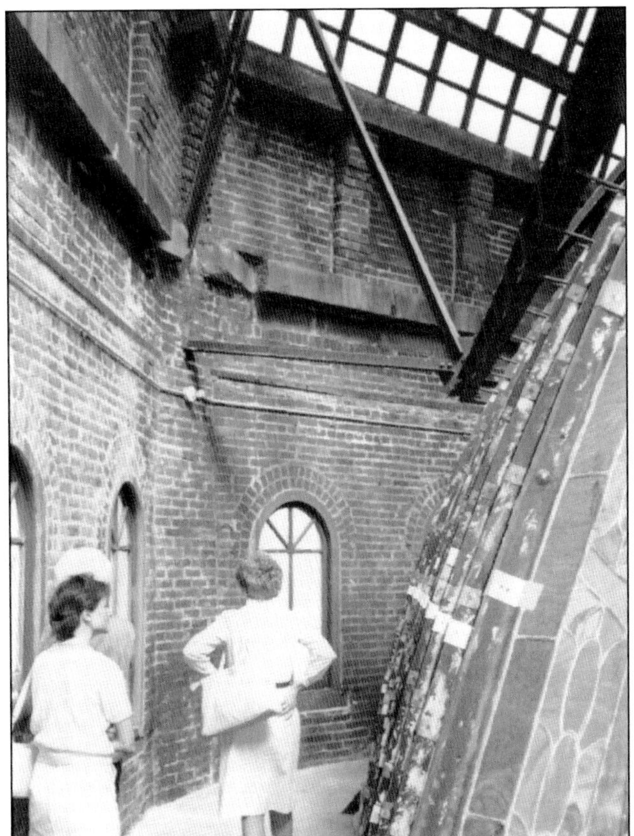

This is a rare behind-the-scenes look at the space between the inner and outer dome of the courthouse. The delicate stained glass in the inner dome is protected from the elements by this exterior cap structure.

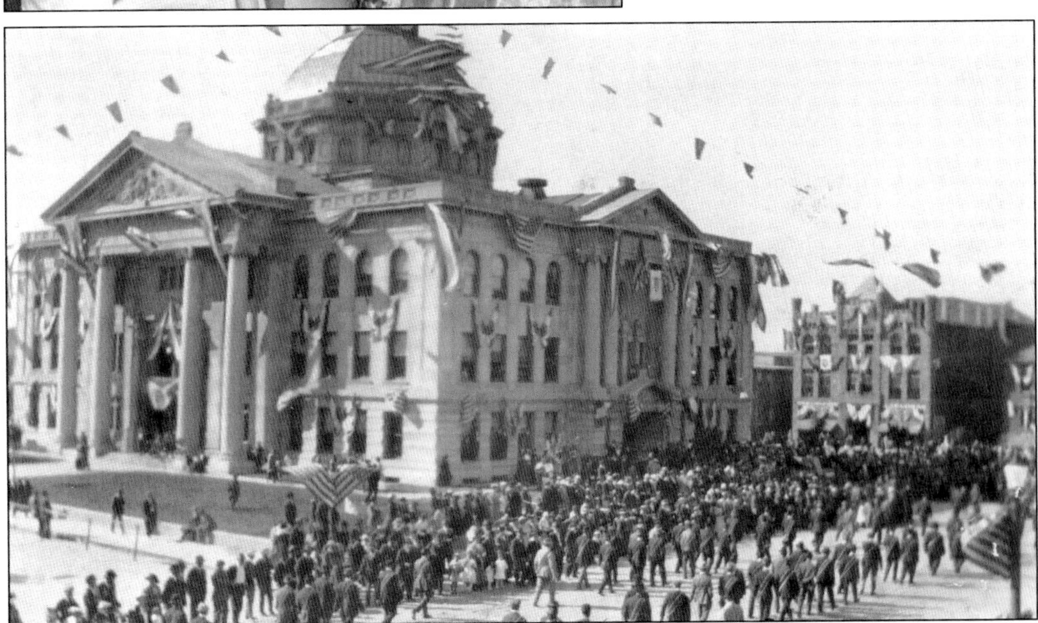

The courthouse dedication on July 4, 1912, brought former vice president Charles Fairbanks out from his Indianapolis home to speak. Lebanon lawyer Samuel Ralston was there, too, heavily campaigning for the governorship he would win that fall.

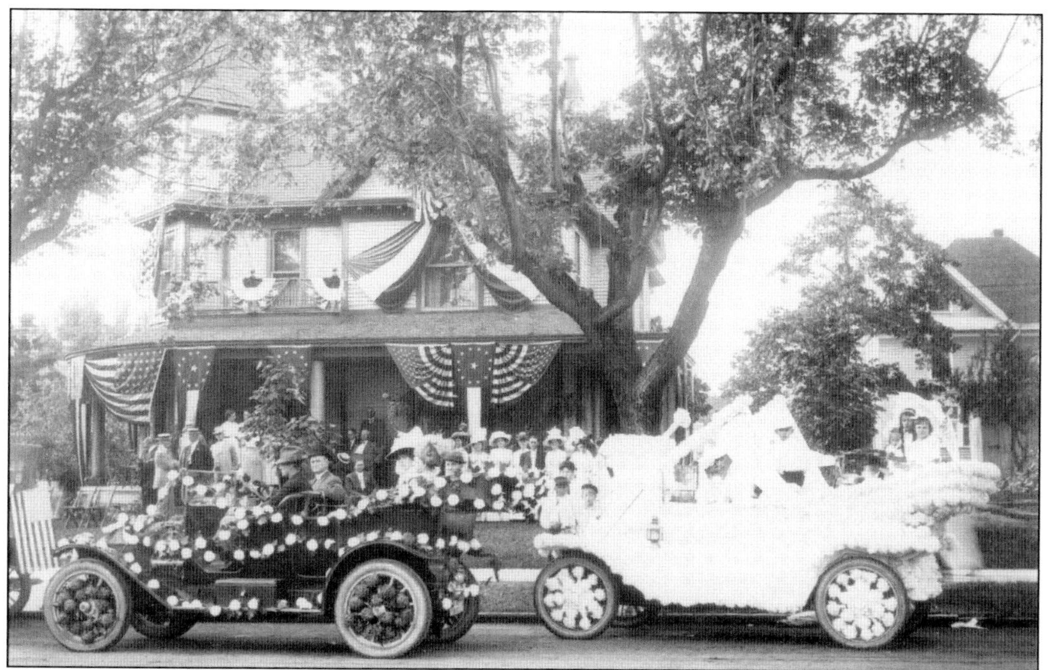

Decorated floats were always a big hit, and paraders could be quite competitive. Here, the Sunshine Society float of 1916 shows off the club's talents.

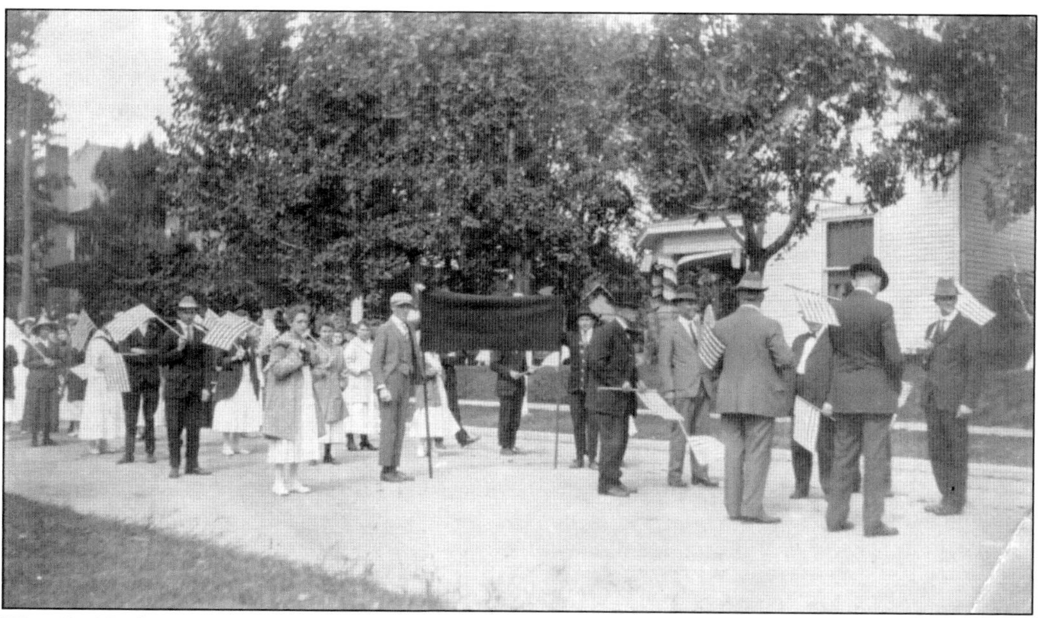

The 1916 Indiana Centennial Parade included all sorts of entries. Here, high school students join the revelry with a simple banner.

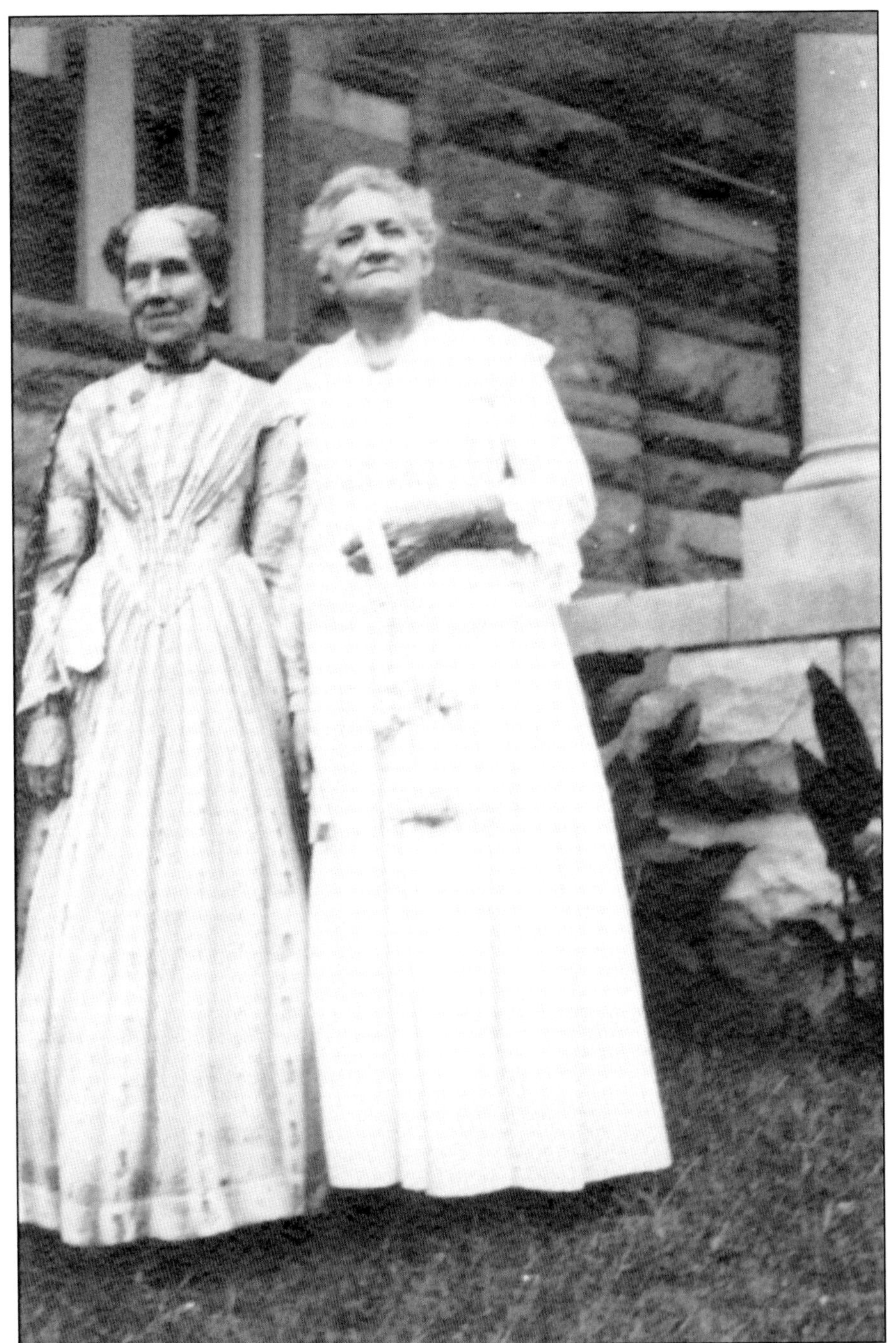

In a 1916 photograph taken during the Indiana Centennial Celebrations at Lebanon, two very influential women of education pose together in period pioneer costumes. Hattie Stokes (left) and Julia N. Harney were both teachers and administrators for many years. When two new schools were added to serve Lebanon's growing populations, the southside building was named Hattie B. Stokes School (erected in 1914), and children on the opposite side of town were given North Side in 1890. North Side was eventually renamed the Julia N. Harney School. Although the original buildings have been replaced, the schools have retained the Stokes and Harney names.

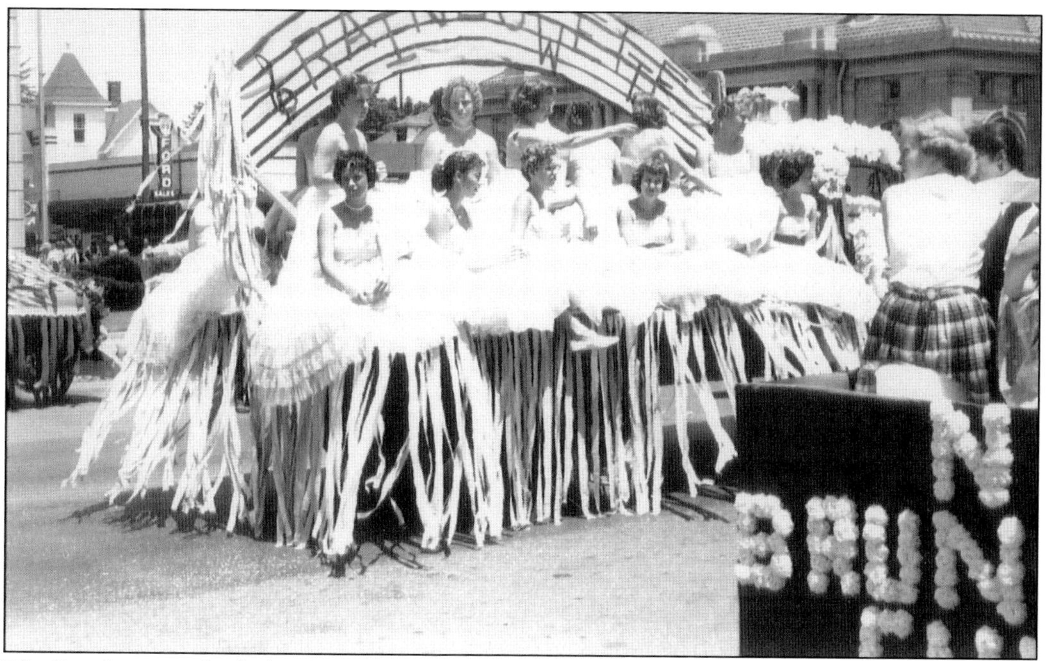

The Rainbowettes had a lovely hand-decorated float in this 1950s parade. The chapter that started in Boone County in 1944 is still active today.

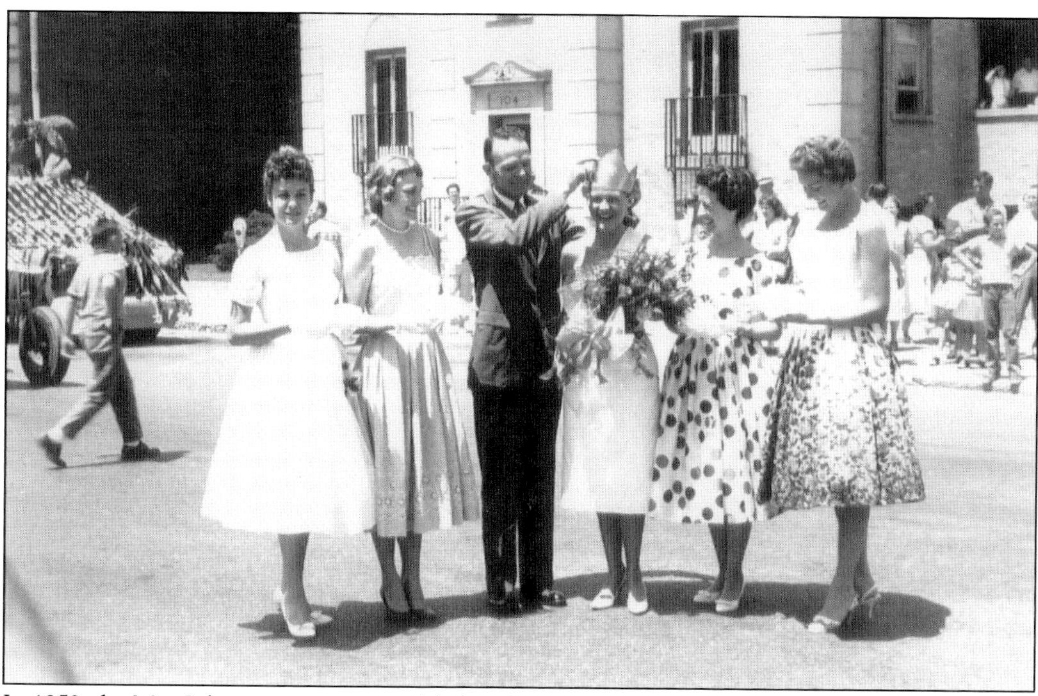

In 1959, the Mrs. Liberty pageant was added to the Independence Day Parade and open to married women over the age of 18 who demonstrated good morals and performed family and community service. Unfortunately, no one ordered a tiara, so the winner was honored with a paper crown. Ann Graham wore the title of Mrs. Liberty quite well.

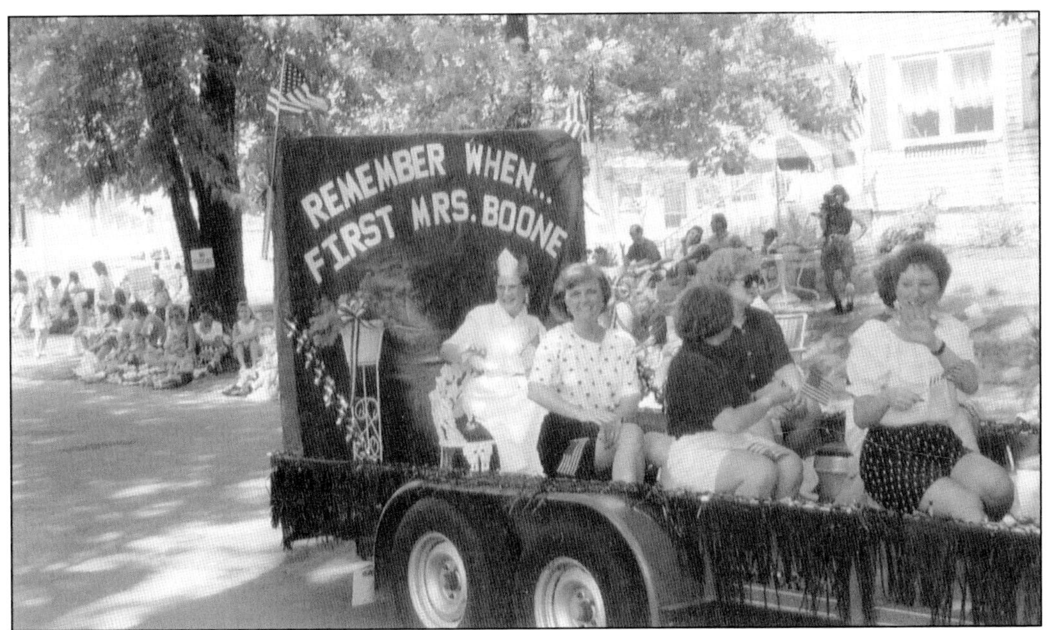

The previous year's pageant was so successful that the next year, a real crown was put on order for the occasion. The title was also changed to Mrs. Boone County. The float pictured here features past winners as a part of a festive parade. In 2016, the 57th queen will be crowned.

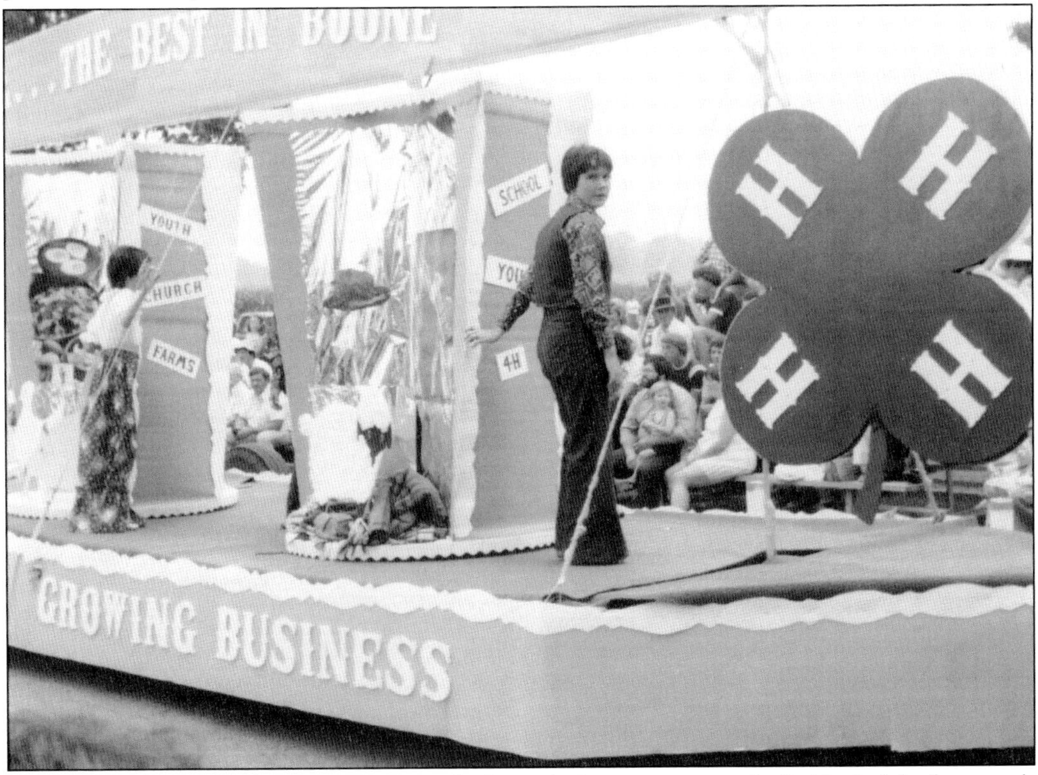

Each year, the 4-H fair begins with a parade through the county seat. Individual clubs from each of the 12 townships enter floats to complement the fair's theme.

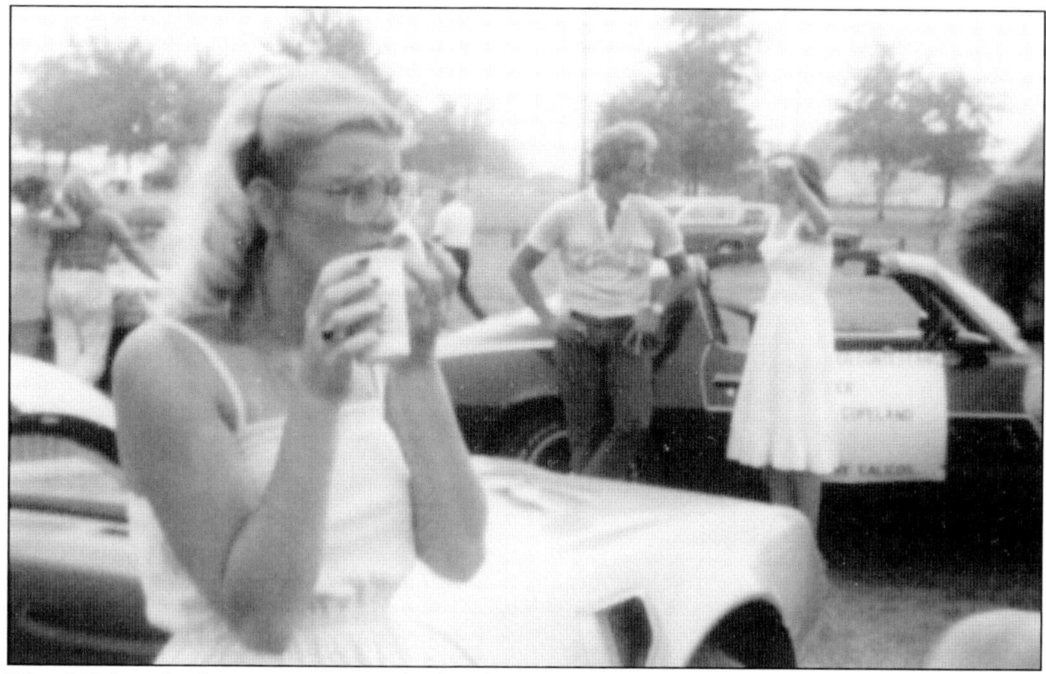

The 4-H fair also hosts a pageant. The local Fair Queen goes on to represent Boone County at the state level, seeking the ultimate title of Miss Indiana State Fair. In 1959, Debbie Smith of Thorntown was crowned the first Miss Boone County. She then went on to bring home the title of Miss Indiana State Fair. Here, 1970s-era Miss Boone contestants nervously await parade time. (Author's collection.)

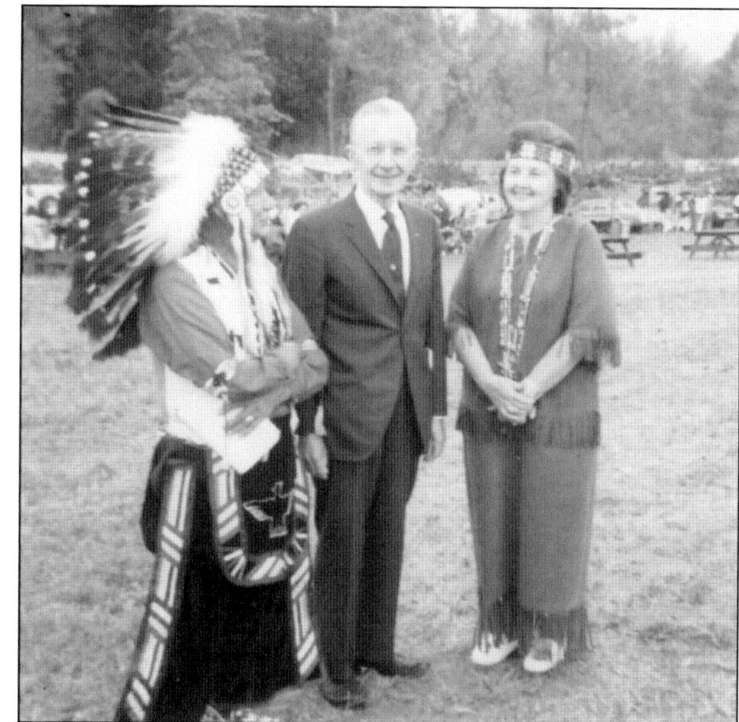

Celebrations are held all over the county for a variety of festivals and events. Here, Ralph Stark poses between visiting Indian Chief Mon Gon Zah (left) and Mrs. Wilbur Bowen for a photograph during the 1974 Festival of the Turning Leaves at Thorntown. Over the years, festivals, fairs, and parades have included Log Cabin Days, Pioneer Days, Brick Street Market, Renaissance Fair, Christmas Teas, fireworks displays, and many more.

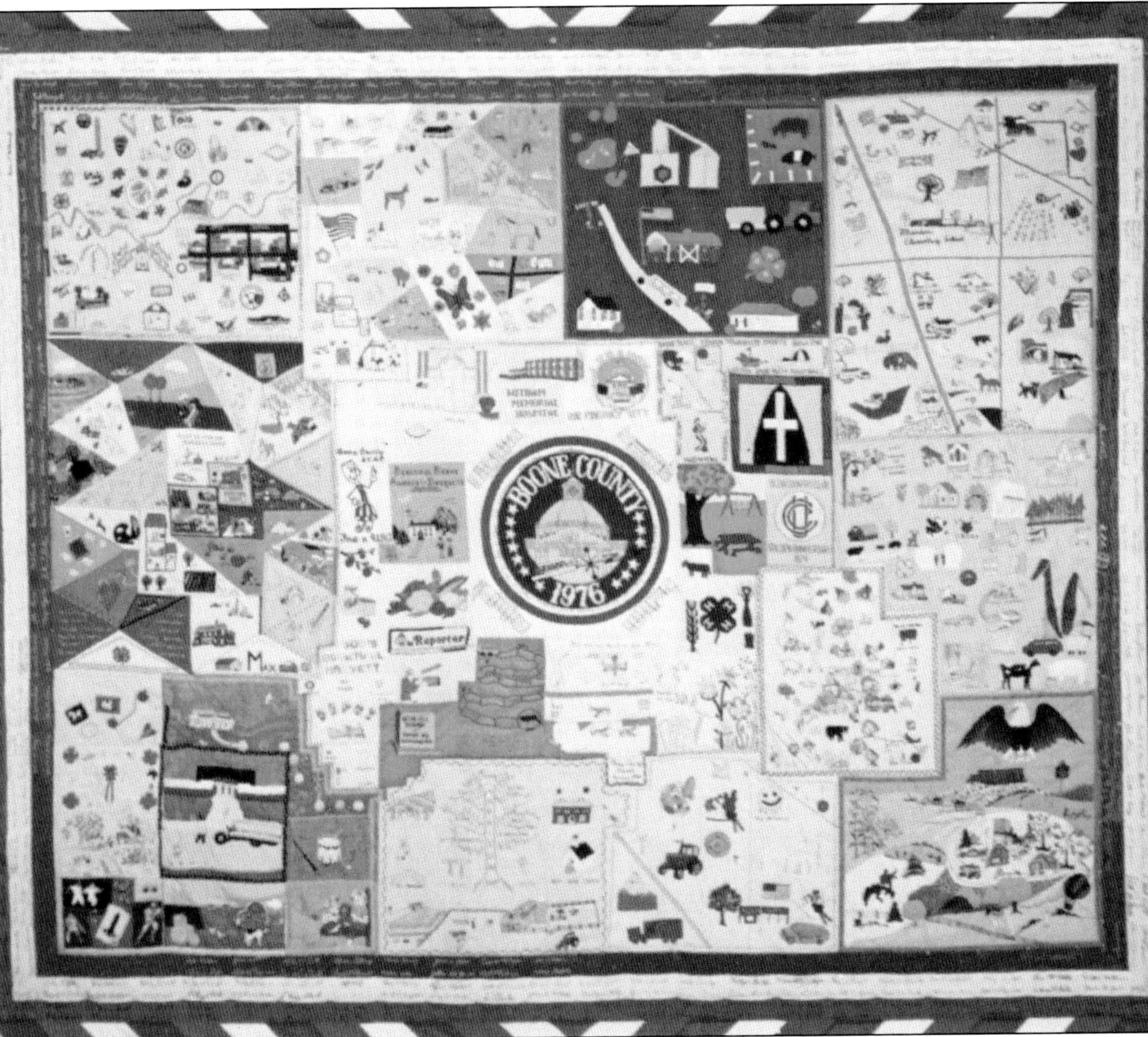

In 1976, Boone County went all out in celebration of the nation's bicentennial. A special subcommittee was formed and headed by Mrs. Wendell Iddings to create this 1976 Boone County Bicentennial Sampler. A chairwoman was appointed for each of the 12 townships, and work began on the collaborative project. All who were interested in needle arts were encouraged to participate. The end product was a 10-by-12-foot sampler showcasing images representing all that was beloved and famous within Boone County. Included were the names of past county presidents for the Boone Extension Homemakers and many more. Although the sampler was planned to be hung from the courthouse rotunda for one year, as of this writing, it has not been removed. As a happy coincidence, the filtered light of the courthouse dome protects the sampler from damage.

Nine

Fondness and Fame in Boone County

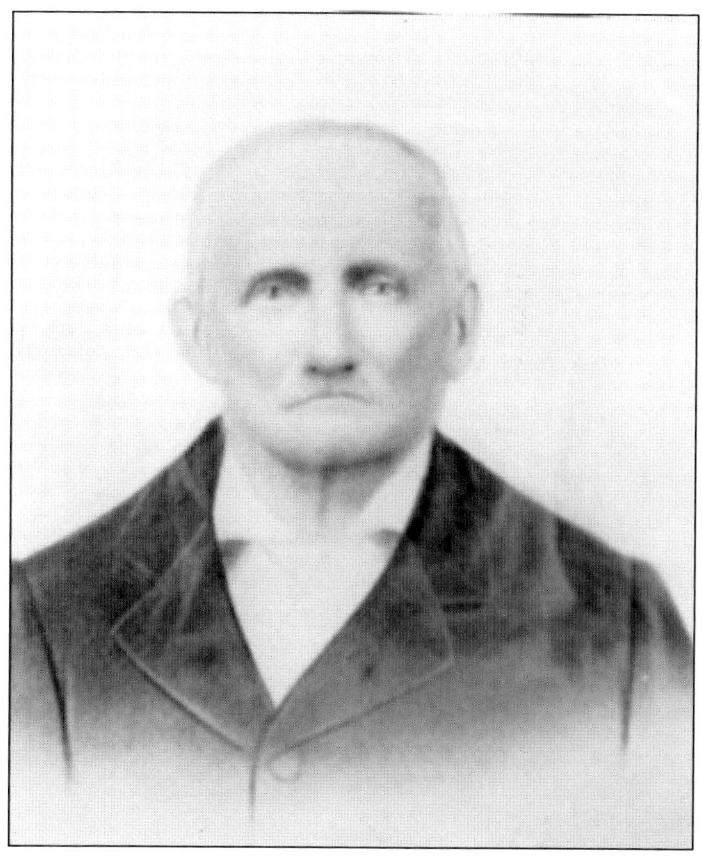

James McCann (1787–1870) served two terms as county recorder from 1836 until 1850. His first office was in the original log courthouse at Lebanon.

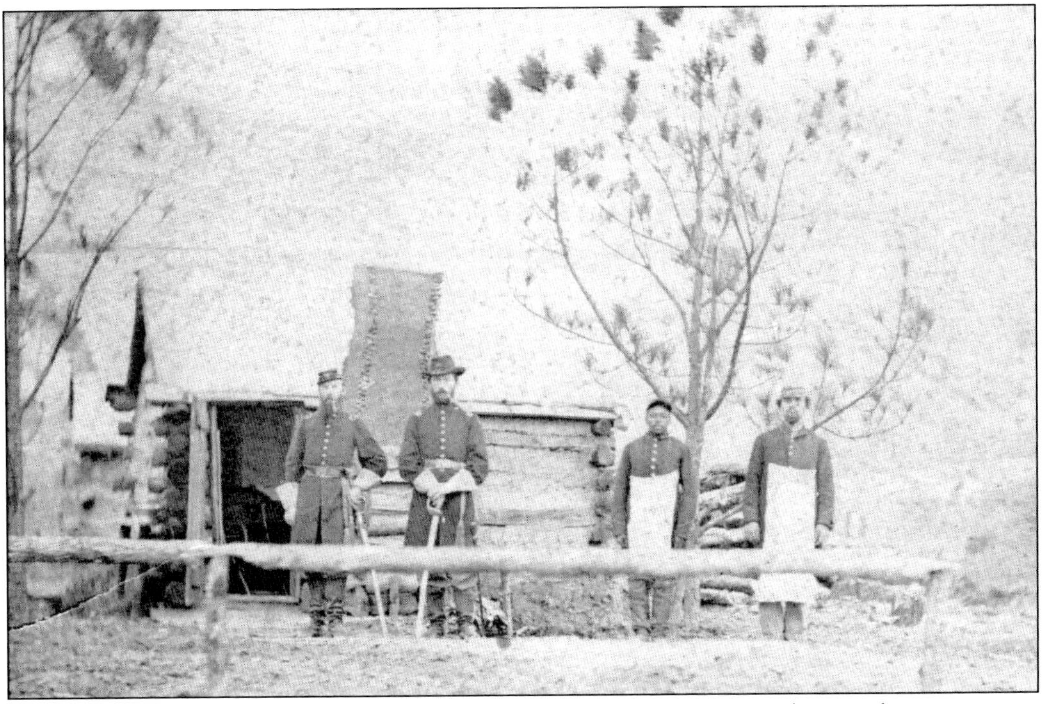

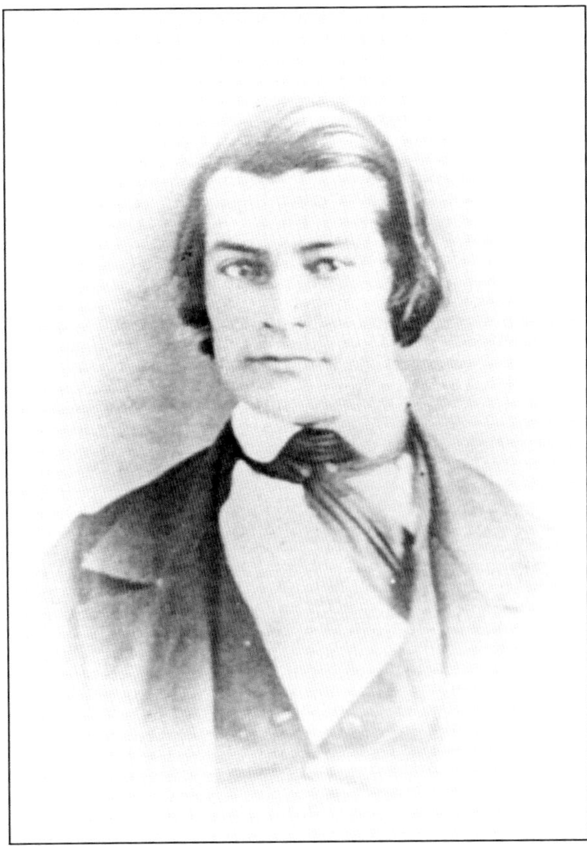

This photograph was taken in 1864 at the winter quarters of Joseph O. Pedigo (far left) in City Point, Virginia, as he was serving as captain of Company D, 28th Regiment of the US Colored Troops. Upon his return to Boone County, Pedigo worked as a lawyer and entered politics, serving as mayor of Lebanon from 1892 until 1896.

Stephen Neal (1816–1904) never attended college; he studied law for a time under Joseph G. Marshall in Madison, Indiana, and was admitted to the bar in 1841 at age 25. Neal was a Boone Circuit Court judge credited with writing the original 1866 draft of the 14th Amendment to the US Constitution. The 14th Amendment guarantees that all persons born in the United States or naturalized as citizens—regardless of race or creed—have the right to vote and to receive equal protection under the law. This 1847 photograph was taken on the last day of the legislative session at Indianapolis when Neal was about 30 years old.

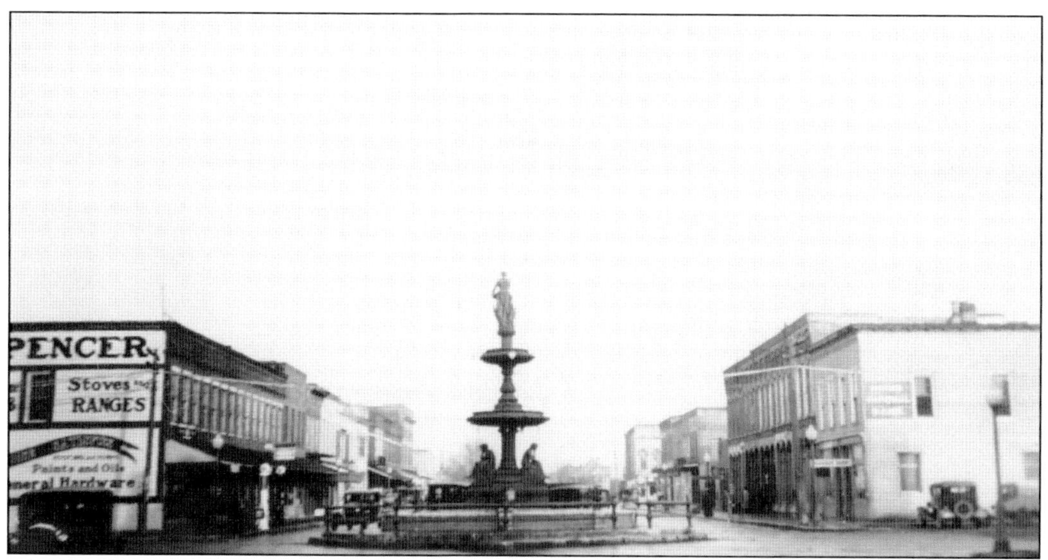

This lovely iron fountain was installed as the centerpiece of Thorntown in 1909 to honor the family and generosity of Anson Mills. Mills, a former Thorntown resident and founder of El Paso, Texas, gifted his boyhood home with money to fund a much-needed modern waterworks. In 1944, residents decided that the metal the fountain was sculpted from could be put to more honorable use, so it was donated to a World War II scrap drive and melted down.

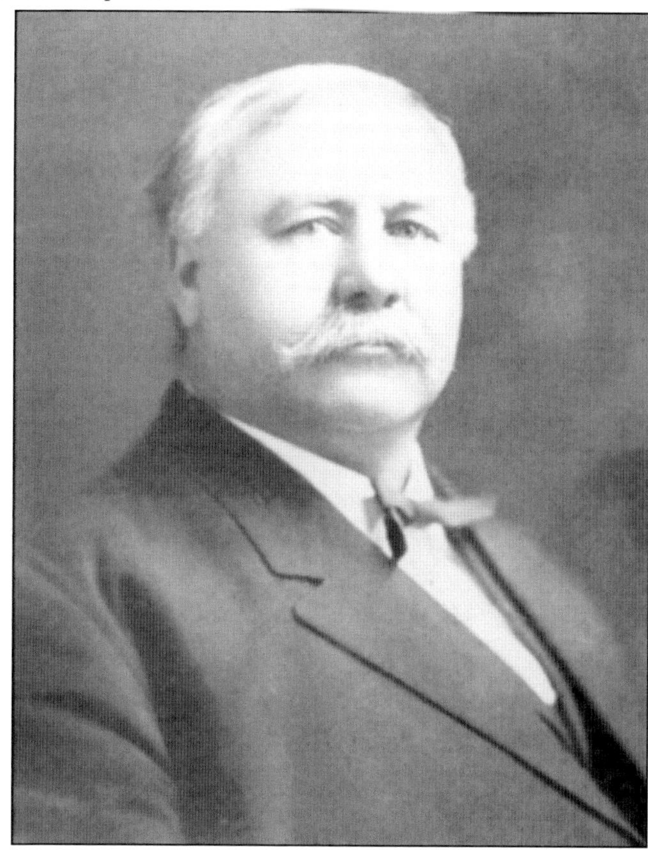

Samuel Moffett Ralston was a Lebanon lawyer. He was elected governor of Indiana in 1913 and served one term during the state's centennial.

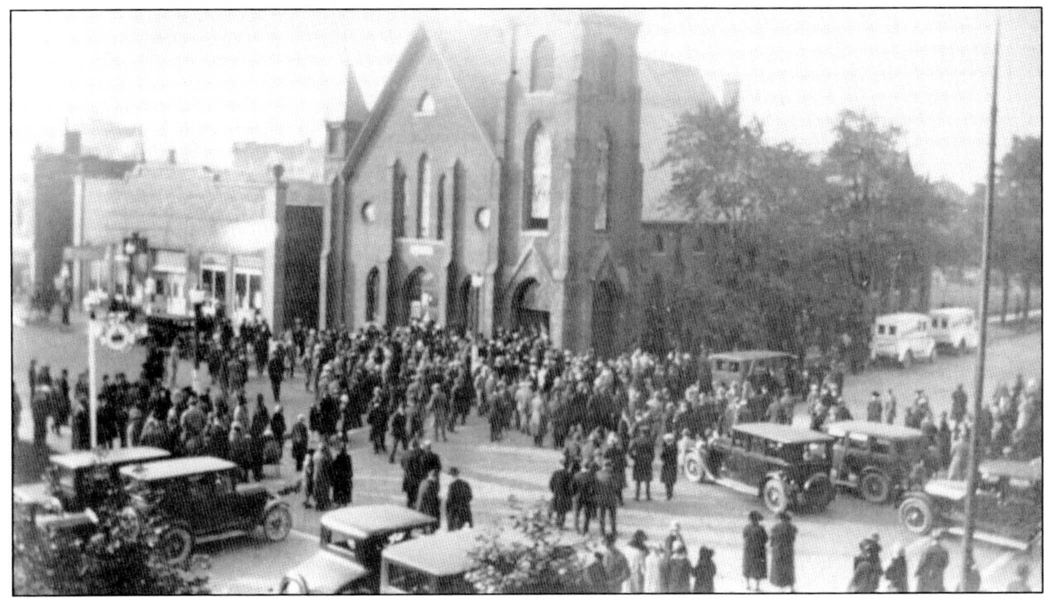

Ralston was elected to the US Senate in 1922 and represented Indiana until his death in 1925. His funeral at the First Presbyterian Church in Lebanon was widely attended. Thousands flocked to Ralston's home city service. The church overflowed, with many quietly listening from the street.

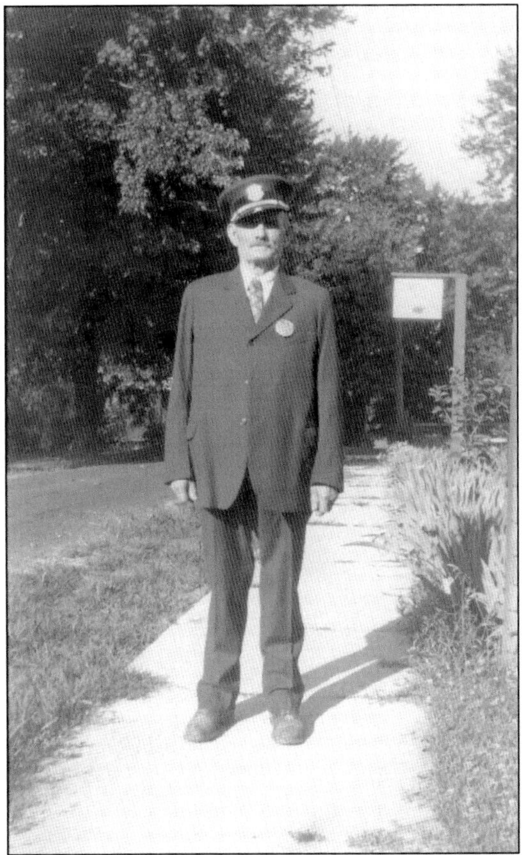

Deputy Marshal Stonsbrough served the town of Zionsville for many years. Others, like Maynard Moore, town marshal for nearly 30 years, also worked as a firefighter and on the street department during the same tenure. (Special thanks to the Zionsville Police Department.)

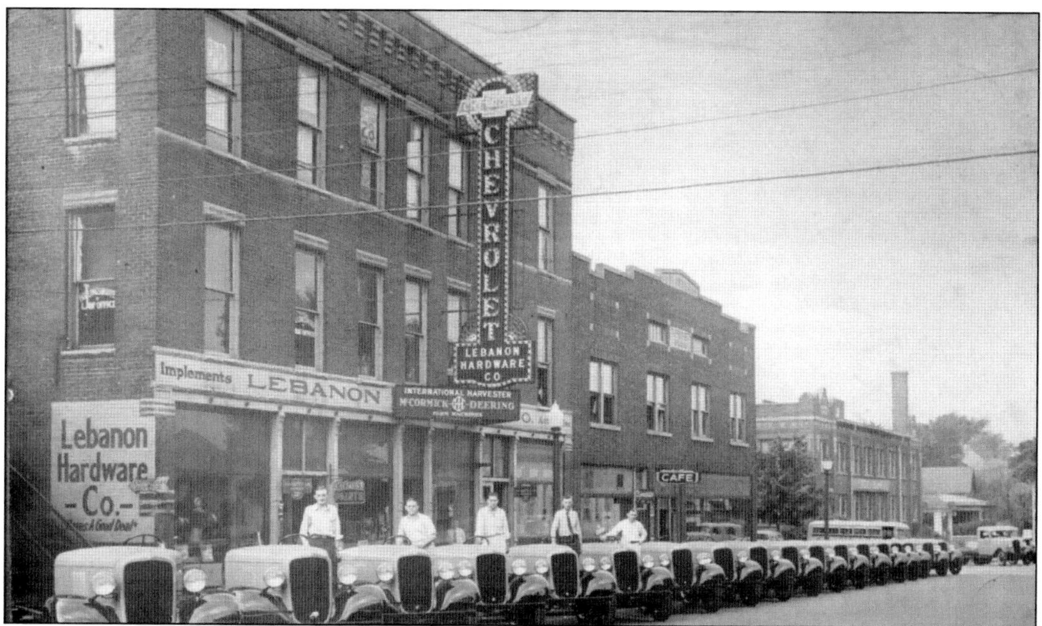

Dillinger gang member and known Prohibition era criminal Harry "Pete" Pierpont robbed Shelby's Lebanon Hardware Company store on December 22, 1924. With his crew of five, he made his getaway in a car stolen from a wealthy Indianapolis family along Meridian Street. Pierpont went on to use the 12 guns, 8 knives, and 50 or so boxes of ammunition from the hold-up the next day while robbing the Upland State bank of $2,500 in cash.

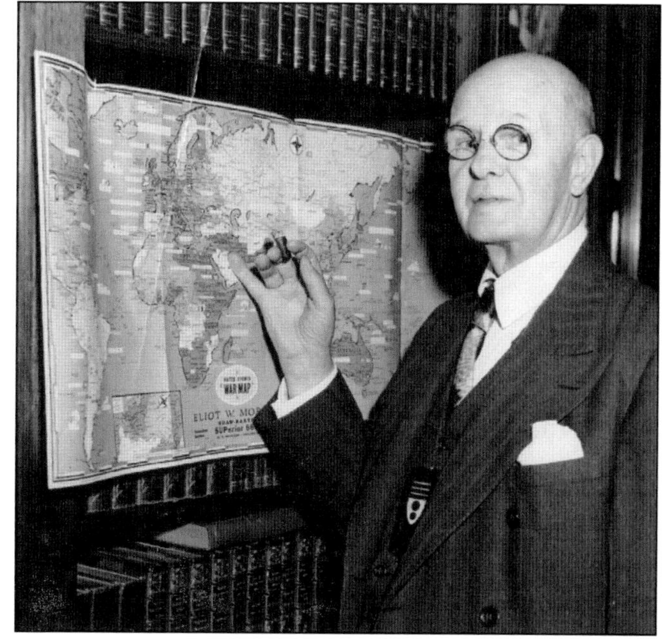

Henry C. "Hank" Ulen was born in Boone County in 1871. He attended school until the age of 14 but did not feel he learned as much in a classroom as he could by just going out and doing a thing. After working odd jobs, including selling newspapers, working carnival concessions, and clerking in a law office, Ulen set out in the building and engineering field. Before his permanent return to Lebanon in 1929, Ulen built enormous projects all over the globe, such as railroads, waterworks, tunnels, dams, power plants, and irrigation systems. His Marathon Dam project in Athens, Greece, is still ranked among Europe's top engineering feats.

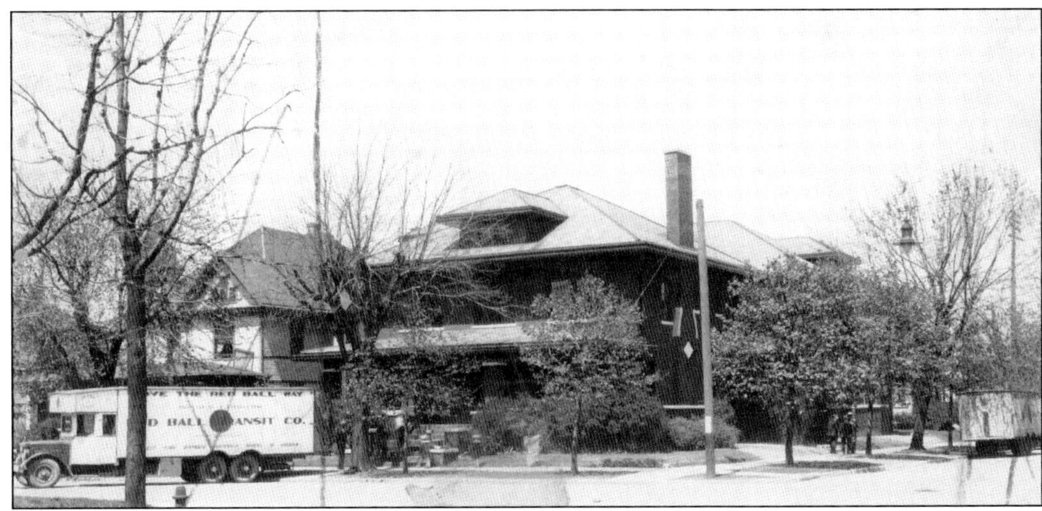

Perhaps one of Henry Ulen's largest projects was his decision to move the headquarters of all world operations back to his hometown of Lebanon. By then, he had gained the title of chairman of the board of the largest engineering and contracting company in the world. Ulen Contracting Corporation moved all executive offices to Lebanon in 1929. He also added a country club with world class golf amenities and a small private enclave of homes, named Ulen, on the outskirts of Lebanon. The little town is now ringed by the larger city of Lebanon.

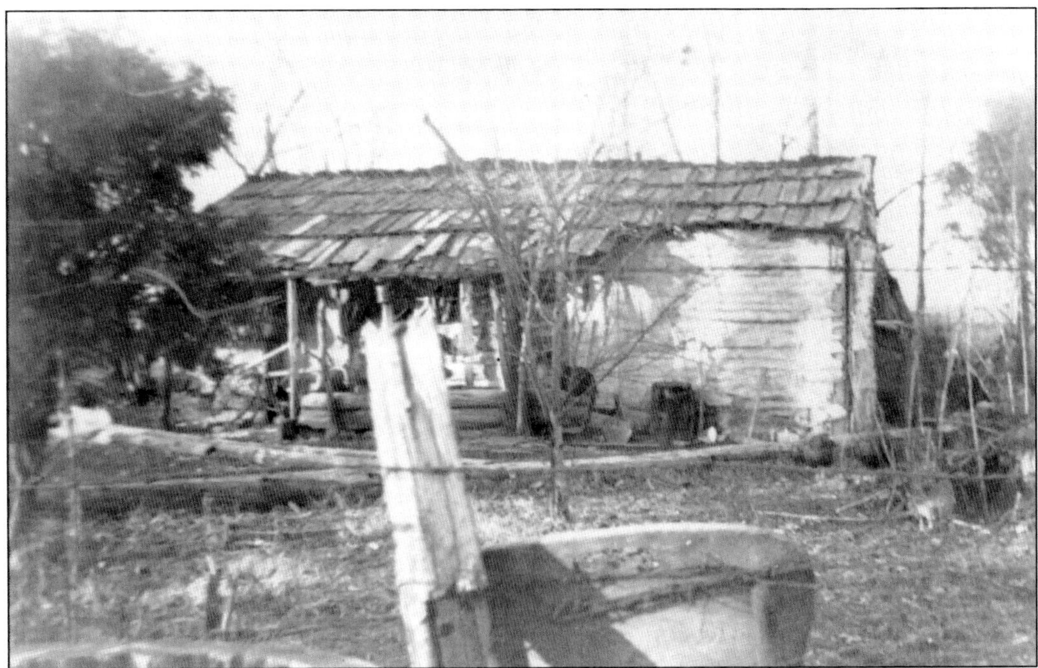

Warren Massey, famous as the "County Hermit," was finally forced to leave his self-sufficient little home in about 1940. His daughter took her aged and ailing father to her home, where she could care for him with modern conveniences such as heat and plumbing. He took along his beloved hunting dog, his fiddle, and little else. Within months, the decrepit cabin collapsed. Massey died about two years later.

Hometown hero and basketball legend Rick Mount was the first high school athlete to ever grace the cover of *Sports Illustrated*. The February 14, 1966, issue features Mount on the cover and includes an in-depth, multi-page article discussing the purity of his jump shot. Rick's dad, Pete, also played for Lebanon and was elected All State in the 1943 and 1944 seasons. Here, Rick lends a bit of his celebrity to advertise his uncle's flower shop. Mount's, a Lebanon staple since 1946, is still in business today under the stewardship of Lana Hale.

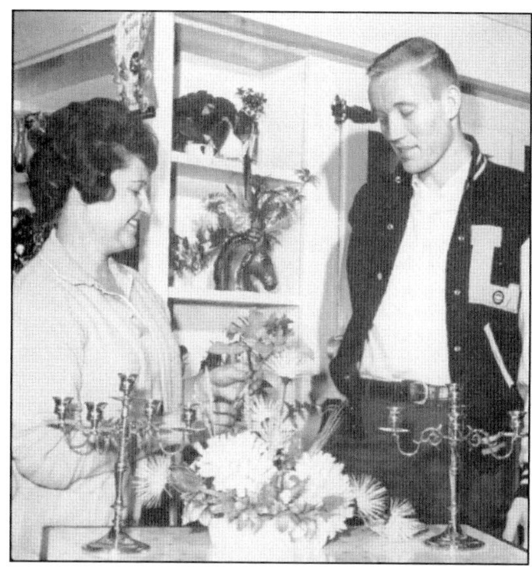

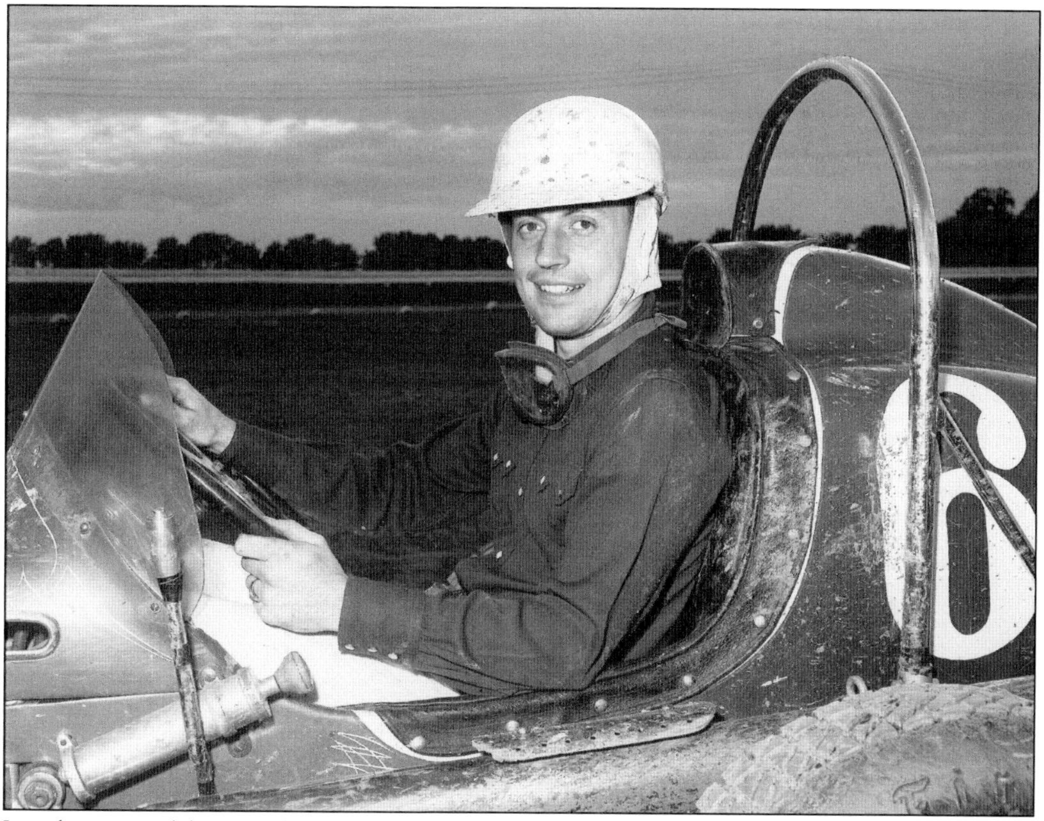

Local racing celebrity Mel Kenyon competed in eight Indianapolis 500 races and is the author of *Burned to Life*. He was most widely known in the motorsports world as "King of the Midgets," being the sport's winningest racer. "Miraculous Mel" was an accomplished dirt-track racer and won seven national championship crowns. He sponsors races (The Classic) and speaks to groups about his deep faith. He is also active as owner of the Mel Kenyon Midget Series. (Photograph by Ralph Hibbard, loaned by Gene Crucean.)

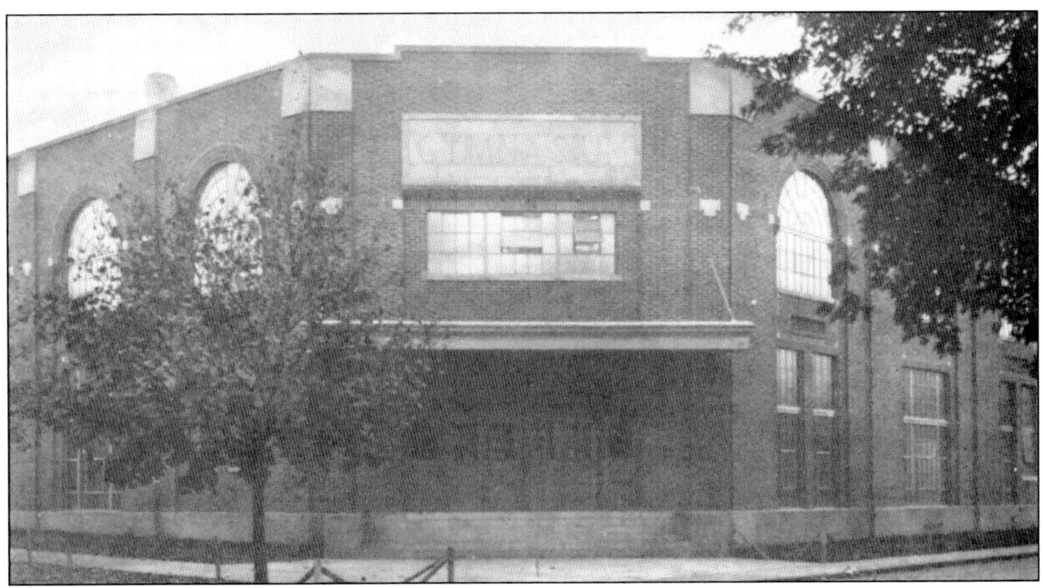

Memory Hall, the gymnasium of the old Lebanon High School, was a filming location for the 1986 movie *Hoosiers*. The scenes portraying the regional championship game were filmed here. Many locals came out in their 1950s best to join the fun as extras. Kent Poole, a graduate of Western Boone High School, landed a role in the movie as Merle. He later played Molly Ringwald's love interest, Stephen, in the 1988 film *Fresh Horses*.

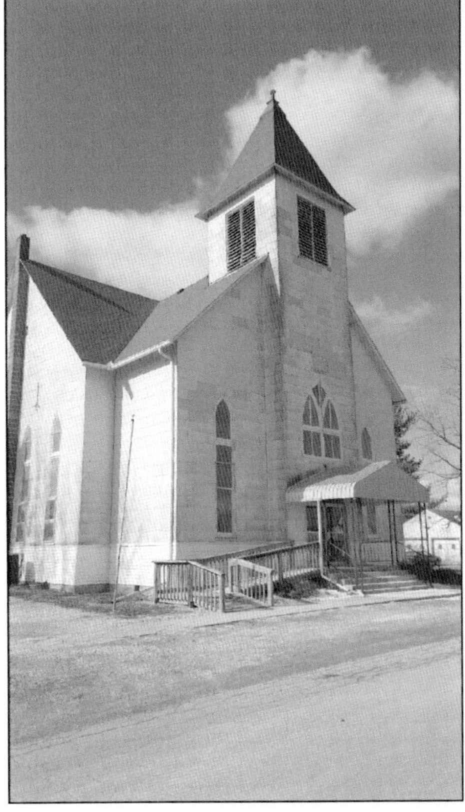

Though the movie *Hoosiers* featured the Elizaville Baptist Church as the site of the town hall meeting regarding the Hickory coach, the movie may have also given a boost to nearby Marion Township's village Terhune. Residents claim the town name was the inspiration for the "Hickory Huskers" rival team.

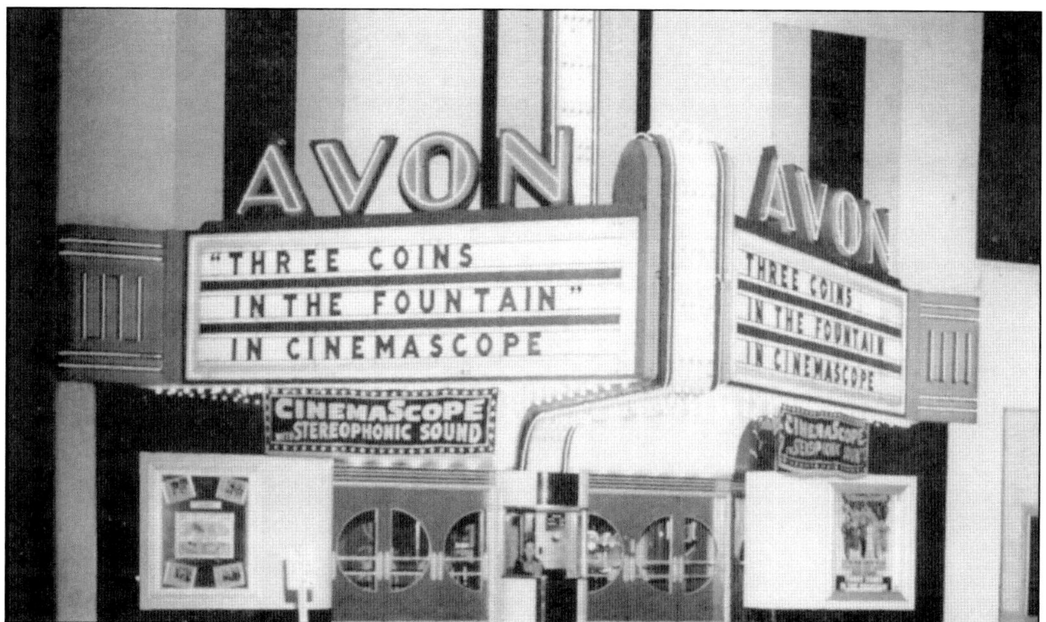

The Avon Theater showed films to generations of Boonites. Its marquee was also featured in a scene in *Hoosiers*. This 1954 photograph was coincidentally taken in the same year as the film's setting.

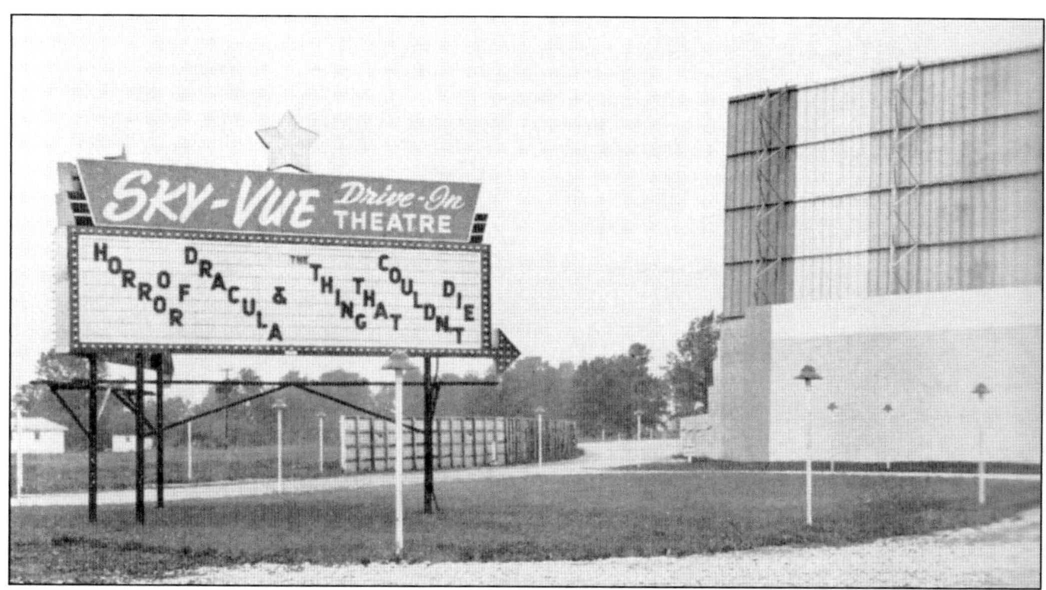

Now closed, the Sky-Vue Drive In Theatre was a fixture for many years, along with the Frankfort-Lebanon theater near Mechanicsburg. Now called Mel's Starlight, the Frankfort-Lebanon Drive In received grant money enabling the costly switch to digital formatted feature films. Mel's is now one of just over 300 outdoor movie theaters in the United States.

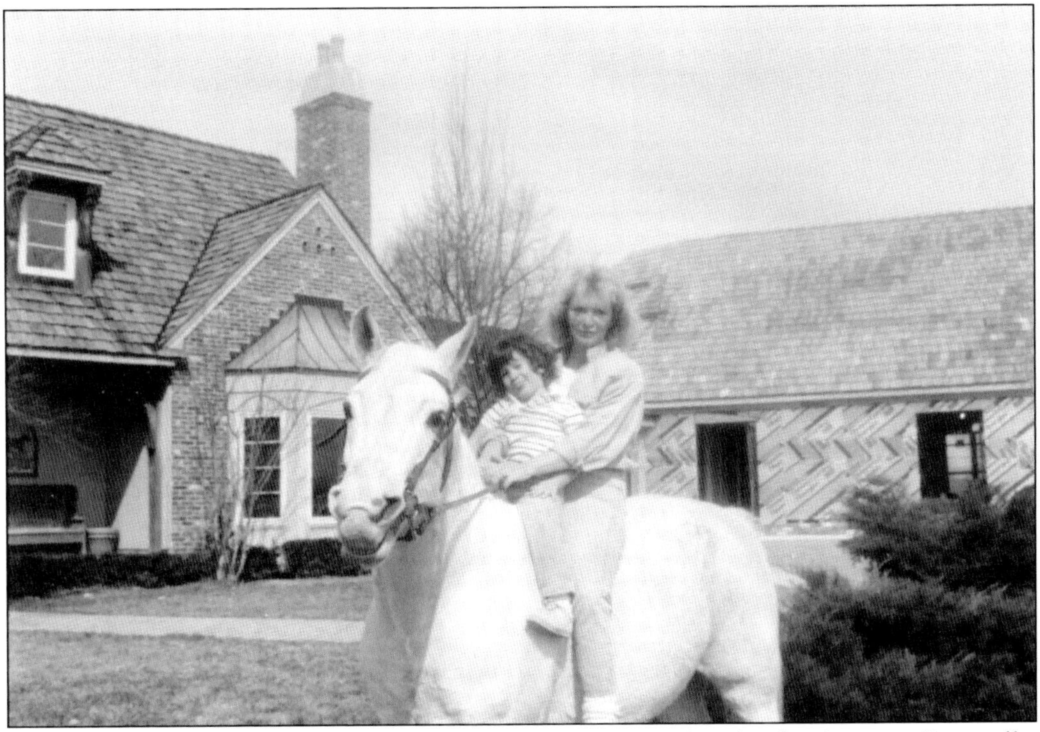

Hoosier-born and internationally acclaimed artist Nancy Noel makes her home in Zionsville. Locals know her for her philanthropy and love of animals as much as her hauntingly realistic paintings of children, angels, and simpler times. (Nancy Noel.)

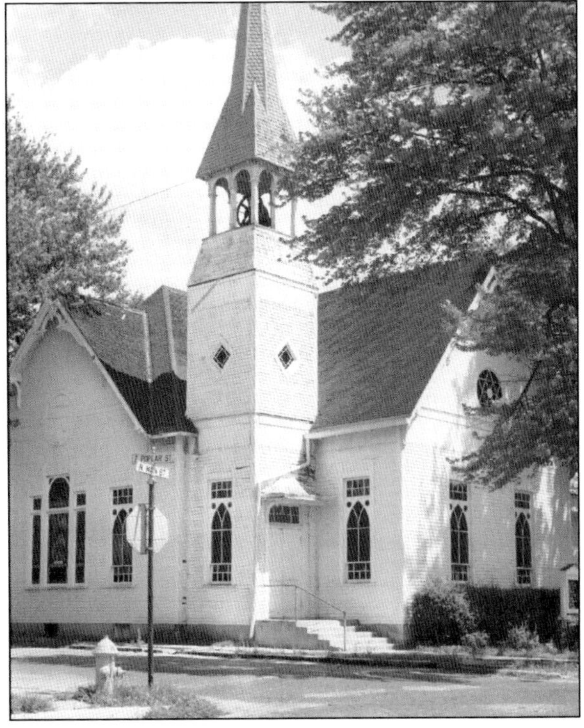

Nancy Noel bought the 1854 First Methodist Church near Zionsville's central restoration district and refurbished it as her gallery. She aptly named it the Sanctuary.

Ann McKay Houston was a singer with Al Cobine's Big Band. A talented vocalist with an incredible stage presence, she joined the ensemble in the early 1950s while studying at Indiana University. She continued on after graduation, as did her husband. Later, the pair settled in Lebanon to raise their three children. (Scott Houston.)

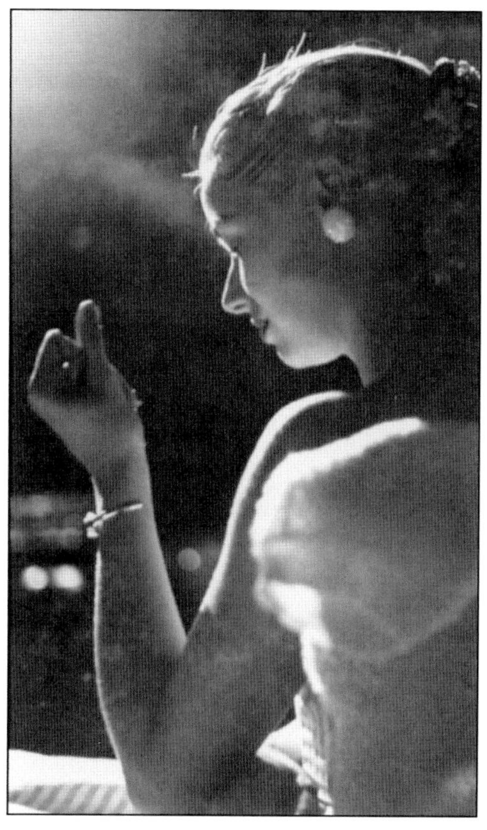

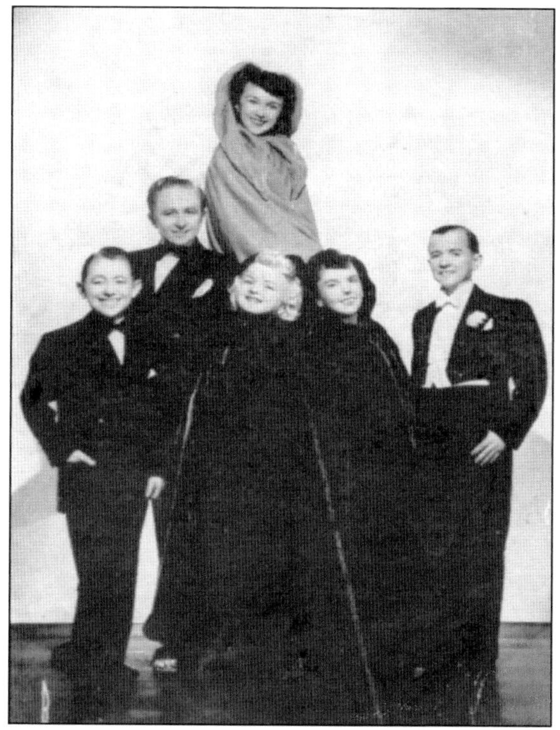

Arthur Noble Roseboom, Hollywood and vaudeville performer, made his fame under the stage name Art Noble. His headline act, Art Noble's Midget Stars, gave him his start. Roseboom, pictured here on a promotional card, is at far left in the front row. (Author's collection.)

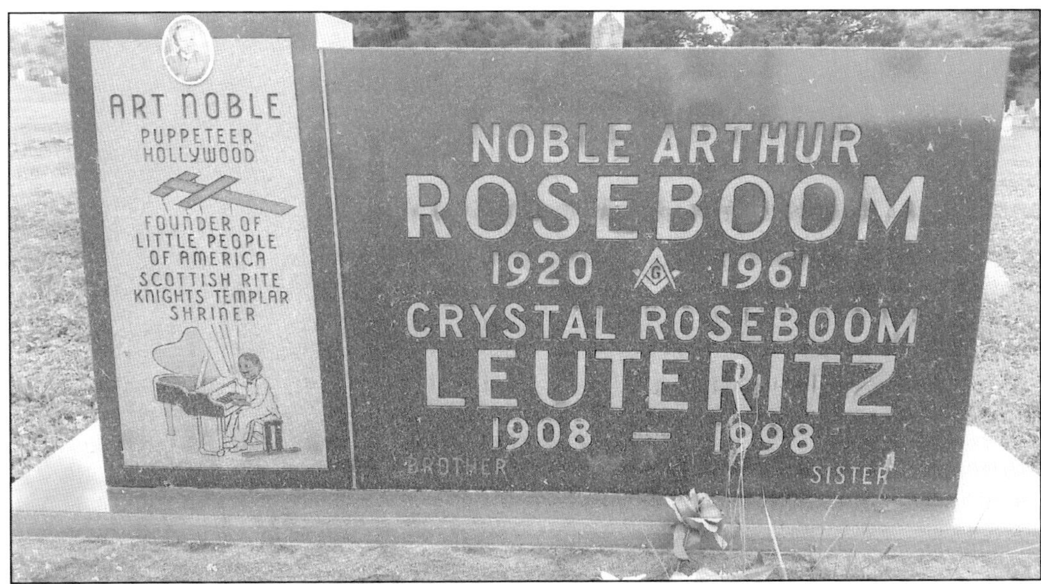

Art Noble died tragically in an auto accident. By then, the world was changing and "little people" were uniting to show the world that they were more than bit players in side shows and feature films. Art was instrumental in the founding of the advocate group Little People of America. He is buried next to his sister near Fayette at Mt Tabor. (Author's collection.)

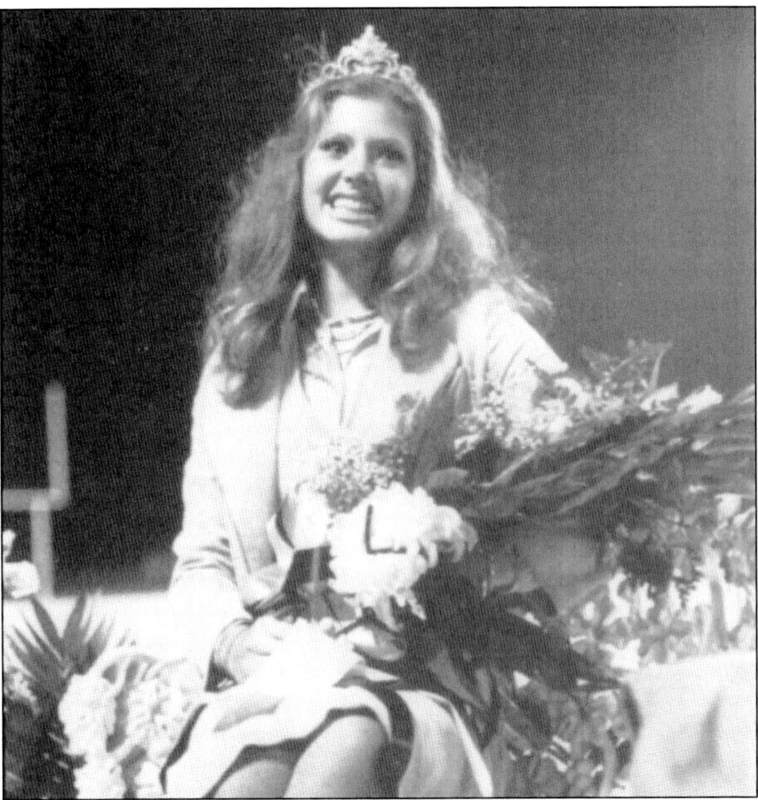

On Valentine's Day 2001, William Shatner (aka Capt. James T. Kirk) beamed up local girl and former homecoming queen of Lebanon High School Liz Anderson. They married in a courthouse ceremony. Elizabeth and William costar on reality television shows such as *American Pickers* and *The Shatner Project.*

If you long to be a darling of the media, then being a Boone County homecoming or prom queen is a good way to start. Julia Moffitt, news anchor for the Indianapolis NBC affiliate WTHR, was crowned during her senior year at Lebanon High School.

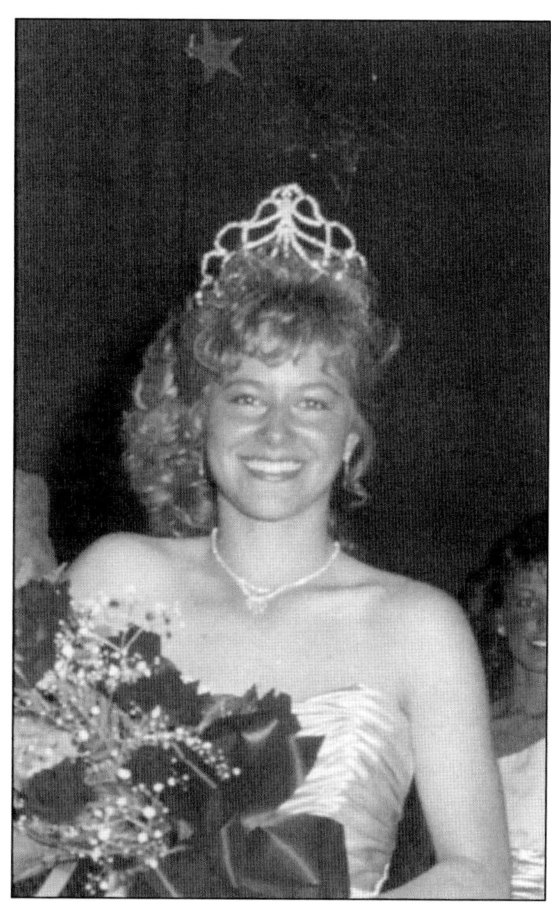

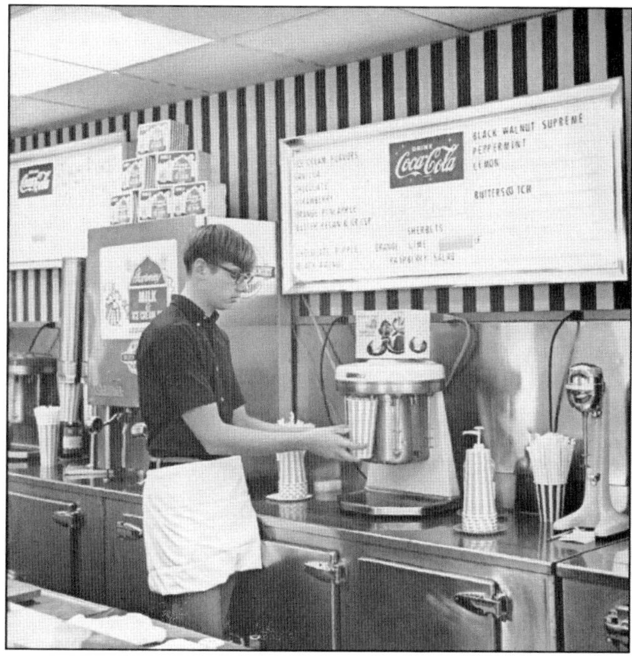

Guernsey's was locally owned and a favorite place to get a dairy bar treat. Their famous milkshakes made them a community favorite.

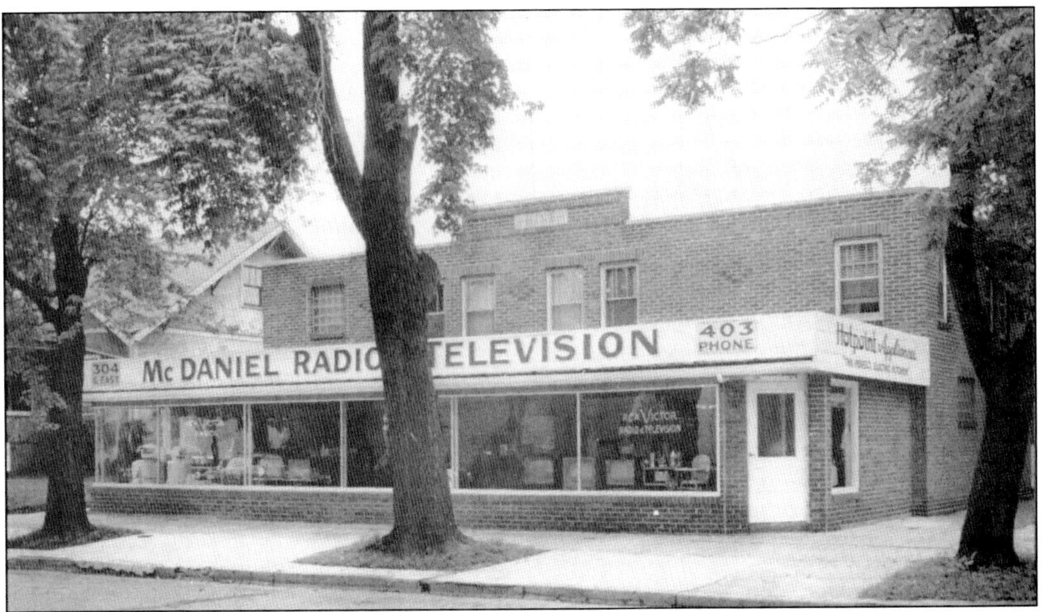

McDaniel's was the first seller of the "Magic Picture Box" most people have grown to find indispensable. Over his years in the business, owner George McDaniel sold nearly every television purchased in Boone County. Folks who purchased one frequently found friends and neighbors wanting to take a photograph of their newfangled appliance.

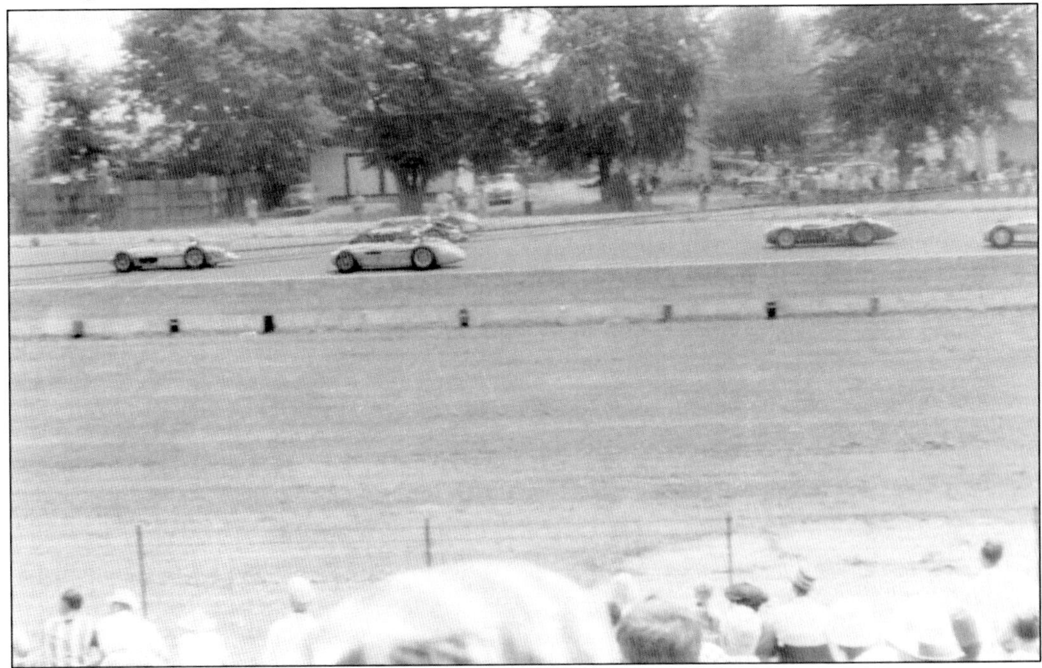

During the live 1949 broadcast of the Indy 500, marketing genius George McDaniel set up three makeshift viewing venues in Whitestown where people could huddle around one of his television sets to watch. That day, WFBM Channel 6 of Indianapolis officially signed on. This was the first and only year the race was ever shown live in the Indianapolis market. This photograph is from the 1957 race. The 2016 event will mark the 100th running. (Miller family.)

Donaldson's Candy has been a hometown tradition since 1966. Founder Fred Donaldson has shipped his sweets to all corners of the northern hemisphere. Over concerns of quality, the company politely discourages orders that would suffer the equator's heat while in transit. (Author's collection.)

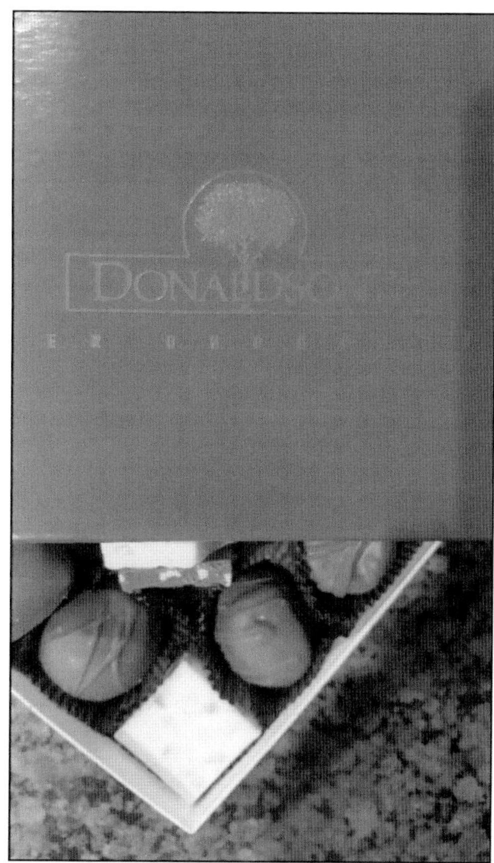

Shown here taking down an old house to make room for "progress," Ratts Wrecking was only one of Col. Noble Ratts's enterprises. He was also a junk dealer and auctioneer. His wife, Frances, long known to her students strictly as Mrs. Ratts, operated the Metropolitan Beauty School for decades.

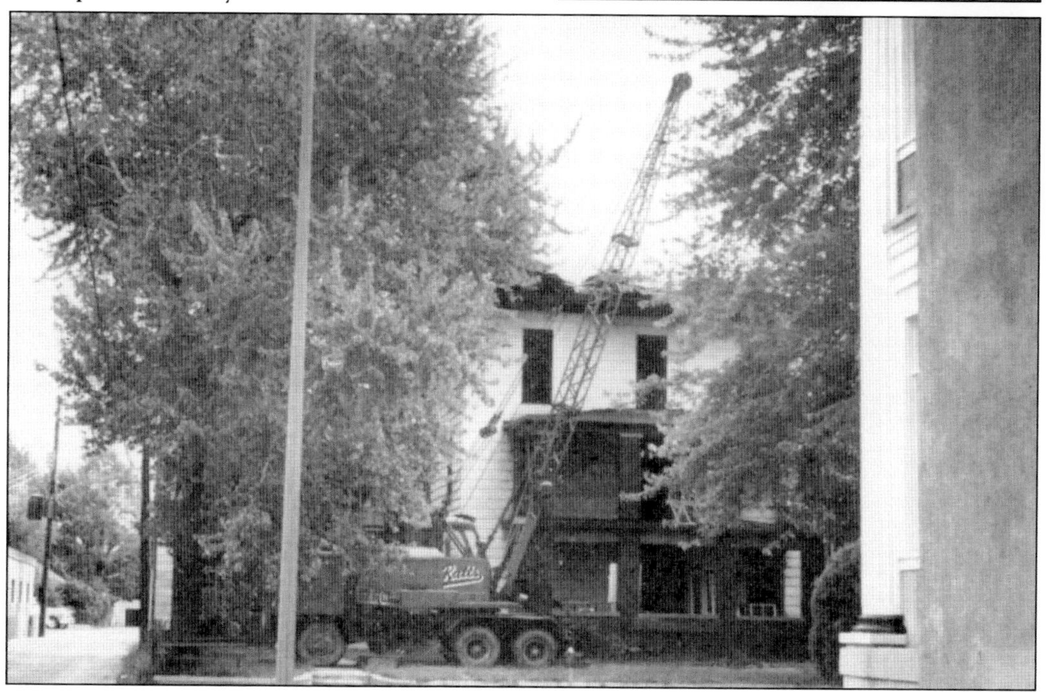

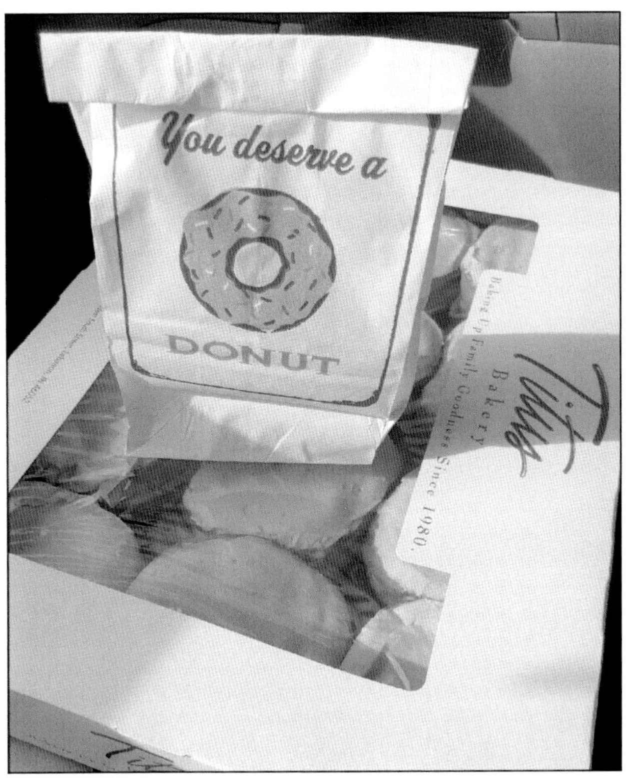

The Titus name has meant sweet treats to generations of Boone residents. Starting in the 1960s, the family has dabbled in donuts for a long time. Recently, the store opened at the site of the old offices for Titus Petroleum near Interstate 65. The cheery exterior is painted with brightly colored and enticing four-foot-wide pink sprinkled donuts. Pershings—a maple iced treat—have been the signature sellout since the store opened. The author prefers their classic glazed. (Author's collection.)

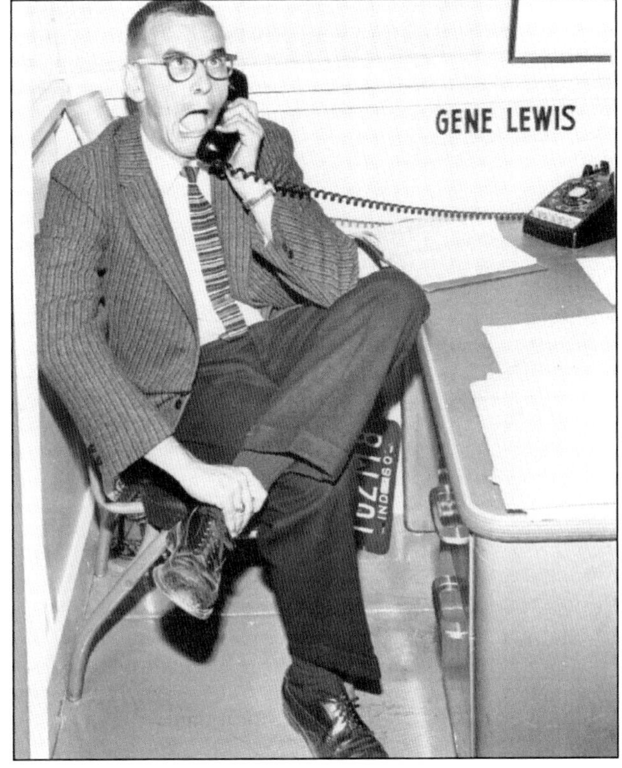

Gene Lewis grew up in the car business. His dad, Perry Lewis, opened his first Ford dealership in Paris, Illinois, in 1902. Setting up his own location in Lebanon, Gene quickly became known for his community involvement, square deals, and wacky sense of humor. (Lewis family.)

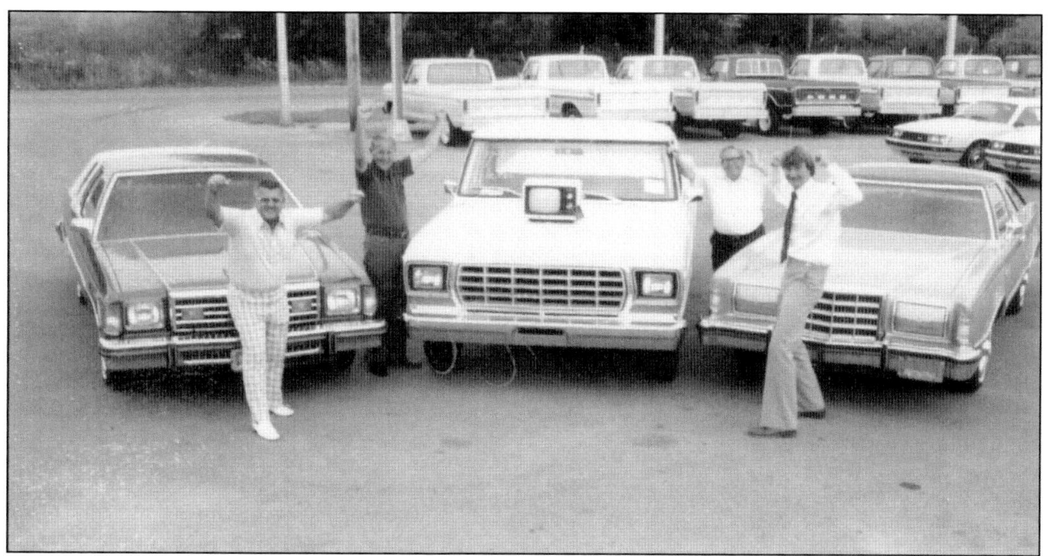

Gene Lewis passed those same traits on to his three sons—David, Steve, and Jim—who continue running Gene Lewis Ford today. Here, the Lewis sales team sweetens car deals by offering a free television with the purchase of a new Ford. (Lewis family.)

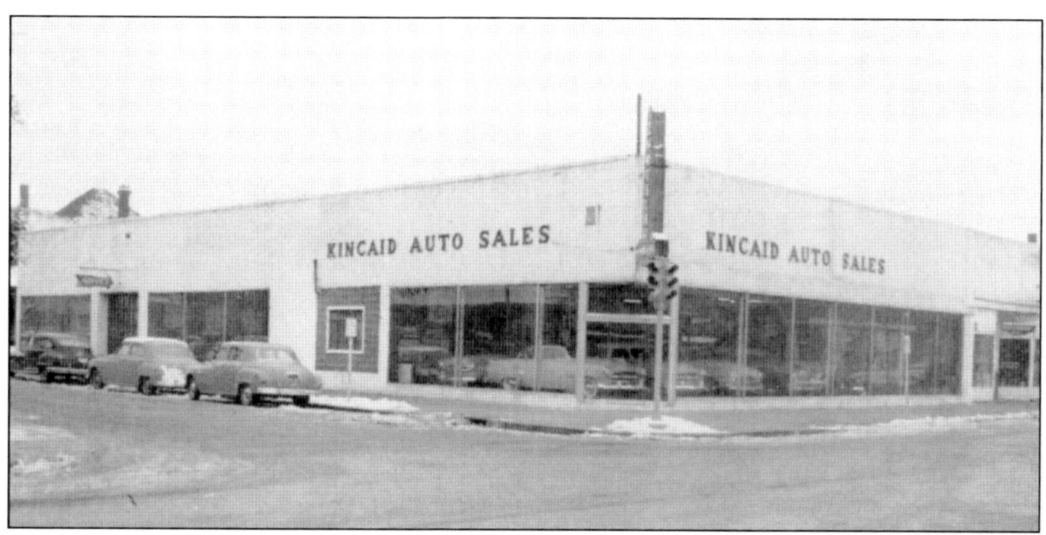

Kincaid Auto sold Chrysler products in Lebanon from the 1930s until 2015. Kincaid also supplied the specially equipped cars driven in high school driver's education classes.

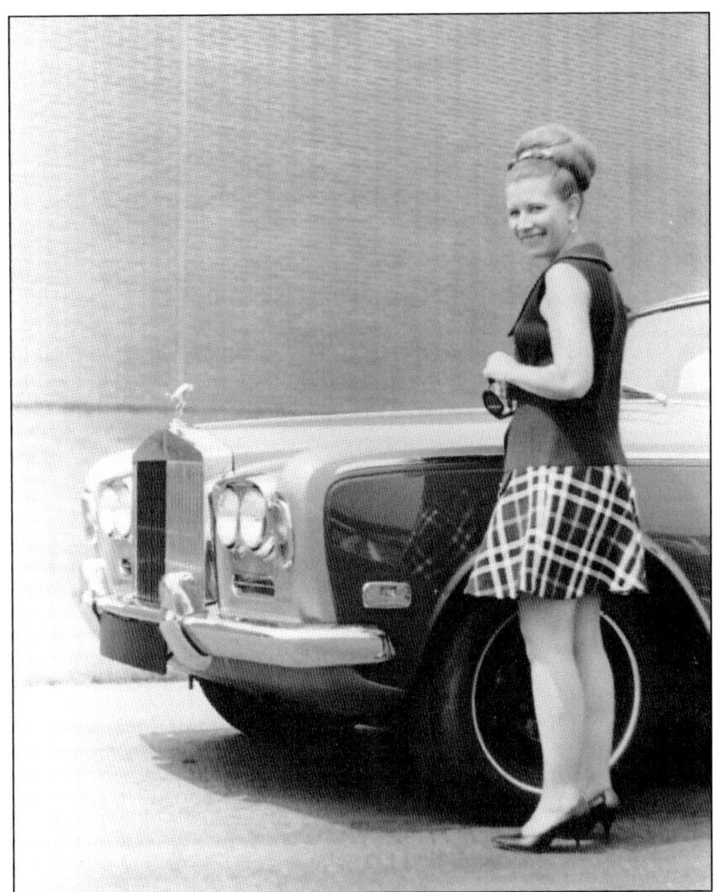

Hermann Albers Rolls-Royce (now Bentley) in Zionsville is the oldest North American dealer for the ultra luxury automaker. Originally located on fashionable Meridian Street in Indianapolis, the Albers family moved the store north in the 1960s. Here, Jerolyn Albers stands next to a car ready to be delivered to the lucky new owner. Hermann and Jerolyn's sons Mark and Greg now run the business. (Albers family.)

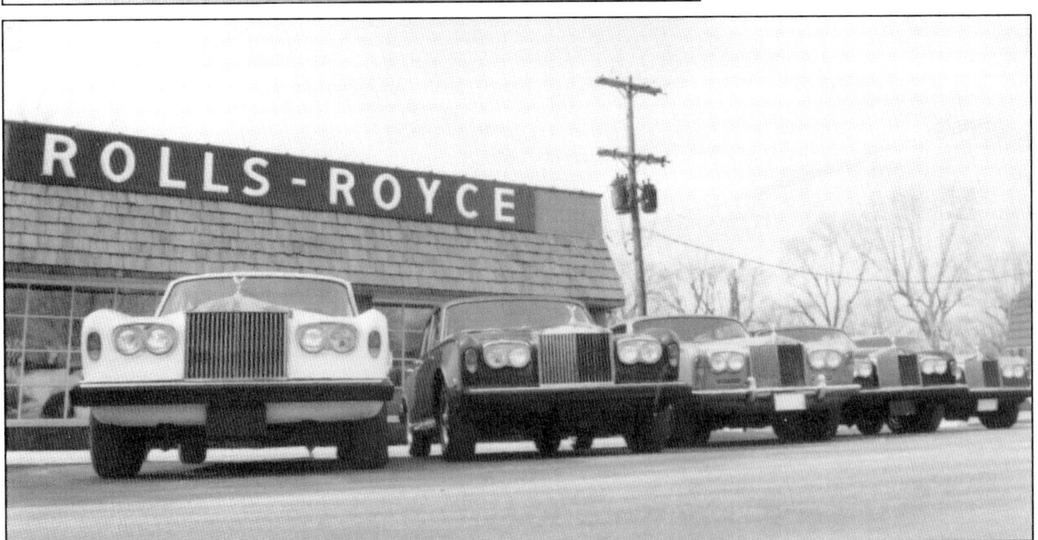

Originally, Hermann Albers and his wife, Jerolyn, met each car at the shipping dock in New Jersey, then had it uncrated and personally drove it to the new owner. Some buyers preferred to come out to Zionsville. This offered an excuse to have dinner at Adam's Rib Restaurant, with its exotic offerings such as ostrich, eel, and rattlesnake. (Albers family.)

For just over 30 years, the Oak Hill gravesite of the Rhodes family was adorned by this impressive cast bronze Tiffany urn. The one-of-a-kind piece was ordered in 1890 for display streetside at the Indianapolis When department store. The proprietor, John T. Brush, also owned the Cincinnati Reds and New York Giants baseball teams. The high Victorian style was considered dated with its griffins and flourishes, so the Brush family sold the urn after closing the store in the 1920s. Unfortunately, due to ongoing vandalism, the Rhodes family removed the artful urn. In order to assure its safe keeping, they gifted it to a long-time family friend.

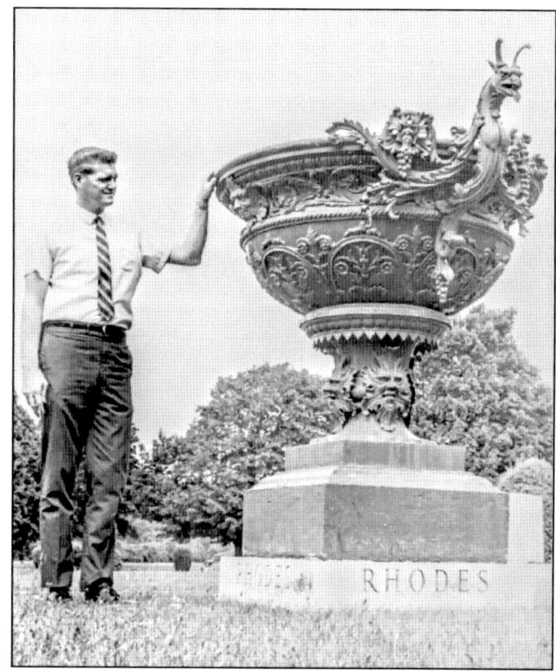

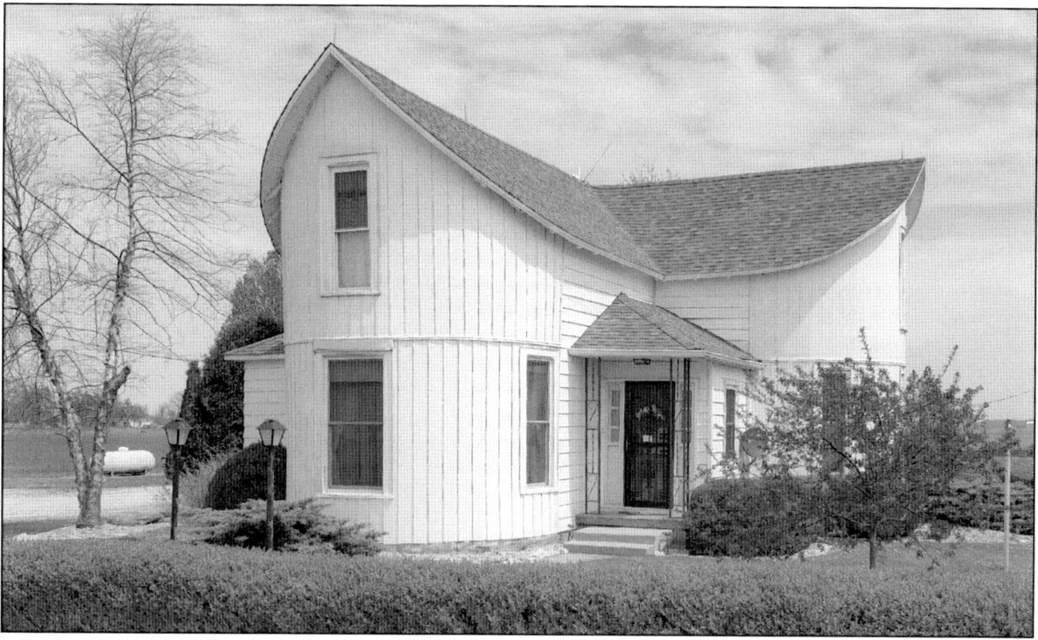

The house built by carpenter and barrel stave maker John Whitecotton was rumored to be the result of an 1880s dare. When viewed from above, the home at the south end of Advance looks like a three-leaf clover. A rectangular section at the back serves as both the kitchen and the clover's "stem." Lore has it that several lard vats were kept full of boiling water in the yard during construction. The steam was used to shape the lumber. When the Dickerson family purchased the farm in 1960, they had the home re-sided. The modern siding had to be applied vertically. Apparently, there were no stave builders on the crew who could properly bend pieces to install them horizontally like the originals. (Author's collection.)

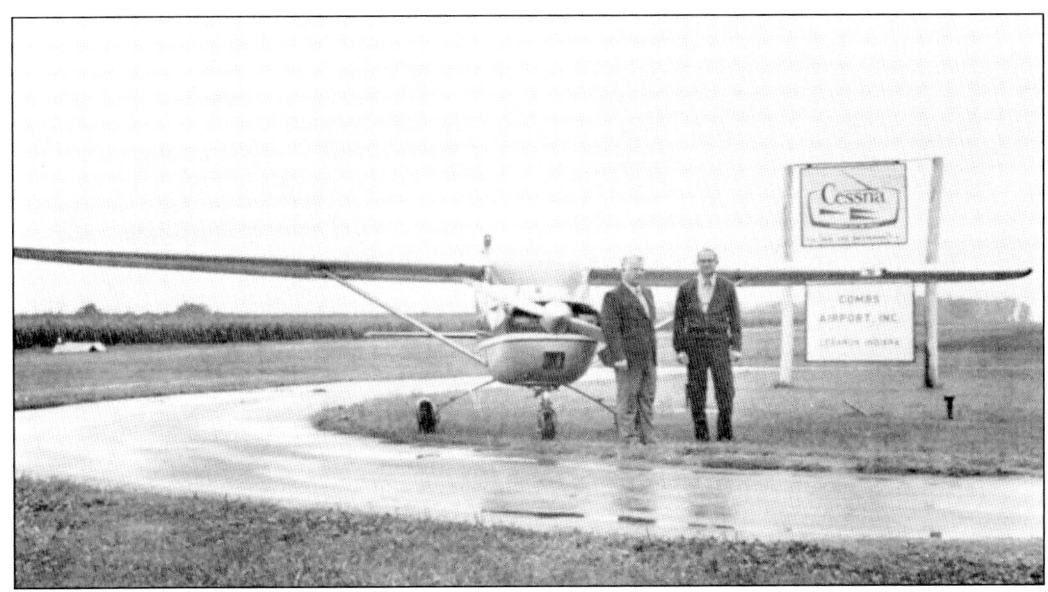

Combs Airport, now known as Boone County Airport, is located just south of Lebanon near the old John Shelburne farm. Shown here are Ralph (left) and Herm Fisher. Ralph was a history teacher at Central Elementary School and was also a World War II fighter pilot. Ralph taught flying lessons and fueled and washed planes. His brother Herm ran the business end of the airport. The Terry Airport, located between Zionsville and Sheridan, was a competitor. Pilot Harmon Campbell named the airstrip after his son Terry, who was also a pilot.

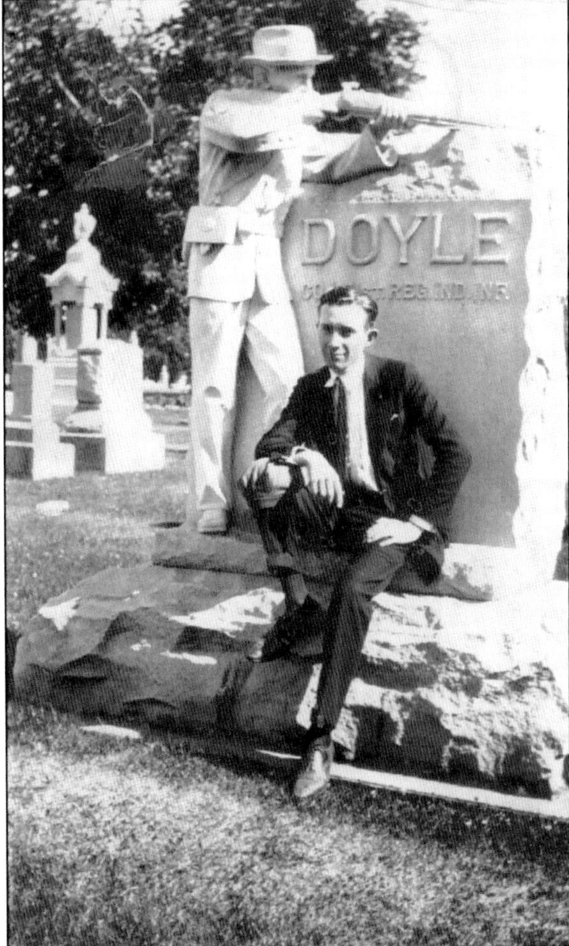

Perhaps no one in the history of Boone County has conjured more dedication to the people, legends, events, and significance of the area than Ralph W. Stark (1901–1984). By resolution of the Indiana General Assembly on February 22, 1980, in conjunction with the sesquicentennial of Boone County, Stark was named honorary historian of Boone. A special area of Lebanon's Carnegie library was set aside to house his entire donated collection. The history portion of the library was officially named the Ralph W. Stark Heritage Center.

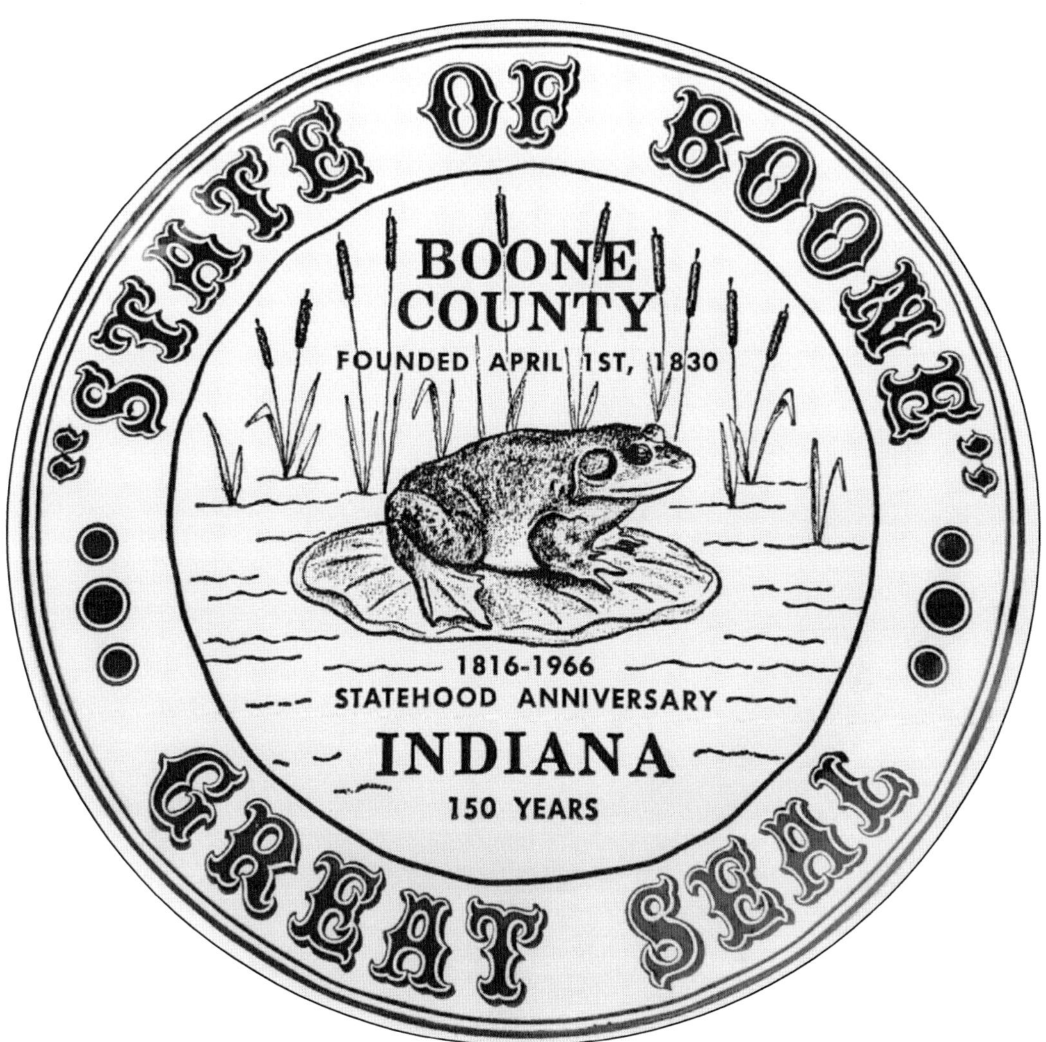

With artwork by local artist Charles E. Martin and design input from Ralph Stark, Boone County issued this commemorative plate honoring the 1966 sesquicentennial of Indiana. Labeled "Great Seal of the State of Boone," the plates were a big hit with Boone's good-natured citizens. Through dogged determination, pioneer homesteaders were rewarded with some of Indiana's finest farmland. Those who took a stake in "the State of Boone" certainly had the last laugh. (Author's collection.).

Consistent with our mission to preserve history on a local level, this book was printed in South Carolina on American-made paper and manufactured entirely in the United States. Products carrying the accredited Forest Stewardship Council (FSC) label are printed on 100 percent FSC-certified paper.

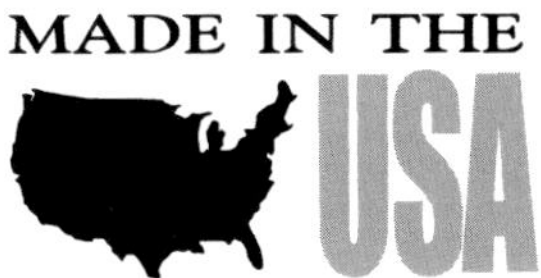